David Lloyd George: The Movie Mystery

CW00821156

1. The film title card for *The Life Story of David Lloyd George*. Note the emphasis on graphics. Drawings featured on many of the film's intertitle cards.

DAVID LLOYD GEORGE
The Movie Mystery

edited by

David Berry and Simon Horrocks

UNIVERSITY OF WALES PRESS
CARDIFF
1998

© The Contributors, 1998

British Library Cataloguing-in-Publication Data.
A catalogue record for this book is available from the British Library.

ISBN 0–7083–1371–X

All rights reserved. No part of this book may be reproduced, stored in a retrieval system, or transmitted, in any form or by any means, electronic, mechanical, photocopying, recording or otherwise, without clearance from the University of Wales Press, 6 Gwennyth Street, Cardiff, CF2 4YD.

Typeset at Multiplex Medway Ltd, Walderslade, Kent
Printed in Great Britain by Gwasg Dinefwr, Llandybïe

CONTENTS

LIST OF ILLUSTRATIONS

THE EDITORS AND CONTRIBUTORS

The Editors

David Berry is research officer for Welsh media agency Sgrîn and the Wales Film and Television Archive. An authority on Welsh film, his comprehensive *Wales and Cinema: The First Hundred Years* was published by the University of Wales Press in 1994 and is now available in paperback.

Simon Horrocks teaches film studies at University of Wales, Cardiff. He was previously cinema education officer at Cardiff's Chapter Cinema.

The Contributors

Neil Brand regularly accompanies silent movies on the piano at the National Film Theatre in London and venues around the world. He is also a radio playwright.

Kevin Brownlow is a film-maker and an internationally renowned authority on silent film. His publications include *The Parade's Gone By* (Secker and Warburg, 1968) and *Behind the Mask of Innocence: Social Problem Films of the Silent Era* (Jonathan Cape, 1991). He is also well known for his work of silent film restoration, notably on Abel Gance's 1926 *Napoleon*.

John Grigg is currently writing the fourth volume of his Lloyd George biography. The first three instalments – *The Young Lloyd George*, *The People's Champion 1902–1911* and *From Peace to War 1912–1916* – are available in paperback from HarperCollins.

John Hardy has composed music for numerous films and television programmes including the Oscar-nominated *Hedd Wyn* (1992).

Nicholas Hiley is head of information at the British Universities Film and Video Council, and a regular writer on silent cinema and its audiences.

Gwenan Owen was a founder staff member and formerly education and outreach officer of the Wales Film and Television Archive.

Roberta E. Pearson has written widely on silent cinema, including the book *Eloquent Gestures: The Transformation of Performance Style in the Griffith Biograph Films* (University of California Press, 1992). She teaches at Cardiff University.

John Reed is the WFTVA's preservation officer. He was principally responsible for the restoration of *The Life Story of David Lloyd George*.

Peter Stead, a former history lecturer at University of Wales Swansea, wrote *Film and the Working Class* (Routledge, 1990) and a biography of Richard Burton.

Sarah Street co-wrote with Margaret Dickinson *Cinema and State: The Film Industry and Government 1927–1984* (British Film Institute, 1985) and her recent work includes *British National Cinema* (Routledge, 1997). She teaches film at the University of Bristol.

John O. Thompson has published articles on many aspects of film and television theory. He currently teaches film studies at Thames Valley University.

FOREWORD

LORD TENBY

When my grandfather, David Lloyd George, visited Hitler in Berchtesgaden in 1936 he was accompanied by members of his immediate family and his personal secretary, the late A. J. Sylvester. 'A.J.', as he was always known, was a committed photographer and for this special occasion was entrusted with Lloyd George's new toy, a home movie camera. Reputations meant nothing to A.J. and he moved Hitler about peremptorily, barking orders at him (to the astonishment of SS guards and ministers alike) as he shot his sequences, which had the added novelty of colour.

My father, Gwilym, inherited all my grandfather's films but the ones we looked at were the home-made family ones and the one of the German visit always figured prominently on such occasions. Accordingly, when I received an invitation from the Wales Film and TV Archive to attend a viewing of a film on this subject, I was intrigued since I was unaware that there was another copy. Unfortunately, a previous commitment prevented me from attending, but for once my chaotic and indefensible answering system – which meant that my reply was so late that it had to be phoned – proved to be an advantage.

During the course of the ensuing conversation I admitted that I had the Lloyd George film collection in a barn at my house in Hampshire but that lack of time, and my fear of damaging the clearly old films, had prevented my assessing the material. Following this chance telephone conversation, the Archive's preservation officer, John Reed, arrived and the whole collection was expertly and, it has to be said, gingerly, conveyed in a van to Aberystwyth. There were many pleasing surprises revealed in the collection. There was a complete set of the so-called Hepworth Cinema Interviews, filmed at the height of the First World War (hitherto thought to exist only in fragments), valuable early *Pathé-Gazette* newsreels of Lloyd George, and so on, but the real prize lay in a heavy lead chest: Maurice Elvey's *The Life Story of David Lloyd George*.

The brilliant and painstaking restoration of the film is described in the following pages. Throughout the process I had the opportunity of seeing video out-takes as each stage was completed, and initial scepticism gradually turned to wonder, both at the scale and technical innovation of the film itself and at the skill and dedication of its restorers. Nothing, however, prepared me for the impact of the finished feature, with a memorable piano or orchestral background, a reaction clearly experienced by all the audiences lucky enough to see this remarkable film.

This privileged number is a comparatively modest one, as it has been possible to arrange few theatrical showings. That is sad, and the same might be said of the television industry's almost total lack of interest in the film and the extraordinary circumstances surrounding its disappearance on the eve of its world-wide launch in 1919, a point tellingly made by Kevin Brownlow in his contribution to this volume.

I feel proud and honoured to be involved in this fascinating story and I warmly congratulate all these talented people – too numerous to name individually in a foreword – who have made what, at first, seemed an impossible dream become reality. My wish, if I may be granted one, is that the artistic and entertainment establishment wake up to the treasure they now have in their midst and that, as a result, this unique film receives the recognition, and acclaim, that it deserves – eighty years after its completion.

ACKNOWLEDGEMENTS

This collection of articles has taken some time to reach the light of day (if not quite as long as the film we celebrate in the following pages). It began to take shape back in 1995 when a group of people gathered to watch a few exciting glimpses of *The Life Story of Lloyd George* in Cardiff's Chapter Cinema. Present that day were two individuals without whom this collection would never have appeared at all: Gwenan Owen and Linda Pariser. As education and outreach officer for the Wales Film and Television Archive, Gwenan was initially my co-editor (until she left Aberystwyth for the sunnier climes of Brittany in 1997) and had a hand in much of what you are about to read. Linda (then film programmer at Chapter) kindly allowed me to devote some of my time to getting the project under way, as well as bringing her usual energy and infectious enthusiasm to the proceedings.

Since 1995 numerous people have helped this collection to become a reality, not least the staff of the WFVTA who offered their friendly advice and assistance throughout – my thanks go to Iola Baines, Jane Davies, Stephen Mason and John Reed. My co-editor, David Berry, also deserves a special mention for giving the project new life with his ideas and tenacity. David has also asked me to extend his thanks to the following people who provided vital help and information: Bryony Dixon and Alison Strauss of the National Film Archive's viewing services department; Luke McKernan of the British Film Institute's Cataloguing Department; the staff of the British Universities Film and Video Council, Denis Gifford and Le Giornate del Cinema Muto, and Tony Fletcher.

Finally, I would like to express my appreciation to the University of Wales Press and two members of its staff, in particular, who have stuck with us through all our prevarications and changes of direction. My thanks go to Richard Houdmont, who showed initial faith in the project, and Susan Jenkins, our editor, for her encouragement, her advice and – most of all – her patience. Like *The Life Story of Lloyd George*, we got there in the end.

Simon Horrocks

May 1998

This volume has been produced with financial assistance from the National Lottery Unit of Wales and the former Wales Film Council.

INTRODUCTION

DAVID BERRY

In 1994 a long-lost and marathon silent film feature never seen by an audience, but pivotal to British cinema history, was rediscovered in remarkable circumstances after seventy-six years. The central figure in this movie drama – on and off screen – was the charismatic politician David Lloyd George, the 'Welsh Wizard', prime minister of Great Britain from 1916 to 1922.

The film, one of the first feature-length 'biopics' and unique in portraying an incumbent prime minister played by an actor, had long been forgotten, consigned to a footnote or two at best in even the most conscientious film histories. Yet it trailed an astonishingly murky history of suppression and proved to be an enthralling work in its own right, particularly in its treatment of Lloyd George's singular political achievements and its handling (and occasional fracturing) of linear narrative. *The Life Story of David Lloyd George* (1918) presented a record of Lloyd George's life and legislation up to and including the last year of the First World War – the apogee of his career, when he was lauded internationally for his crucial role in helping to inspire the Allies to victory. It can also now be seen as a film vital to any study of silent movies in Britain, as a biopic (however partisan and subjective) which attempted to carry that subgenre – still in its embryo stages – further than ever before, and as a feature which has prompted a total reassessment of the status of its director, the nation's most prolific film-maker, Maurice Elvey. He made more than 200 movies in a forty-four-year career, yet died relatively forgotten in 1967, dismissed as a journeyman at best.

This book examines, from a variety of standpoints, the implications and repercussions of the surprise 'exhumation' of *The Life Story of David Lloyd George*, produced by the Ideal company of London's Wardour Street and withdrawn before its intended Cardiff trade show in November 1918 following false and hysterical magazine allegations that the film's producers were 'Hun' sympathizers. The offending article's publication may not, as we shall show, be the sole reason why the film's release was aborted.

In this collection we seek to examine the film's value as part of the British and silent film heritage and as a social/historical document. The importance of the film for UK screen historians has already been recognized. In 1997, the year after its world première in Cardiff, the Lloyd George film was shown at Le Giornate del Cinema Muto – the world's leading silent-film festival, at Pordenone, near Venice – as the centrepiece of a seven-film season of Elvey work, which went far in rehabilitating the director. It was a season which could never have been contemplated with such confidence had the Lloyd George film remained in limbo. It also proved conclusively that Elvey, at his best – in parts of the Lloyd George film and in a fistful of British silent films he directed after returning from a 1924–5 stint in Hollywood with Fox (most notably *The Flag Lieutenant* (1926), *Hindle Wakes* (1927), *Palais de Danse* (1928) and *High Treason* (1929)) – was, at the very least, on a par with Hitchcock's mentor Graham Cutts, and lagged not too far behind the master himself.[1] Film historian/theorist Barry Salt has noted that Elvey's editing was far more confident and mature after his Hollywood sojourn, but the seeds of improvement can be discerned in his handling of bravura set pieces in the Lloyd George movie, notably the suffragette riots outside London's Queen's Hall. In his article in this volume, Kevin Brownlow, who advised the Wales Film and TV Archive on its restoration work for the film, comments on the significance of the Lloyd George film then and in the present television age of political drama-docs. He relates it to Elvey's *œuvre* in the wake of the valuable Pordenone showcase and writes of the film's impact on him as a critic, film-maker, restorer and historian. The social measures shown in the film and the images illustrating Lloyd George's anecdotes and speeches might be expected to fascinate the author of *Behind the Mask of Innocence*, which has shed much new light on the considerable social content of American silent movies of the 1910s and 1920s (and shamed those writers most prone to regurgitate other critics' preconceptions).[2]

No debate on *The Life Story* or its genesis should, of course, be carried out without assessing the status of the British film industry in silent days and the perceptions (of both observers at the time and today's critics), of the indigenous pre-sound cinema. The sad fact is that the British film hierarchy and the bulk of its screen historians are ashamed of Britain's movie legacy from those years, if they bother to think about it at all. Only 2 per cent of British features from 1918 are extant, an appalling example of the industry's own neglect of its history, but surely a low enough figure to prompt a certain amount of caution in reaching general conclusions about the merits of the national output. The bulk of the features and the fictional films made in the last decade before the introduction of talkies are lost or rarely summoned up from the vaults of the National Film and Television Archive.[3] Too many of the survivors are, to use a screen analogy, like those retarded or scarred relatives in innumerable horror movies – only whispered about and left for decades in locked, darkened rooms. Some of these films are on nitrate, unpreserved. The NFTVA has neither the money nor the staff to disinter them. The received opinion is that after the outstanding Victorian pioneering work in cinematography, trick and special effects and narrative construction of pioneers like Williamson, G. A. Smith, R. W. Paul and Cecil Hepworth, British cinema went into a precipitous decline only arrested in the late thirties.

The majority of current UK screen historians allude briefly to the contempt felt by other nations for British silents from the 1910s onwards. They skitter dismissively over the work of studios such as Cricks and Martin, Stoll, Clarendon and the London company (in its pre-Korda manifestation), pausing only for a few sniffy obsequies. Many disdain empirical research and take their lead from Rachael Low with her robust dismissal of Stoll company films in general and Elvey films in particular, for example, and the derisive view of British fiction production held by such fundamentally blinkered patrician critics as Paul Rotha. Many ignore British silent film altogether, save for the odd genuflection to the pictorial qualities of surviving Hepworth melodramas or to the work of one or two directors such as Graham Cutts, or directors who sealed their reputation with sound, for example Hitchcock, Victor Saville and Anthony Asquith (son of Lloyd George's great Liberal adversary).

The standards of research into very early projected cinema or cinema prehistory in Britain has risen immeasurably in the past decade, thanks primarily to the contributions of John Barnes and his brother William in chronicling the technological developments and the initial screenings, and such specialists and enthusiasts as David Robinson, Stephen Herbert and Luke McKernan.[4] The early British narrative cinema, from 1903 to (say) the end of the US Nickelodeon era – around 1908–9 – developed enterprisingly, with the films of Paul, Hepworth and such 'provincials' as Mottershaw, Bamforth and Haggar, all displaying technical innovation and/or ingenuity, and the form of these shorts has been best illuminated by perceptive critics such as Noël Burch.[5] But criticism of the domestic films of the 1910s and 1920s remains largely a void. Until recently no one has attempted to build on the invaluable but schematic recordings and assessments of Rachael Low in her first four volumes of British film history.[6]

Little of significance had been written about Maurice Elvey in his native country prior to 1994, even though he worked extensively for most of the more significant companies including London and Ideal (both at Twickenham studios), British and Colonial, Stoll and Gaumont. Even the British Film Institute's dossier, *The Commercial Imperative in the British Film Industry: Maurice Elvey, a Case Study*, published in 1987 and reissued at Pordenone in 1997, damned Elvey with very faint praise. The interview with Elvey conducted by the socialist film-maker Ralph Bond in the 1960s and preserved through the BECTU History Project is revealing for its insight into British studio conditions in the silent era. More valuable, however, is the (long-unpublished) interview with Elvey conducted by Denis Gifford in the same decade and recently exhumed by the Italian magazine *Griffithiana*, which reveals some obscure recesses of the director's career.[7] The extracts we publish as an appendix here dealing with *The Life Story* (admittedly nearly fifty years after the fact) illuminate Elvey's philosophy and working methods and tell us as much about the Lloyd George filming as we could glean from the trade press of 1918.

Screen historians have been bafflingly mute and incurious about this most mysterious, notorious chapter of Elvey's career – his shooting, in the last months of the First World War, of his hagiography of David Lloyd George. The politician at that time found himself, somewhat incongruously, as Liberal prime minister in a Tory-dominated coalition, and arguably the most powerful statesman influencing Europe's conduct of the war. The non-appearance of the film, to judge from the contemporary trade press (principally the *Bioscope* and *Kinematograph Weekly*), aroused no concern then and prompted little research before *The Life Story* finally surfaced. It proved to be an extraordinary two and a half hours long – the legacy, perhaps, of the company's intentions, stated as late as October 1918, to release it in ten weekly instalments from December of that year.[8]

The feature, starring the then well-known London stage actor Norman Page as the prime minister, was collected by the Wales Film and TV Archive from the Hampshire home of Lord Tenby, Lloyd George's grandson. The negative, a virtually complete roughcut, was soon restored with the help of the NFTVA to near-pristine condition. The random order of its later scenes on arrival at the Aberystwyth archive gave some corroboration to the memoirs of Harry Rowson, Ideal's co-founder, which are partly reproduced in this book. The story behind Rowson's observations is developed in this book's first section – 'A Mysterious History' – by Sarah Street, the screen historian who lighted on them in the British Film Institute library in 1987, and wrote up her find in an academic journal, little thinking then that the movie would be recovered just a few years on.

In his memoirs Rowson claimed the film was effectively seized after Lloyd George expressed his wish that it should not be released.[9] Lloyd George's views, which remained hearsay to Rowson all his life, were apparently expressed soon after the publication of a libellous article by Horatio Bottomley in the fiercely patriotic British magazine *John Bull*, asserting that the film-makers were 'Hun' sympathizers and unfit to make the film. Rowson claimed he had sold the feature (under duress and after intolerable pressure to withdraw it) to solicitors Lewis and Lewis – presumably acting for the government or the Liberal party – who purchased the feature for £20,000 in £1,000 notes and took away the only known copy and the negative. That copy – if it existed – is still untraced. It was only the negative that surfaced in 1994.

Kevin Brownlow's article, which concludes this collection, attempts to extrapolate, assessing what the film tells us of the state of British silent film during the First World War and how the Lloyd George film might have boosted the confidence of the indigenous industry and affected others' perceptions of our home-grown movies had it been released at that time. The British film, then as now, found itself under enormous pressure from US imports. Brownlow also stresses Rowson's comments that friends of Lloyd George regarded the cinema as 'infra-dig' and had persuaded him also that the status of the cinema would be enhanced if the film was shown. Their comments implied that the whole country would be in danger if cinema gained ground and aired the kind of views expressed in the Lloyd George film, Brownlow surmises.

The Life Story of David Lloyd George is also invaluable, inevitably, as an insight into government propaganda of the day and how Lloyd George was perceived at the time by sympathetic film-makers. How far did that reflect the views of more shrewd political observers? How did the 'Great

6　　　　　　　　　JOHN BULL.　　　　　OCTOBER 5TH, 1918.

SO the ex-Prime Minister has made *his* speech—and it leaves me quite cold. His "attitude" towards the war has, with certain exceptions, always been correct, and his Manchester views are very much like those he expressed at Bristol and Edinburgh. But when he talks politics I find that, like the Bourbons, he has learnt nothing and forgotten nothing. For instance, after all that has been revealed to us, he is still the old "Free Trader." Of course, he hedges—as is the way of the politician. He is against tariffs, but he doesn't mind—in certain exceptional cases—State subsidies. That is something, but it is a process of economic reasoning that does not appeal to me. If I know anything of my countrymen, we have not fought this war, and nearly won it, in order to begin all over again our quibbles and our shibboleth worship at the respective shrines of "Free Trade" and "Tariff Reform." Those phrases stink in the nostrils of sensible men.

The War's First Lesson.

If there is one lesson we have learnt, or should have learnt, it is that the Hohenzollerns and all their bestial crew tried to ruin us before fighting us. They have again and again boasted that before the war they were effectively crippling our commerce and grabbing our trade ; and it was only territorial greed which induced them to strike the blow on the field of battle, before they had won their triumph in the economic war. Thank God, in their impatience they showed their hand too soon. Those of us who had gone about the country with warning cries were denounced and derided. They who to-day claim to be the nation's counsellors were ready to stigmatise as an enemy to his country everyone who refused to bow the knee to Berlin, and to acclaim the Kaiser as the arch-apostle of peace. Sometimes I am inclined to use the pages of this journal for no other purpose than to print the utterances of the politicians who laughed at danger. When I read their past speeches and see their impudent attempts to-day to guide and instruct the people, I marvel at the short memory of the public. But, at the same time, nothing will convince me that we shall ever again tolerate the parrot cries of pre-war days. Business Government, as properly understood, will be the new policy of the nation. That, indeed, is the first lesson of the war. This much should be said for Mr. Asquith—he was not among those who blatantly proclaimed their disbelief in the inevitable war. But in the matter of German "penetration" he was one of the blind leaders of the blind. Like Mr. Lloyd George and his brave British henchman, Sir Alfred Mond—the alkali monopolist—he was an eloquent exponent of the merits of our old fiscal system ; but whilst the Prime Minister has "come on," we find his predecessor unmoved by the logic of events, untouched by the lessons of the obvious, still ready to plead with all the arts of the practised advocate for the maintenance of that system which very nearly ended in our national ruin. I care nothing for theories ; I have always entertained supreme contempt for copy-book maxims—which are for children. I try to judge everything by the stern logic of the realities ; and to-day I find that we are once more confronted with the old, crude, absurd theories which men like Cobden and Bright—being, as they were, true patriots—would have thrown to the winds to-day. And if Mr. Asquith and his "Liberal Federation" do not yet realise the truth, they will find themselves left behind in the hour of national reconstruction. Remember that whilst Germany was endeavouring to kill us economically, prior to crushing us by the might of her military power, it was this Liberal Federation which, through its president, Sir John Brunner—Sir Alfred Mond's partner—not many months before the war, tried to force upon us a reduction of the Navy ! Just as, obsessed with the same ideas, it was Mr. Lloyd George himself, who, on New Year's Day, 1914, actually proclaimed to the world that never had there been a more propitious moment for a reduction in our armaments ! But now we know.

Britain for the British.

Now, I am certainly not going to blame the gallant little Welshman and his friends for having made mistakes which might have ended in Imperial ruin. They simply didn't understand. But I am going to suggest that just as they were wrong—hopelessly, terribly wrong—in 1914, so Mr. Asquith, once the exponent of the best political thought in Britain, is to-day pointing the way to

disaster. We have to realise this fact : that the war has upset all our theories and beliefs ; that the German menace, for the time transferred to the arena of war, will in due course return to the fields of trade and commerce. We allowed the Hun to steal our trade and creep into our markets. We bought his goods, and with the money he built his Navy and equipped his Army so that when ready he might fall upon us and slay us. But Foch and Haig and Pershing, and the glorious array of British battleships, have foiled his fell design. Still, the purpose and intent were there. Only by the blood of brave men and the combined might of the Allies have we stemmed the tide of his arrogant aggression. And when I read the ex-Premier's fatuous declaration of faith in "Free Trade," which made all these horrors possible, I despair of the sanity of our so-called statesmen. We will have no more "Free Trade" after the war, if "Free Trade" means freedom for the Hun to invade our markets, undersell the products of our industries, dump down upon us his surplus goods—and keep our workmen poor. What is more, I warn the Politicians who still have the temerity to wave the discredited old Party banners that their doom is certain. "Britain for the British" is the cry of the man who has fought that we may live ; and the returned soldier, full of scars as of honour, will not stand idly by and see the errors of the past repeated.

The Lloyd George Film.

Take this much-advertised film of the life of the Prime Minister. It is being produced by the Ideal Film Renting Company—against which, as a trading concern, I have nothing to say ; I believe it enjoys a first-class reputation. But what is the composition of the Company ? I have before me the latest Return filed with the Joint Stock Registry, and this is how the Board is described :—

NAME.	FORMER NAME.	OCCUPATION.
Harry Rowson	.. Harry Rosenbaum ..	Director
Simon Rowson	.. Simon Rosenbaum ..	Statistician
Sara Wilmot	.. Sara Wohlgemuth ..	Widow
Simon Gilbert	.. Simon Gelberg ..	Journalist
A. M. Kay	.. A. M. Koppel ..	Secretary.

It is only right to say that they all declare themselves to be British. Then take the present list of shareholders ; it is dated January 11th, 1918 :—

H. Rowson (Rosenbaum)	.. ..	1,050
Jane Burnstein	.. ..	500
S. Gilbert (Gelberg)	.. ..	515
A. Gardner	.. ..	285
E. Rowson (Rosenbaum)	.. .. ..	315
S. Wilmot (Wohlgemuth)	.. .. ..	200
Hilda Jacobson	.. ..	150
S. Rowson (Rosenbaum)	.. .. ..	100
Jacob Wilmot (Wohlgemuth)	.. ..	100
D. Rowson (Rosenbaum)	.. .. ..	85
A. M. Kay (Koppel)	.. .. ..	130
Rose Boodson	.. ..	30
Nathan Boodson	.. ..	20
Leslie Rowson	.. ..	1

Here, again, it may be that each of these persons—despite the remarkable Teutonic flavour of their original patronymics—is a thoroughly loyal British subject, but the fact remains that, by some blood affinity, they were all drawn together into a trade organisation in competition with firms of a truer All-British ring. And the irony of it is that one of the Rosenbaums was for some time a leading light of the Tariff Reform League—you see, I am assuming for the moment that Mr. Lloyd George is still a Free Trader ; he is, too, I believe connected with the War Topical Budget, whilst either he, or his brother, has been given a commission in the Army ! Well, I have no desire to labour this point ; but I do say that the composition of the Company is an object lesson for the business community

THE KAIS
The Lessons of the War—Britain

2. Horatio Bottomley's inflammatory article in *John Bull*, 5 October 1918.

OCTOBER 5TH, 1918. **JOHN BULL.**

7

CAVING IN.

British—The Prime Minister's Film.

ITOR.

of the country. In the same way, I do not suggest that the Company is directly responsible for all the details incidental to the production of the film. Otherwise I should ask the Directors to explain the facts disclosed in a Statutory Declaration of one John Dwyer, of 40, Ravensbourne Road, Catford, now before me. Here it is :—

I, JOHN DWYER, of 40, Ravensbourne Road, Catford, do solemnly declare and say as follows :—

I am and have been for some years an actor and have lately been employed as one of the " crowd" in one of the scenes of the proposed Life of Lloyd George film, viz., the scene inside the Town Hall, Birmingham. The film is being produced by the Ideal Film Company and I got the job in the following manner. When not otherwise engaged, I call at the office of the Elite Film Actors' Bureau—of whom I am informed a Mr. Warren is the manager—of Whitcombe Court, Leicester Square, and on this occasion I was taken on as before stated. There would seem to have been a crowd of about 450, including many men who took the part of soldiers and sailors. I noticed on this occasion, and have noticed on other occasions when I have taken part in a crowd of supernumeraries, that there were many foreigners of various sorts—mostly so-called Scandinavians—and I particularly noticed on this occasion a little clique of 5 or 6 men talking together previous to going into the studio where the scene was filmed. These were among those who were taking the part of soldiers and sailors and they wore various military and naval uniforms, and my attention was called, apart from the fact that they were talking in a foreign language, to the fact that one of them wore the uniform of my old regiment, the Royal West Kents.

I questioned one of the men, and he admitted to my surprise that he was a German and I replied, " if I thought he meant it I would punch his head." The man thereupon retracted what he had said and declared he was a Dane.

Well, I know these Danes—and so do you. But I respectfully direct the attention of Messrs. Rowson to the matter. Meanwhile, I must assume that Britishers were not available—discharged soldiers, for instance. It is all very puzzling.

Thick-Skinned Ministers.

Then, too, I have been reading some remarkable allegations against one of Sir Alfred Mond's Companies—of having been guilty of a gross infringement of the Trading with the Enemy Act. But, so far, like Mr. Leverton Harris (who *was* to have had a peerage), this Minister of the Crown is silent. I have been very definite in my allegations against the Parliamentary Secretary to the Ministry of Blockade. It is by no means a small thing to suggest that a Minister of the Crown has used his official position for personal profit. Moreover, I have challenged the firm of which Mr. Harris was, until quite recently, the largest shareholder, to produce its books. Why has the right hon. gentleman made no attempt to answer the allegations, and why have Harris and Dixon, Ltd., made no reply to my challenge ? And now we have this other Minister, the First Commissioner of Works, publicly accused of offending against the law—of doing things which impugn his position as a member of His Majesty's Government. This is the charge, as set forth in the *New Witness* ; there is nothing vague about it : Sir Alfred Mond is Chairman of the Mond Nickel Company, and he and they are accused, in connection with the process of re-construction, of allotting shares to Germans after the declaration of war, and subsequent to the issue on September 9th, 1914, of a Trading with the Enemy Proclamation which warned every subject of the King against entering into "any transaction or completing any transaction already entered into with an enemy in any stocks, shares or securities." Whoever did so was deemed guilty of a crime and liable to punishment and penalties accordingly. The contention of our contemporary is that Sir Alfred Mond has been guilty of a grave offence : it makes very specific allegations ; it calls upon the Public Prosecutor to act.

What is done ? Whitehall does not move. Sir Alfred Mond does not reply. Perhaps, when Parliament re-assembles, Mr. Bonar Law will get up in the Commons and assure us that *he* would have acted " in precisely the same way " ! What a game it is ! Each of these members of the Government has been charged with the gravest offences—and each of them sits silently under the charges. In the old days, Britain's Prime Minister would have called upon his colleagues to clear their honour—but, you must understand, an election is in the air, and rich supporters must not be lightly thrown aside. *Non olet*—"it does not smell "—is the Politician's motto where Party funds are concerned. " It is not in the public interest " that they should take any notice of allegations which, once established, would tend to deplete the coffers. " Bring your money—and no questions asked," is the order of the day.

The Kaiser Caving In.

But now let me turn to a much more congenial aspect of the situation. Following upon Austria's feeble effort for peace, comes Bulgaria's request for an armistice—whilst who shall say how long we may have to wait before the deluded Sultan also throws up the sponge ? These things, however, are but pointers; preparing us for something very much bigger—and something which I have sound reason for believing is not outside the sphere of probability. I do not know whether many of my readers see the German, Swiss and Dutch papers. The extracts from them which are from time to time published in our own Press are very incomplete, and frequently badly translated. It is no exaggeration to say that to-day a deep gloom has settled over Berlin—Vienna, we know, has " got it badly." And with the fall of Cambrai imminent, with Metz to follow, and the fulfilment of Foch's promise that during the present offensive he will go " straight to the Rhine "—to say nothing of the havoc being wrought by the Allied air services—the Kaiser is undoubtedly in for a rough time with his own people. He cannot pretend that a wholesale retreat of his army back into Germany, accompanied by the daily and nightly bombardment from the skies of the principal Rhine towns, is "all according to plan" ; and I venture to predict that when Metz falls to the glorious American army, and the Allied forces for the first time put their feet on enemy territory, a cold shudder will go down the back of the All-Damnedest—who will have to acknowledge what he already realises, that the game is up. *And then he, too, will cave in.* Of course, the surrender will be camouflaged in every possible way. First of all, we shall have the Pope once more on the scene, pleading for the cessation of hostilities in the name of Humanity. And then, through various circuitous channels, the compassion of President Wilson will be beseeched. Contemporaneously with these machinations, subterranean efforts will be made to effect a separate peace, first with Italy and then with France. But all to no avail. And finally will come the appeal to Britain direct to cease hostilities pending the discussion of peace. From one point of view, all this is very encouraging—for it means that the war is won. There is, however, a terrible and sinister aspect, for the Politicians will then come in, and Heaven alone knows what mischief they may contrive !

Get Ready the Peace Terms.

I hold, therefore, it is high time that the people themselves began to take in hand the question of peace ; and unless any untoward incident should occur in the war—which is now unlikely—I think that, in the proud *rôle* of Tribune of the People, I had better from this time forward concentrate attention upon this matter. Next week, therefore, I shall ask you to consider with me what should be the Allies' minimum Terms ; and when we have agreed upon them, every Member of Parliament and of the Government, and every candidate at the next election, must be bombarded with the mandate. Personally, I see no need whatever—at any rate, at present—to talk about a Peace Conference. Apart from the fact that we should dictate, and not discuss, our terms, I should be extremely apprehensive of the politicians who would go to such a conference as our delegates. The only conference needed is one between the Allies, and before that takes place, each of them should be fortified with the knowledge of the irreducible minimum which will satisfy its People. But there is no time to be lost—the Kaiser is caving in ! We must get ready with *real* peace terms.

3. Elvey's robust re-enactment of the Queen's Hall suffragette riots, shot during a London policemen's strike.

Man' version of history dispensed here by Elvey and his screenwriter, Sir Sidney Low, square with the facts? These are some of the issues raised in this critical anthology.

The release of *The Life Story* in 1918, assuming it had remained in the public domain in subsequent decades, would – at the very least – have discouraged later historians from dismissing Elvey quite so summarily. More significantly, perhaps, they would have looked with a less jaundiced eye, and delved more deeply into the work of other directors of the later silent period (Walter Summers, for instance, with his startlingly evocative reconstructions of war incidents).[10]

The Lloyd George film reveals its director's undoubted flair for punctuating his film with documentary-style detail before the term 'documentary' was even used. The director also choreographed, with great daring, set pieces and crowd scenes (for example suffragette 'riots'

...e Birmingham Town Hall fracas of 1900, re-created on location – with as many as 10,000 extras ...ide and inside the hall, according to a contemporary trade paper.

in London and the Birmingham Town Hall fracas when Lloyd George donned a policeman's uniform to escape the mob). The London suffragette skirmishes were even shot during a policeman's strike, with numerous Elvey extras (mainly 'recruited' from local labour exchanges) forced to pose as actual police to control the 'rioters' during shooting. The persuasively violent scenes outside London's Queen's Hall were shot outside the venue at the time of an actual Lloyd George visit there (according to Elvey in his Gifford interview). The felicitous moment when Lloyd George dashes into the town hall and down a corridor, in shadow, towards the camera, has an immediacy we almost never see in political reconstruction scenes or even actuality footage of the period.

It is true that the film's opening stutters a little. It resembles a bad educational film at times and Low has no command of working-class argot but the early scenes also provide ample evidence that the film's

5. Shadow and light: Lloyd George on a factory visit.

editing had not been completed at the time of its 'seizure'. Some location scenes of Lloyd George's youthful life are nevertheless, superbly shot, and Elvey soon hits his stride. The later continuity cutting in *The Life Story* leaves a little to be desired at times (notably in those town-hall skirmishes which seem jerky and repetitive) but the film's grasp of *mise-en-scène* is often extraordinary, notably during Lloyd George's visits to munitions and aircraft factories which have an almost uncanny veracity (thanks partly to Norman Page's natural demeanour).

Elvey uses light and shadow with great precision and employs diagonal movement (sometimes picked out with intelligent use of overhead camera), as Lloyd George and his entourage pass factory benches, rows of aircraft or men employed in smelting and other industrial processes. These moments gain much from the film's modern colourization (courtesy of the Wales Film and TV Archive) following the 1918 tinting and toning instructions to the laboratory on the leaders of the film. One of the most visually striking of all the Lloyd George sequences in the feature is the factory oration as, caught in sunlight from the window, he addresses workers in shadow. Fortuitous or not, the chiaroscuro lighting effect adds to the messianic flavour of the war sequences, as Elvey presents Lloyd George as a man who galvanizes production and inspires the nation's confidence in the eventual outcome of the conflict. Elvey observes the factory processes lovingly – almost achieving a symbiotic relationship with Lloyd George as he casts an approving eye over the industry which has adapted to war conditions so quickly after his instructions as minister of munitions.

There is no doubt Elvey was inspired by his subject's social reforming zeal. In his youth the director was recruited into Fabian socialism, fell under the spell of both Bernard Shaw (while producing one of his plays in America) and the great left-wing editor Robert Blatchford. Elvey even flirted with journalism for a while, writing front-page pieces for Blatchford's *The Clarion*. As a young theatre actor-director, prior to entering the film industry, Elvey was infused with enthusiasm for trade unionism as a weapon against poverty. 'I'd always known the underdogs, the underprivileged, had a damned awful time. I determined that trade unionism was the only way out for people like me – the worker.'[11] Certainly some affinity with the 'underdog' can be discerned in *The Life Story*'s robust and intense dramatization of the effects of financial hardship. In one scene, when a policeman bursts into a man's home to arrest him for stealing a loaf of bread to feed his family, a small child of the hapless culprit throws up on screen.

The film also illustrates Elvey's willingness to lard the narrative with flashes backwards and forwards, as Lloyd George spices his speeches with liberal use of anecdote – regaling politicians with past tales of hardship or projecting in his mind images of the future. Elvey also is not afraid to jettison the film's strict interior narrative logic, when he moves from Lloyd George (the schoolchild visualizing the David and Goliath battle as he hears the story from a teacher), and creates *his own* visual analogy, as the biblical adversaries dissolve and metamorphose into Lloyd George as middle-aged statesman and the Kaiser, respectively. The low-angle shot of the biblical David flexing his muscles against the sunlight – strangely suggestive to modern audiences of the Aryan supremacy cult of the physical propagated on screen by Leni Riefenstahl – is followed by a similar angled shot privileging Lloyd George as statesman.[12] At these moments Elvey is far from the journeyman. Above all, perhaps, it is the sweep, ambition and bravado of the film which impress, for all the reservations one might have (and which are expressed by some writers here), about the overall cinematic achievement or structure.

The essays in this book will show just why the Lloyd George film's disappearance in 1918 must be seen as a tragedy for a British movie industry which had produced no comparatively ambitious and authoritative feature that year (or indeed, up to that time) and which remained, in consequence, retarded in the eyes of outside observers for years. In the book's first section we speculate on the reasons for *The Life Story*'s post-production fate which must remain open to conjecture eighty years after its intended release. Ironically, Ideal, a medium-size firm perhaps fifth or sixth in the pecking order of British production companies, had not initially conceived their great war feature as a paean of praise to Lloyd George. Their original idea was to capitalize on the derring-do reputation of the young MP, author and sometime Boer War correspondent Winston Churchill, distilling events through his consciousness and opinions. The finished script was to be furnished by Eliot Stannard, the company's regular scenarist, who collaborated with Elvey on more than twenty films.

When Churchill returned to the Cabinet the film was postponed, but Harry and his brother and fellow Ideal executive Simon Rowson revived the war-feature concept later, transforming it into a biography of Lloyd George which would simultaneously reflect, and boost, the national spirit and stress the crucial role of the British political leader. The working title, according to the trade paper the *Kinematograph Weekly*, was, significantly, *The Man who Saved the Empire*.[13] Pre-production was thorough. Elvey trailed the prime minister around various functions, including the Welsh National Eisteddfod, assimilating telling detail. Norman Page reputedly visited the House of Commons repeatedly to study the great man's mannerisms, while the historian Sir Sidney Low, of King's College, London, spent seven weeks in north Wales writing the screenplay. *Kinematograph Weekly* ran double-page advertisements hailing the film as the most ambitious Ideal feature yet. The company claimed that 1918 would be 'the year of the Lloyd George picture' which, they surmised, would be as successful as their hits of previous years: *My Old Dutch*, the film from Hollywood actress Florence Turner's company which Ideal distributed in 1915, and Ideal's own productions *The Second Mrs Tanqueray* (1916) and *Masks and Faces* (1917). The Rowsons proclaimed that the Lloyd George feature would bring 'dignity to the picture palaces' and 'lift the kinema onto a level of national importance . . . never reached before'.[14]

In the summer of 1918 Maurice Elvey was forced to re-shoot part of *Nelson* – the second of his unofficial heritage trilogy after his 1915 *Florence Nightingale* – when the film was damaged in a fire at the laboratory at St Margaret's Studio, Twickenham. This near-catastrophe meant Elvey was not available for shooting the Lloyd George movie until the last week of August at the earliest, and it almost beggars belief that by November he had apparently all but finished the film and it was advertised in October for a 12 November trade show.[15]

On 5 October the blow fell. Bottomley's article in *John Bull*, *Kinematograph Weekly*'s Odhams Press stablemate, insinuated that the executives of the Ideal company, Harry and Simon Rowson, were Huns or Hun sympathizers and scarcely fit people to make such a film. The claims by Bottomley, *John Bull*'s editor, were based on the fact that the Rowsons, Jews of eastern European extraction, were by birth Rosenbaums and had changed their name, like countless others in and around the war years, to avoid vilification and suspicion. The poisonously paranoid and xenophobic atmosphere of 1918 can be gauged from even the most cursory study of Hansard. Questions were repeatedly asked in the Commons about the origins of businessmen and individuals who had changed their names. In this climate the government introduced the Naturalization of Aliens Bill, which tightened up restrictions on aliens, even from friendly countries.[16]

British film historian Sarah Street deserves much credit for focusing attention on those Rowson memoirs which give us some flavour of the prevailing paranoia. His papers, held separately in the British Film Institute's special collection, also reveal, sadly, that as late as 1945 Harry Rowson was so obsessed with shooting another Lloyd George biography that he communicated with the politician's private secretary, A. J. Sylvester. On hearing of the politician's death he even suggested that he had enough cuttings and obituary notices to assemble some kind of documentary.

Street's subsequent article was, strangely, not seized on by other journalists or historians, for the memoirs were genuinely revelatory.

Harry Rowson claimed that considerable pressure was brought to bear from the government (and the chief whip, Captain Guest) and the industry to withdraw the film. Rowson contended that Lloyd George, who had originally provided full co-operation, now opposed the film and Ideal faced a 'worldwide scandal' if they flouted Lloyd George's desires.[17] The Rowsons, prominent members of the Jewish community, also feared a damaging anti-Jewish backlash. The memoir – written decades after the events and deposited at the BFI by Janet Davis, Harry Rowson's daughter, in the 1970s – says that the company agreed to withdraw the film, and a Lewis and Lewis solicitor, Reginald Poole (on a date unspecified by Rowson) paid over £20,000 in £1,000 notes in return for the film. In January 1919, Ideal predictably won a libel action against *John Bull* and Odhams Press.[18]

The negative emerged again when Lord Tenby, impressed by the archive's work in helping to restore the film taken by A. J. Sylvester of Lloyd George's 1936 visit to Germany and meeting with Hitler, invited the archive to take for storage and preservation a collection of Lloyd George films. These included actuality items from the cinema news magazines such as *Topical Budget*, the coloured original of the Sylvester Hitler movie, the *Cinema Interviews* of Cecil Hepworth (which included a Lloyd George interview) – *and the Lloyd George feature*.[19] Viscount Tenby had no idea that the reels handed over contained the long-lost Lloyd George biopic. Indeed he had never heard of it, such was the secrecy about the movie post-1918.

Street suggests that Lloyd George, in the throes of campaigning for the 1918 election in December that year, might have worried about the potential damage to his prospects of the 'Huns' allegation in a powerful magazine with a weekly sale of 1.7 million. The 'People's Paper' at that time had not been tarnished by Bottomley's scandalous behaviour and was renowned for championing the cause of the 'little man'. It would be some years yet before Bottomley's spectacular tumble from grace with the 1920s exposure of his *John Bull* lottery fraud and seven-year gaol sentence.[20] Yet could Lloyd George have been frightened of Bottomley's influence *per se*? Bottomley had, after all, been declared bankrupt twice by 1918 and been forced to defend himself – successfully – against one allegation of corruption. Lloyd George could surely have crushed Bottomley, particularly in the wake of the court decision and the successful election outcome of December 1918 when the coalition was returned with a crushing majority. There seems much more to it than that. *John Bull* was a powerful tool of political influence in Bottomley's hands, and the editor was a noted public speaker and polemicist who often appeared on platforms disseminating coalition propaganda. He obviously had powerful allies including the Information Minister, Beaverbrook.

Sarah Street and Kevin Brownlow both suggest that the film's socialist thrust might have been anathema to Basil Thomson, assistant commissioner of the Metropolitan Police and soon to be director of the Special Branch. If Thomson, with his huge influence, considered the film might have given working men returning from the war 'socialist' ideas, this could be a significant reason for suppression.

Another factor comes into play. By the war's end many exhibitors were openly antagonistic to propaganda movies, and they were determined not to be used for political purposes in the 'khaki election' in December 1918. Herbert Brenon's so-called 'national film' (working title *The Invasion of Britain*, but later called *Victory and Peace*) was based on the fiction that the Germans had overrun Britain (a forerunner of the Kevin Brownlow/Andrew Mollo feature *It Happened Here!*). Brenon's movie was nearing completion at the Armistice, but was shelved. It had no 'mission to fulfil' when completed, said the cinema trade's 'unofficial' representative in the Commons, A. E. Newbould, former chairman of the Cinema Exhibitors' Association.

The trade's hostility to what they regarded as political propaganda manifested itself in a campaign by various exhibitors orchestrated by *Kinematograph Weekly* to prevent the screening of specially made slides of members of the Lloyd George coalition. Newbould advised CEA members to resist exploitation and said he had written to newspapers seeking publicity for this stance but a section of the press 'with a Coalition bias' had ignored him. The trade press was full of vitriolic views from exhibitors who thought cinemas had suffered a surfeit of war material and special pleading.[21] Despite all the alternative scenarios about the film's fate, is it not also just as likely that Lloyd George felt he had overreached himself? He could have sought to suppress the feature personally, to forestall the charges of fellow politicians (who might have regarded the film as mere government propaganda or self-aggrandizement) or even to foreclose investigations into the funding of the film. Was it backed by Liberal party funds, Lloyd George's own

personal fund (perhaps, more likely) or through the government War
Aims Committee (despite denials in the Commons by its chairman, the
apparently ubiquitous Captain Guest)?

During the movie's production some MPs were not slow to make jibes
at the film's expense.[22] Harry Rowson's memoirs state only that Ideal had
been guaranteed that debts would be covered through the bank. No
documentation has so far been found on the financing of the movie or the
deal struck by Rowson with Lewis and Lewis (our inquiries via the Law
Society and with partners in the firm at a later date and successors of the
company have all drawn a blank). So we can only speculate. Elvey
himself claimed, in the Gifford interview, that the film had 'eventually
been destroyed' but also that Simon Rowson had told him the film was
considered 'an unfair use of Liberal Party funds for political propaganda'.

Today's generation must make what it will of the film's retrieval from
the Lloyd George family. It arrived in Aberystwyth in cans sealed in 1920,
which adds spice to the assertion by Lloyd George's mistress and future
wife Frances Stevenson that she saw a copy in that year and pleaded with
him to suppress it. Stevenson's observations are noted by Lloyd George's
biographer John Grigg, in his article in this book. They suggest that as late
as 1920 Lloyd George could have been contemplating acquiescing in the
release of the film – or was Frances Stevenson simply mistaken about the
year?

Grigg offers numerous theories for Lloyd George's alleged vacillation
over the film, and also stresses the potential influence on public opinion
of The Life Story's emphasis on Lloyd George's progressive social
legislation and the implication of those measures for living standards,
mores and morality in Britain during and after the war. Britain was
certainly in industrial and social turmoil in 1918, with shipbuilding, the
buses and police hit by strikes – and the success of the Russian Revolution
had fuelled the establishment's concern that it might inspire emulators in
Britain. Lloyd George was no Bolshevik, and as both Grigg and Street
point out, soon drifted rightwards in thrall to his Tory coalition
colleagues, but, as Brownlow says, the film could have sparked a desire
for radical changes among dissenting working-class audiences. There
were clearly many who might have wished the film's suppression, not
least politicians resentful of Lloyd George gaining most credit for victory
in the war. Some MPs doubtless saw in the film the manipulations of
Beaverbrook and Northcliffe, unpopular appointments by Lloyd George

in the Information Ministry, and desired to control their power and keep these press magnates at arm's length from the nation's executive.

The Rowsons' fears for their own position in the film industry, given the climate of 1918 and the possibility of an anti-Jewish backlash, might explain why they apparently surrendered so meekly. The Naturalization Bill must be seen against the background of recurring questions in the House about immigrants or aliens running British businesses. No one seemed to be sacrosanct. Even Viscount Milner, an erstwhile Boer War hero and in 1918 Secretary of State for War, was asked in the Commons about his 'foreign' origins. Screenwriter of *The Life Story*, Sir Sidney Low, knighted in 1918, head of the Information Department's radio section and a member of Northcliffe's Propaganda Committee for Enemy Countries, resigned both roles before the year was out – apparently finding his situation untenable – after a seemingly anonymous letter to Lord Northcliffe asking about *his* European roots.[23] In this atmosphere of wartime paranoia the MP Noel Pemberton Billing – later to write the stage play which inspired Elvey's 1929 spy drama *High Treason* – figured in a scandal when his publication, *The Imperialist*, alleged that the Germans had a list of 47,000 so-called perverts (mainly homosexuals) who were supposedly vulnerable to blackmail.[24] It is also odd that Elvey, given his knowledge of the harassment of the Rowsons and Sidney Low, should in his movie *Comradeship* (1919) have reinforced stereotypes, presenting a German working in a London tailor's shop as a sinister First World War spy.

The Rowsons' worries were probably more justifiable than they might seem from the comfortable standpoint of the 1990s – witness an astonishing film released in 1918 (and promoted vigorously by *John Bull* in almost the same week as the proposed but aborted Cardiff trade show of *The Life Story of David Lloyd George*, and *after* Ideal's decision to take libel action against *John Bull* had been publicized). No one has hitherto drawn attention to the sinister implications for the Rowsons of the release, late in 1918, of *The Hidden Hand*, effectively a shortened five-reel version distributed by Gaumont, of a ten- or twelve-reel Union Jack Company 'patriotic' production, *It is for England!*, released in 1916 and directed by Laurence Cowen from his screenplay (which employs the film's title phrase as a regular refrain). Cowen had written a stage play based on the 1916 film and playing in the West End two years later – at the time of *The Hidden Hand*'s release. The extant print in the National

Film Archive (actually from the Library of Congress in Washington) of *It is for England!* is printed on 1917 stock and seems to be incomplete. But here is the rub: the villain of this film is a Jewish businessman (an odious hunchback, with a goatee) who seeks to sabotage the British fleet. His name is revealed in intertitles as Rosenbaum. British prints of *The Hidden Hand* also named the German spy-villain as Rosenbaum, as the *Kinematograph Weekly* review confirms.[25]

What does the re-release of *It is for England!* precisely at this juncture in 1918 tell us, especially when Bottomley had sent out a notice to the press stating that he wished to speak at its première, ostensibly about returning to the Commons and representing the film trade there?[26] How on earth did anyone at the time fail to 'read' *The Hidden Hand* as a scarcely veiled attack on the Rowsons or 'Rosenbaums'? Did Bottomley think he could libel the Rowsons with impunity, and could the piece in *John Bull* provide evidence of a much more concerted campaign against the Rowsons and all associated with Ideal than we have suspected hitherto? It is just possible that Bottomley, in order to deflect attention from the gross implications of *The Hidden Hand*, or to safeguard that film, ensured – with his article – that Lloyd George did not want *The Life Story* released, and that there was less likelihood of the Rowsons, having succumbed on that front, attracting more attention by bringing legal action against *The Hidden Hand*. We may be in the realms of conspiracy theory here but the racial tensions of the day are clearly vital to any understanding of the Rowsons' position.

One might in ordinary circumstances have expected the Rowsons to kick against the pricks and seek legal advice about the Cowen film – even if we cannot be surprised that Lloyd George did not intervene, given subsequent developments on *The Life Story*. Even if we were convinced that Lloyd George realized *The Hidden Hand*'s full implications – and *that* evidence is not forthcoming – any attempt by the prime minister to interpose or chastise the film-makers might have given his detractors more fuel. There is no doubt, as my own essay in this volume indicates, that Bottomley approved of *The Hidden Hand*'s anti-Jewish message and condoned attacks on 'aliens', friendly or otherwise.

I would like to advance another theory, particularly after reading John Grigg's allegations that Lloyd George was an anti-Semite.[27] Is it not conceivable that the prime minister initially gave permission for the Elvey feature with little idea who ran the Ideal company and was only fully apprised when *John Bull* printed a list of executives and shareholders, and the names suggested the Jewish roots of all the company's principals? It seems highly probable that Lloyd George was far less worried by Bottomley's 'Hun' rantings than the more realistic vote-losing possibilities, on the election eve, of making a film for a Jewish concern in such xenophobic and racist times. The danger to his career from this ethnic association might have been uppermost in his mind, *whatever* his personal views on the Jews in 1918.

One should not underestimate Bottomley's capacity for duplicity. He would have been quite capable of a 'hidden agenda', especially if he knew of Lloyd George's anti-Semitic prejudice. In the guise of reporting individual changes of name by Ideal's allegedly 'Teutonic' shareholders and hinting at a potential for disloyalty, he may have intended principally to discomfort Lloyd George and/or his advisers by making them aware, however obliquely, of the Jewish connections. Their names, in many cases, were enough to indicate their roots (at least in the minds of prejudiced readers). The tone of *John Bull* articles in 1918 suggests that Bottomley would have had little compunction about harassing or targeting the Rowsons. At one point the magazine even printed a list of Russian Jews who had changed their name since 1914. The mere fact that no one spoke up against *The Hidden Hand*, despite its clear linking of the Rowsons to the plotline, hints at the fertile ground in which dog-in-the-manger xenophobes operated.

Bottomley certainly seems to have felt himself immune from reprisals. It is highly significant, in hindsight at least, that the Birmingham businessman Reuben Bigland, enraged by Bottomley's *John Bull* lottery scandal, felt the government had been deliberately protecting the magazine's editor in the early 1920s. Bigland, as one Bottomley biographer, Julian Symons, makes clear, embarked on a near-suicidal course to expose the MP as a fraud, printing scurrilous pamphlets of his own and circulating them personally in London and Cardiff, wearing a mask. It was Bigland who provoked Bottomley into the court action which led to his downfall.[28]

There appears to have been a conspiracy of silence after *The Life Story* was shelved. The principals (Elvey, Page et al.) *could* have signed some kind of agreement with the government that they would not breathe a word about the film's fate. Sidney Low, if we are to believe his biographer, was genuinely baffled by the film's demise and trailed around government departments seeking an explanation. It is passing strange, if such an agreement was not signed, that Elvey should remain so reticent in retrospect about a film which was clearly his most ambitious to date. After all, he told Gifford nearly fifty years later that the film was the most important of his career and 'one of the best films I made or shall ever make'. Yet in a trade-paper interview in January 1919, a week or two after his last known connection with the Lloyd George film, he ignored *The Life Story* altogether and opined that *Nelson* (inferior to the Lloyd George film by any criterion) was the kind of epic the British cinema had long needed.[29] Norman Page had significant roles in only seven or eight films – including three for Elvey – but the Lloyd George role was the consummate performance of his career and might have been his passport to Hollywood had the film been distributed by Carl Laemmle at Universal or any other of the companies which had expressed interest. Harry Rowson, as far as we know, confined his comments on *The Life Story*'s suppression to the memoirs deposited in the British Film Institute after his death.

The 'Mysterious History' section of this book concludes with my own article on British First World War propaganda movies in which I seek to place the Lloyd George film in the context, primarily, of domestic fiction production and of Elvey's considerable wartime contribution. I also try to give some brief insight into Ideal's contribution, the industrial climate, the preoccupations of the film-trade press, and the attitudes towards and role of the government's Information Ministry in that last year of the war.

The book's second section, on the Lloyd George movie's rediscovery and restoration opens with an article by the Wales archive's former education and outreach officer, Gwenan Owen, and WFTVA preservation officer John Reed, the man responsible – above all others – for restoring *The Life Story of David Lloyd George*. It details work on the rediscovered negative after it arrived in Aberystwyth, charting the problems of assembling and reordering the material – in consultation with professional historians – and explores the moral and ethical issues involved in seeking to keep faith with the director's assumed intentions and the chronology of Lloyd George's career. The article also explains the archive's decision to reintroduce out-take intertitles in the interests of clarity. The piece sheds light also on the archive's work in resolving the colourization issue by using modern laboratory methods to reproduce as far as possible Ideal's tinting and toning colour instructions to its own laboratory.

The Elvey film has only academic and historical value if it does not work with 1990s audiences and those into the next century. Fears that it would be seen as a mere anachronistic curio were allayed by reactions at the film's first preview screening in Pwllheli, north Wales, the world première in Cardiff – on 5 May 1996, the exact hundredth anniversary of the first projected screenings in Wales – and at two screenings of the film at the National Film Theatre in London and its single Pordenone performance on 15 October 1997.

The role of music in popularizing the movie in the present is explored in the article by John Hardy, whose specially commissioned score for the Lloyd George feature's Cardiff première was performed by an orchestra assembled for the occasion. Hardy reveals the technical problems in marrying, with great precision, the tempo of the music to the screen action as well as the obligations he felt to temper the film's uncritical tone with a nuanced score reflecting hindsight knowledge of Lloyd George's career and the divisive Versailles treaty which effectively scuppered any hopes of a permanent peace in Europe.

National Film Theatre pianist Neil Brand who has accompanied *The Life Story* live on at least nine occasions (including at Pwllheli, the NFT and Pordenone) writes of the particular challenges posed by the film's refusal to conform to the norms of narrative drama, and the often staccato rhythms inevitable in a film so concerned with chronology and the sequence of 'known' events. Brand's virtuosity and dexterity were also tested by the wartime battle scenes and the prolonged munitions factory-visit sequences in which Elvey proved an exemplar, and pioneer, of documentary-style veracity rather than a born dramatist of events. Brand writes emotionally of surrendering, to an extent, to the film's own intrinsic passion and momentum.

The feature's worth as a film *per se*, its narrative devices and its relevance as we approach the millennium are explored in part III, 'Screening Lloyd George'. Peter Stead considers the film in the context of other screen political biographies over the decades, particularly those of the Hollywood cinema. Nick Hiley, from a close study of *The Life Story*, extant newsreels and the remarkably detailed British Universities Film and Video Council-based newsreel database, offers a fascinating argument. His contention is that Maurice Elvey, in portraying the public life of Lloyd George, generally chose to reconstruct the formal style of news magazine or newsreel interviews (with their limitations on camera placement) rather than adopt a style more familiar from fictional representations. Hiley points out that Lloyd George was the first British prime minister whose image in newsreels was a significant part of his political identity – so Elvey felt impelled to re-create how Lloyd George 'looked and behaved in the newsreels'. A key part of that representation involved filming Lloyd George outside the studio, just as he was seen, for instance, on the screen at outdoor ceremonies or leaving and entering public buildings. This newsreel mode of presentation accorded with Elvey's professed preference for simulating the factual.

John Thompson writes on the film's highly unorthodox heavy reliance on, and deployment of, speeches and thought to trigger the action through flashbacks. After all, the concept of a silent film about a great orator is a curious one, as he points out. What late 1990s screenwriter would concentrate so shamelessly on his hero's speeches, he asks. Thompson also raises, interestingly, the question of what we, the modern audience, might remember of Lloyd George's deeds now. There are analogies we might make, he says, with Britain's welfare state and the Attlee era, had the Liberals' 'near-total mid-century eclipse' not fostered what he describes as 'our collective amnesia'. Thompson examines scenes involving the young Lloyd George, in which the actions of Lloyd George as adult are 'not presented but prefigured'. We are privy to glimpses of a future already known to the audience but not to the film's putative national leader and, as Thompson reminds us, the point of the film's emphasis on David's childhood games of the Franco-Prussian war is 'prospective rather than retrospective'. The audience of 1918-19 was supposed to make the connection with the current conflict and, by implication, hope that in the Great War, in contrast to 1870, the German arms would 'sustain a crushing defeat'.

The American early cinema expert and theorist Tom Gunning (who has Welsh roots) expressed fascination in Pordenone both with Elvey's use of what he termed 'the future inevitable' in scenes such as the transformation from David/Goliath to Lloyd George/Kaiser and with the admittedly problematic way Elvey often seemed wilfully to spurn innate dramatic possibilities. Gunning cited, for instance, Elvey's 'failing', or unwillingness, to follow through on the church and school recriminations against the youthful Lloyd George for refusing to say his catechism. Like Thompson, Gunning was also clearly intrigued by Elvey's insistence on revealing Lloyd George's worth almost entirely through his parliamentary acts, or key speeches. *The Life Story* rejects the usual biopic's exploration of the 'cult of personality' in which often the hero or heroine is revealed through family/domestic situations. There is little emphasis on Lloyd George's private life, perhaps not surprising given his domestic situation. 'In this film', said Gunning, 'Lloyd George *is* his legislation.'[30]

In his article, Thompson also considers the difficulties the film presents in implying the prime minister's value and deeds through his speeches, rather than action (what might be termed an anti-cinematic stance) and he defines the film's achievements and problems in the context of André Bazin's theories in opening up the discourse on the photographic image – how it captures or fails to capture reality and 'overcomes mortality' (as *The Life Story* does by presenting Norman Page as surrogate Lloyd George). Thompson uses Bazinian theory as a springboard for his explorations of how Low and Elvey tried to 'open up' their screen biography or 'life-in-words'. He also cites the writings of David McDougall in his reflections on the weight of memory – and the film's 'efforts to approximate the process by which the mind represents experiences to itself'. Thompson talks of the contradictions in photographing 'thought and speech . . . the general and conceptual rather than the existent' and the efforts Low and Elvey make to overcome the problems. He also examines the film's use of metaphor and considers the rupture in the time continuum of Lloyd George's life with the David vs. Goliath/adult Lloyd George vs. Kaiser analogies.

Roberta Pearson considers *The Life Story* in relation to early screen history, and the cult of the biopic developed in later years. The film, she concludes, is 'Janus-faced', looking both backwards and forwards 'to a genre not yet invented'. In a combative essay, she acknowledges that some sequences seemed, at her first viewing, 'astonishing in the context of a war-weakened British film industry already coming under the domination of Hollywood', and she concedes that the 'film does history on a grand, spectacle-intensive scale' with 'vast crowds of extras' and 'amazing' location work. Yet she finds that, compared with Griffith's epics of the 1910s or 'even more modest features', it is formally retrograde in some respects. She compares its devices to early modes of representation in biographical material and its style and iconography to Edison and Vitagraph screen biographies, and turn-of-the-century cinema Passion Plays.

Pearson also discusses the film's pronounced focus on key events in Lloyd George's life and stresses the movie's lacunae – the comparative absence of narrative action and any 'psychologization' of the politician. She also highlights the film's dependency on intertextual references (with conventional narrative information elided in deference to a contemporary audience's presumed familiarity with Lloyd George's career). The film relies on its audience's prior knowledge, but some frames of reference available to the 1918 audience inevitably elude spectators today, Pearson points out. The striking scene when the poor materialize out of the wall, liberated by the Old Age Pensions Bill, works 'quite well' for a 1990s audience, while other attempts are less successful, and the author assesses the limitations of intertitles in conveying emotion at certain points in the narrative.

This volume's appendices include extracts from Elvey's *Griffithiana* interview, profiles of the chief players in the Lloyd George film drama, together with the film's credits, and brief notes on the Ideal company and its studios and a synopsis of the film (adapted from the official published programme produced by the Wales Film and Television Archive for its first screenings in 1996).

Clearly, *The Life Story of David Lloyd George*, whatever its shortcomings or problematic elements, offers us not merely a mystery which may be decades in the solving but, more pragmatically, the chance we had scarcely expected after its many years in limbo, to see (and assess) how one significant company planned to represent the politician to audiences at the time. We can also compare the 'laundered' view of Lloyd George here with television versions made after the politician's death – such works as John Hefin's nine-part 1981 BBC *Life and Times of David Lloyd George*. It remains intriguing today to reflect on the apparent fascination of film-makers *in silent days* with the charisma of Lloyd George, a man known to the world mainly through his oratory but denied a voice by the limitations of the medium. Before talkies Lloyd George was always in huge demand, and he figured in no fewer than fifty of just over 400 *Topical Budget* newsreel items relating to Wales and the Welsh.[31] Elvey's screen hagiography can also be compared with Lloyd George's own war memoirs and the various biographies, notably the three-part chronicle of his life by John Grigg.[32]

As we have suggested, *The Life Story* also gives film historians and enthusiasts a compelling reason to revisit and reassess the work of

Maurice Elvey, and to begin to recover from near-oblivion the British silent cinema of the 1910s and 1920s – and those films which have not been preserved on acetate and/or have no viewing copies. British cinema has lacked the kind of detailed overview provided by Eileen Bowser and Charles Musser et al. in the groundbreaking and monumental History of the American Cinema series.[33] The Lloyd George film's rediscovery and its merits remind us that we should be wary of, and adopt a much more rigorous attitude towards, the judgements of previous generations. We must also be less prone to write off directors on the basis merely of extant films which often comprise a slim proportion of their *œuvre*. It is time now to do some honest digging of our own.

Notes

[1] For information on Elvey see Denis Gifford's article 'The Early Memoirs of Maurice Elvey' in the film-history journal *Griffithiana* (La Cineteca del Friuli/Le Giornate del Cinema Muto), 60–1 (October 1997), 76–125; Linda Wood (ed.), *The Commercial Imperative in the British Film Industry: Maurice Elvey, a Case Study* (British Film Institute, 1987). Graham Cutts (1885–1958), is best known for *The Rat* (1925) and *Woman to Woman* (1923).

[2] Barry Salt, *Film Style and Technology: History and Analysis* (Starword, 1992 edn); Kevin Brownlow, *Behind the Mask of Innocence: Social Problem Films of the Silent Era* (Jonathan Cape, 1991).

[3] An estimated 80 per cent of all silent films are lost – and very little 1918 material survives. The only 1918 'British' feature films listed in Denis Gifford's *British Film Catalogue 1895–1985* which survive in their entirety are *The Life Story of David Lloyd George* and the Film Company of Ireland's *Knocknagow* (director Fred O'Donovan). D. W. Griffith's *Hearts of the World*, another survivor listed, was, essentially, an American co-production with Britain's War Office Committee. Elvey's extant *Nelson* was made in 1918 but released in 1919.

[4] See in particular John Barnes's 'The Beginnings of the Cinema in England 1894–1901' series, five volumes, starting with *The Beginnings of the Cinema in England* (David and Charles, 1986). The next three volumes (*The Rise of the Cinema in Great Britain: Jubilee Year 1897, Pioneers of the British Film: The Rise of the Photoplay 1898*, and *Filming the Boer War*) were all published by the Bishopsgate Press, between 1988 and 1992.

[5] Burch, *Life to Those Shadows* (British Film Institute, 1990) and *In and Out of Synch: The Awakening of the Cine-Dreamer* (Scolar Press, 1991).

[6] Low, 'The History of the British Film' series (Allen & Unwin). The first four volumes were published between 1948 and 1971.

[7] Elvey interviewed by Ralph Bond, London, 1 October 1963, for BECTU History Project (tape at BFI Library, London); Linda Wood, op. cit.; *Griffithiana*, 60–1, October 1997.

[8] *Kinematograph Weekly*, 3 October 1918.

[9] Memoir of Harry Rowson, and Rowson special collection, both in BFI library, and Sarah Street, article from the *Historical Journal of Film, Radio and Television* reprinted in this volume.

[10] For example, in films such as *Ypres* (1925) and *Mons* (1926).

[11] Elvey interviewed by Ralph Bond, London, 1 October 1963, for BECTU History Project (tape at BFI Library, London).

[12] See Riefenstahl's *Triumph of the Will* (1934) and *Olympische Spiele* (1936).

[13] *Griffithiana*, 60–1 (October 1997); Wood, op. cit.

[14] The publicity was crystallized in an article by the film's agent, S. Gilbert, 'The National Aspect of the Lloyd George Film', *Kinematograph Weekly*, 3 October 1918.

[15] *Kinematograph Weekly*, 17 October 1918.

[16] In his memoir Harry Rowson (b. 1875) says his father arrived in Manchester from Russia. Rowson grew up in the Hebrew community in Manchester. As a young man he went to New York and there sold celluloid as scrap. Later he sold film and set up the Ideal business as a renter in London in 1911 with a chemist named Kay as partner.

[17] Street, op. cit.

[18] Ibid.

[19] See article, 'Buttonholing the Cabinet', *Bioscope*, 14 September 1916, p.1022 for a fascinating critique of the Hepworth interviews. The NFA previously held only a few of the thirty-six interviews which were in the Lloyd George collection in their entirety.

[20] Julian Symons, *Horatio Bottomley* (Cresset Press, 1955).

[21] *Kinematograph Weekly*, 15 August, 5 and 12 December 1918.

[22] Hansard, 5th series, 106, War Aims Committee entry, 13 May 1918.

[23] Desmond Chapman-Huston, *The Lost Historian: Sidney Low 1857–1932* (Murray, 1936).

[24] The articles were both written by a Captain Harold Spencer though purporting to be the work of Pemberton Billing. Pemberton Billing was sued by Maud Allan – among those referred to in the *Imperialist*, following her appearance in a controversial production of Oscar Wilde's *Salome* – but won the case. See author's notes in Pat Barker, *The Eye in the Door* (Viking, 1993/Penguin Books, 1994), 278–80. Pemberton Billing himself asked parliamentary questions about aliens (Hansard, 5th series, 105, 15 April 1918).

[25] *Bioscope*, 28 September 1916; *Kinematograph Weekly*, 7 November 1918. NFA database material on print in the Archive. I am indebted to Luke McKernan for this material. Harry Rowson was still calling himself Rosenbaum in 1915, as trade press reports confirm.

[26] *Kinematograph Weekly*, 7, 14 and 21 November 1918. Bottomley regained South Hackney at the December 1918 election, as an independent beating the coalition Liberal candidate, Henri – but he did not represent the film trade in any sense.

[27] See John Grigg, *The Young Lloyd George* (Eyre Methuen, 1973), 260, and Peter Rowland, *Lloyd George* (Barrie and Jenkins, 1975), 140–1. Grigg proposes that, at the turn of the century, Lloyd George respected the Boers but had nothing but contempt for the Uitlanders ('outsiders' who flooded the Transvaal, mainly to mine for gold), owing 'in large part to his anti-Semitism'. Grigg cites a Lloyd George speech in Carmarthen in 1899 when he said: 'The people we are fighting for, those Uitlanders are German Jews – 15,000 to 20,000 of them. Pah! – fighting for men of that type.'

[28] Symons, op. cit.

[29] Chapman-Huston, op. cit.

[30] Conversation with the author, 18 October 1997.

[31] Figures supplied by Nick Hiley of the British Universities Film and Video Council. Luke McKernan's *Topical Budget* (British Film Institute, 1992) also touches on Lloyd George's appeal.

[32] Grigg's first three volumes are *The Young Lloyd George: The People's Champion 1902–1911*, and *From Peace to War 1912–1916* (Eyre Methuen, 1973–85; paperback edn, HarperCollins, 1997). There are two other projected volumes – one (due in 1999) taking Lloyd George's career to 1919, the other embracing the rest of his life. Both will be published by HarperCollins.

[33] The first three volumes of the series (published by Charles Scribner's Sons, New York) embraced the silent-film period. They were Charles Musser, *The Emergence of Cinema: The American Screen to 1907*, Eileen Bowser, *The Transformation of Cinema 1907–1915* and Richard Koszarski, *An Evening's Entertainment: The Age of the Silent Feature Film 1915–1928*.

PART I

A Mysterious History

*T*he *Life Story of Lloyd George* is just one – albeit highly distinctive – example of a silent film which might have been consigned forever to the dustbin of celluloid history. With so many silent movies either destroyed or quietly decaying in sheds or lofts around the world, there is a serious danger that, but for the work of dedicated film researchers and archivists, future generations may have little access to this crucial period of the cinema's development.

This section starts with Sarah Street's article from 1987 which began to investigate what happened to a film about Lloyd George which disappeared in 1919 under mysterious circumstances. Street's research into British silent cinema – conducted when she was an archivist of Oxford's Bodleian Library – led her to the unpublished memoir of Harry Rowson, co-founder of Ideal, and the extract which she includes in her article is indicative of the wealth of information about pre-sound cinema which is waiting to be uncovered. That said, even the author must have been surprised by the chance to view the film in question when it surfaced a few years later, something Street reflects on in her 'Postscript' which she wrote for this volume.

John Grigg's contribution could easily have found a home in Part III, 'Screening Lloyd George', as he concerns himself largely with the portrait the film paints of the 'Welsh Wizard'. The article is included here, however, as Grigg goes on to speculate why *The Life Story* may have been suppressed. Arguably there are few people in a better position to make such educated guesses than Lloyd George's biographer.

'A Mysterious History' concludes with David Berry's article placing *The Life Story* in the context of British wartime film production. Basing his work principally on exhaustive reference to periodicals of the time, Berry shows that it is possible to establish a detailed picture of the cinema's social significance even without access to many of the movies themselves. In their own way, then, each of the articles in this section demonstrates both the necessity and the potential of research into silent cinema while, along the way, helping us to render the fate of *The Life Story of David Lloyd George* just a little less mysterious.

S.H.

1

*The Memoir of Harry Rowson: David Lloyd George, MP – **The Man who Saved the Empire** (1918)*

SARAH STREET

The extract below tells the strange tale of a film that was made, was never shown and is now lost. Harry Rowson's unpublished memoir[1] reveals that in 1918 Ideal Films produced a picture about the life of Lloyd George that never reached the cinema screens. The mysterious circumstances surrounding its 'suppression' have been difficult to follow-up. The major sources of potential documentation have yielded surprisingly little about the incident,[2] nor have I been able to trace a copy of the film.[3] The following introduction to Rowson's memoir together with explanatory notes to the document attempt to piece together some of the clues and shed light on the remaining questions about *The Man who Saved the Empire*.

Harry Rowson was born in Manchester in 1875 and died in London in 1951. In the early 1900s he went to America with Dr Emanuel Lasker, the German world chess champion, to assist in running a chess magazine. It was in the United States that Rowson started to deal in films for scrap, soon realising that there was more money to be made from exhibiting films. When he returned to Manchester Rowson decided to establish the Ideal film renting company in 1911. Four years later the company branched out into production, headed by Simon Rowson[4] and Fred Paul. Ideal's first productions were adaptions of plays, using Elstree and later Twickenham Studios. Maurice Elvey directed the majority of Ideal's pictures and Eliot Stannard was their key scenario author.[5]

The scenario of the Lloyd George film was written by Sir Sidney Low who had an interest in film and was an early advocate of a statutory quota for British films. When he took on the Lloyd George project Low was a member of Northcliffe's Propaganda Committee for Enemy Countries, a post from which he soon resigned because of pressure of work. Low went to north Wales to research his subject and produced a script in seven weeks. Maurice Elvey was director, Lloyd George was played by Norman Page and Megan by Alma Reville, who later married Alfred Hitchcock.

News of the forthcoming film caused considerable excitement in the trade press and Ideal had many inquiries about when it would be released. S. Gilbert, at that time one of the principal publicity agents in the film industry, was pushing the film energetically through his hiring agents before Low had started to write his scenario. Gilbert continued to report on the film's progress and when filming was almost completed wrote that 'the Lloyd George picture will give a new dignity to the picture

6. Harry Rowson, executive and co-founder of the Ideal Company. He saw the Lloyd George feature as a coup which could change the face of the British film industry.

palaces. It will be useful to the Nation as a chapter of vivid history.'[6] Particular attention was paid to the pursuit of accuracy and realism. Simon Rowson believed that 'all political allusions should be presented in a simple and knowledgeable way'.[7] In May it was reported that furniture and other items from Lloyd George's old house in Criccieth had been filmed, his birth certificate had been reproduced and Lloyd George's brother William and his election agent had given Ideal valuable assistance. *Kinematograph Weekly* ran an eight-week advertising spread on the film – each week revealing a new aspect of its contents. Apparently the film included a scene depicting the riot in Birmingham in December 1901 when Lloyd George was accused of being pro-Boer.[8] At £20,000, the film was supposed to have cost more than most British pictures at that time, and was insured for £197,000 against various contingencies, for example if Lloyd George's popularity declined in the event of him failing to remain prime minister until the end of 1918.[9]

Rowson's memoir tells of how on 5 October 1918 Mr Elias,[10] managing director of the publishing firm Odhams, showed the Rowson brothers an article attacking Ideal in *John Bull*,[11] edited by Horatio Bottomley[12] but published by Odhams.[13] Elias was embarrassed because Odhams also published *Kinematograph Weekly*, the trade paper that had run the advertising campaign for *The Man who Saved the Empire*. *John Bull* accused Ideal of being a German-constituted company with no right to produce a film about Lloyd George. The Rowsons had changed their name from Rosenbaum in the war, and this had presumably given Bottomley the idea of attacking Ideal. Bottomley's article was a typical example of the jingoism and virulent anti-Germanism frequently found in the pages of *John Bull*. Bottomley had called for a vendetta against all 'Huns' in Britain, naturalized or not.[14] After the attack on Ideal the company began proceedings against the magazine for libel.

The next stage in the saga was to have profound repercussions on the fate of *The Man who Saved the Empire*. According to Rowson, Captain Guest[15] informed Ideal that Lloyd George did not want the film to be released, claiming that the decision had nothing to do with the article in *John Bull*.[16] Of course Ideal was not compelled to halt the picture's release, but Rowson hinted that the likely result of exhibiting *The Man who Saved the Empire* in such delicate circumstances would be an embarrassing 'world scandal'. Sir Sidney Low's diary, however, claims that the film was suppressed by the Home Office (because of Lloyd George's objections), at the instigation of Lord Milner and Sir Basil Thomson, assistant commissioner of the Metropolitan Police. At the end of November 1918 Low was informed that the home secretary disapproved of the picture and Lloyd George was 'determined that the film should not be produced'. In the event Low's only consolation was a private viewing of the film at the studio. He bitterly regretted the 'short-sighted view' taken by the 'bureaucrats' over the whole affair.[17] Rowson's memoir does not mention the alleged intervention of the Home Office, nor does it provide a convincing explanation of exactly why the film was not released. It was all set to do well in America, and Carl Laemmle of Universal was anxious to see the film and market it in the States. The £20,000 obtained by Ideal in the financial settlement of January 1919 must have been little compensation for the loss of potentially high box-office receipts.

Even though it deepens rather than solves the mystery, there is an interesting postscript to this intriguing story. At the end of the extract from the memoir directly dealing with the story of *The Man who Saved the Empire* Rowson attached correspondence between himself and A. J. Sylvester, Lloyd George's private secretary, dated 1945. A second film of the life of Lloyd George was planned but this time never produced, let alone exhibited. There are several questions that remain unanswered: how much did Lloyd George know or care about the first film? Was

Lloyd George afraid that Bottomley might cease to support him in the pages of *John Bull* if he allowed the film to go ahead? What was the extent of Home Office intervention?

The full story may never be revealed but this extract from Rowsons's memoir provides us with an intriguing account of how a film company tried to exploit interest in a contemporary political figure but was thwarted, apparently by the intervention of another powerful medium of persuasion – the press.

*   *   *   *   *

Extract from the Memoir of Harry Rowson

Suddenly it was discovered that pictures of stark reality and the horror of war could be exceptionally attractive in cinemas, even bring many new patrons.

[Some films] issued under the aegis of The Canadian Ministry of Information, under the control of Lord Beaverbrook, were so sensationally successful that hundreds of cinemas, over every part of the country, showed them twice and three times as often and as long as was their usual practice, smashing and shattering all past records.

Somehow, pictures like these continually brought to the front the cause of the war itself – the just cause – and with that, a little consolation to the widows, the orphans, the fathers and mothers – whose losses were irretrievable.

When, therefore, after I had 'joined up', my brother [Simon] suggested the making of a picture showing the origin of the war, itself, and its justice, which was my belief – and practically the whole country's – from the day Belgium was invaded, I agreed immediately.

Always involved in the consideration of topical subjects is what happens in the event – in this case – of the war being over before the picture was out. Every member of 'The Ideal' knew that was involved, each of us understood that what happened to our films or us was unimportant when considering the end of the war.

I agreed to the suggestion immediately that 'Ideal' should prepare a picture on the cause of the war and overjoyed when I learned that Winston Churchill would write a story on the 'origin of the war', for I was certain that besides being accurate – it would also be interesting.

Special Engagement of Winston Churchill
by A. Wiener, M.A., Cambridge

Here is the story of what happened, told by another historian who was to
assist him.

In January 1916, after the resignation of Mr Asquith (later Lord Oxford
and Asquith) from the premiership, the 'Ideal' had decided on making
a film to demonstrate the causes of the war, and had engaged the
Rt Hon. Winston Churchill – who had followed his leader into the
political wilderness – to write the story. Though no longer a member of
the Government, he was still a busy man, and asked for someone to
'devil' for him, dig out the relevant facts of international relations from
1870 to 1914 that could be illustrated pictorially. Accordingly I was
recommended to Mr Churchill by Simon Rowson, who arranged an
interview for me.

On the day and at the time arranged, I presented myself at
Mr Churchill's house. I then heard what Mr Churchill had to say,
offered my own suggestions, and we agreed upon the outline of the
story that Mr Churchill would write from the facts I submitted. Mr
Churchill then showed me around his library, where we had had a
preliminary discussion, and then arranged that as soon as I had
collected sufficient material I should bring it to him. This occasioned
two further interviews at Mr Churchill's house.

I had then completed my task and was asked by the 'Ideal' to meet
their scenario writer, Eliot Stannard and give him an idea of what the
subject matter of the story was . . . But when Mr Churchill returned to
the Government as a member of Lloyd George's Cabinet he naturally
could not give any time to writing a film story, and 'Ideal' dropped the
whole proposition, as provided for in the very beginning of the
negotiations.

The Man who Won the War

Having aimed so high when we approached Winston Churchill; now we
aimed higher.

Most readers can carry their minds back to the end of the last war, to
the day after it was over. Imagine cinemas showing a picture of the Life
of Winston Churchill, full of incidents in which he played big and little
parts. Then imagine the 'run' on cinemas from a grateful people, before

disillusionment and new factors have had time to creep in, people relieved from the anxiety which pervaded every home in the country, people who endured courageously and were fortified by the belief that they were all the time fighting, struggling and making sacrifices to be able ultimately to control their own destinies and realise all those freedoms which, for hundreds of years Britishers have fought and have been determined to maintain. Fantastic, isn't it, even to suggest such a picture at such a time? Yet, that is what we were ready to show at the end of the Great War, when armistice was declared on 11 November 1918.

Yes, it was ready, but never shown!

Such a story must be told from the beginning.

While working for the Ministry of Information, whose function was to issue propaganda, which then meant desirable news, after hearing what had happened to our Winston Churchill story, I suddenly got the idea that the life of Lloyd George, our Prime Minister, contained unlimited material for a film story, a story which had been told thousands of times in fiction. This, however, would be a real-life story of a poor boy who made good, and became the Prime Minister of this country and the most important man in the world.

I had been a follower of his all my life, and thought that showing such a film to the country and the outside world would enable everybody to understand the architect of the Social Legislation which he steered through Parliament and laid the foundation and basis for a new standard of living. It would be well worth showing. This should not be misconstrued as introducing party politics. I am writing of something which took place forty years ago. Those of us who have been through the two wars might well look upon this now, as history.

When this idea reached my colleagues, members of all parties, one after another, I was somewhat astonished to learn of their enthusiasm for it.

From now on, this became completely my brother's affair, for it was right up his street.

The first step was to 'sound' Lloyd George; for, without his consent, we could not possibly begin. My brother was still in close contact with the Unionist Party and its members; among them being Balfour, Bonar Law and Lord Beaverbrook. Long standing differences between them and Lloyd George were cast aside completely; winning the war was their only consideration, and anything towards achieving it had their unequivocal support.

Everybody concerned must have acquiesced to the proposal, including, of course, Lloyd George, because my brother arranged for Sir Sidney Low, political-historical journalist, to go to North Wales, fortified with the necessary letters of introduction which enabled him to scour the district where Lloyd George was born, and had spent his earliest years, and to discuss him with whomsoever he desired.

Lloyd George's uncle, the blacksmith, who had reared David Lloyd George, became Sir Sidney's guide. When he returned, after about a month, he brought with him an outline of the early life of Lloyd George, containing material suitable for cinema audiences which my brother had particularly requested him to collect.

This was submitted to 'somebody' [Captain Guest] who approved it. We then made the following announcement:

> The Man Who Saved The Empire
> The Life Story of
> David Lloyd George,
> specially written by Sir Sidney Low,
> Lecturer on Imperial and Colonial
> History, King's College, London University

The same 'somebody' – I really don't know who it was – made arrangements for our banker to provide us with a sufficient overdraft to finance the production of the picture, so that we had less financial worry than with any we had ever made. We, in return, undertook that nothing would be spared to make it worthy of the subject.

There was no commercial arrangement of any kind, on a par with that 'bill' which was handed over to me a few years before. It was to be our picture and our responsibility. I didn't have any idea who was the man behind the scenes and I never enquired; but I can't help thinking that my brother knew.

We were now in the fourth year of the war. Periodically, every able bodied man under 40 was 'called up', and the labour position was very difficult. We therefore decided to put everything else aside, and concentrate on this one picture.

The scenario contained all the well-known highlights in Lloyd George's career. There was the house in which he was born; the school in which he assimilated 'the three R's'; his first successful fight in the Courts, defending the people's rights; his election as Member for

7. A typical intertitle from *The Life Story of David Lloyd George*, with an Ideal logo beneath the text.

Caernarvon, and his entry into Parliament at the age of 24. There was his first meeting with Gladstone, in the House of Commons in 1892; his opposition to the Boer War; his escape, disguised as a policeman, from Birmingham Town Hall, and his great opposition to Joseph Chamberlain, after the [Boer] war, against his proposals for Tariff Reform. When Asquith became Prime Minister in 1906 Lloyd George became a Member of the Cabinet and Chancellor of the Exchequer. There was the story of his tremendous fight in the House of Commons for that Social Legislation which changed the whole basis and standard of living in this country.

Always there was his pacifism – until the day Germany entered Belgium. John Morley, John Burns and others resigned from the Government because they couldn't eat their own words, and were too old to turn over a new leaf. But Lloyd George was transformed, finally to be recognised as The Man Who Won The War.

Who was to direct this Life of Lloyd George? We invited Maurice Elvey, who made *Florence Nightingale*, our first picture. Of course he was most enthusiastic to do this, making it clear that 'terms' were a secondary consideration.

The theatrical profession was searched for the man to enact the part. This was finally offered to that grand West End actor, Norman Page, who had the big advantage of being built on Lloyd George lines.

From the day Norman Page was engaged, he visited the House of Commons every day Lloyd George was there, and followed him about, observing and taking notes of his mannerisms.

Whether Lloyd George knew it or not, he was followed by Elvey and two or three cameramen to the 1918 Eisteddfod, where with Megan and that big dog, they were all photographed amid scenes of enthusiasm such as even the Eisteddfod had never seen or heard before.

Almost quite naturally, some sections of the Press and members of the House of Commons were suspicious of the Government regarding this picture, as this quotation out of a trade paper indicates:

[*Kinematograph Weekly*, 15 August 1918, p. 58]

The Premier Film

The Ministry of Information is having a bad time of it in the House, and the Press their digs, and it is the film that is being blamed, as usual. This time they have hit upon the *Lloyd George* picture as the butt. The film being entitled *The Man who Served the Empire* [*sic*].

Mr Leif Jones, during the debate in the House on the Ministry suggested that Lord Beaverbrook having control of the film could put in any name he wished such as Lloyd George, Admiral Beatty or Lord Beaverbrook . . . Of course he could, Mr Jones, only that the story of the film happens to be the story of Lloyd George and you would be up against difficulties in trying to fit it into somebody else's life history. Try again, Mr Jones.

While the picture was in production the interest in it became intense. Enquiries came from every part of the world. Nearly every representative of the big American companies in Wardour Street had approached us in regard to purchasing it. When could they see it?

The end of the war was in sight . . .

'Serials' were at the height of their popularity. Exhibitors' interest in the Life of Lloyd George was so great that many who were afraid they would be cut out from showing it at all, actually suggested that we should issue it in parts on what amounted to the defunct 'open' market system. Smaller cinemas would then have a better chance of showing it earlier, as with newsreels. Instead of having one big week when showing it all at one time, they could have six or more weeks.

This rather interested us, both from the financial and the public's point of view. We asked our branch managers for their estimates of our receipts if it should be issued in six parts or as a whole. It was clear that it would have yielded more as a serial, when it could have been booked in ninety per cent of the cinemas of the country and in all the best...

The picture, when finished, exceeded every expectation. Elvey excelled himself. Lloyd George came to life in the impersonation by Norman Page. The picture had everything to be expected from a 'boy makes good' story –

8. Horatio Bottomley, knave and *bon viveur*. His article led Ideal to take court action.

plenty of drama and humour. Tears would be plentiful, but relieved by laughs.

It didn't take us long to decide how we were going to put it out. If serials would have realised ten times as much, not one of us would have been willing to change the effect of seeing it as a whole, the cumulative reaction of seeing a poor little boy growing up to become the Prime Minister of this country, merely for the sake of better returns.

On 5 October 1918 a message was sent to Wardour Street, requesting my brother and I to see Mr Elias (later Lord Southwood), Managing Director of Odham's, as early as possible, in his office. There was also a copy of *John Bull* on my desk, published by Odham's and edited by Horatio Bottomley.

I am telling this story in full, otherwise it might be thought that I am hiding something.

5 October 1918, *John Bull* [vol. 24, no. 644]

Headlines: 'The Kaiser Caving In.
    The Lessons of the War – Britain for the British.
    The Prime Minister film'. [See appendix.]

Here, again, it may be that each of these persons – despite the remarkable Teutonic flavour of their original patronymics – is a thoroughly loyal British subject, but the fact remains that, by some blood affinity, they were all drawn together into a trade organisation in competition with firms of a truer All British ring. And the irony of it is that one of the Rosenbaums was for some time a leading light of the Tariff Reform League – you see, I am assuming for the moment that Mr Lloyd George is still a Free Trader; he is, too, I believe, connected with the War Topical Budget, whilst either he, or his brother, has been given a commission in the Army! [When I was in the Army I was offered a commission, but I asked to be excused (Harry Rowson).] Well, I have no desire to labour this point; but I do say that the composition of the Company, is an object lesson for the business community of the country. In the same way, I do not suggest that the Company is directly responsible for all the details incidental to the production of the film. Otherwise I should ask the Director to explain the facts described in a Statutory Declaration of one John Dwyer, of 40, Ravensbourne Road, Catford, now before me. Here it is:

I, John Dwyer, of 40, Ravensbourne Road, Catford, do hereby declare and say as follows: – I am and have been for some years an actor and have lately been employed as one of the 'crowd' in one of the scenes of the proposed Life of Lloyd George film, viz. the scene inside the Town Hall, Birmingham. The film is being produced by the Ideal Film Co., and I got the job in the following manner. When not otherwise engaged I called at the office of the Elite Film Actors' Bureau – of which I am informed a Mr Warren is the Manager – of Whitcomb Court, Leicester Square, and on this occasion I was taken on as before stated. There would seem to have been a crowd of about 450, including men who took the part of soldiers and sailors. I noticed on this occasion, and have noticed on other occasions when I have taken part in a crowd of supernumeraries, that there were many foreigners of various sorts – mostly so-called Scandinavians – and I particularly noticed on this occasion a little clique of 5 or 6 men talking together previous to going into the studio where the scene was filmed. These were among those who were taking the parts of soldiers and sailors. They wore various naval and military uniforms, and my attention was called, apart from the fact that they were talking in a foreign language, to the fact that one of them was wearing the uniform of my old Regiment, the Royal West Kents. I questioned one of the men, and he admitted to my surprise that he was a German, and I replied that if I thought he meant it, I would punch his head. The man thereupon retracted what he said and declared he was a Dane.

Well, I know those Danes – and so do you. but I respectfully direct the attention of Messrs. Rowson to the matter. Meanwhile, I must assume that Britishers were not available – discharged soldiers, for instance. It is all very puzzling.

The rest alleging corruption of members of the Government 'all high up' and finishing with that politicians don't care a hang for the country so long as money comes into party funds, that's all that matters. 'Bring your money – and no questions asked – is the order of the day . . .' which then pointed out that because the directors of 'Ideal' had changed their names by deed poll the Lloyd George Film ought to be stopped . . .

When we saw Elias he was such a picture of abject misery, we couldn't help being sorry for him. He said, 'I suppose you have seen *John Bull* . . . I heard about it too late to stop it . . . Whatever steps you take against us, I won't blame you.' We believed what he said and went straight to our solicitors, who immediately began proceedings against *John Bull* for libel and slander. We then published as an advertisement the following letter to the editors of the Trade Press:

Dear Sir,
    With reference to the attack made upon this firm in the columns of *John Bull* last Wednesday, we beg to inform you that we have issued a Writ for libel against the proprietors and publishers of that Journal.
    We beg to remain,
    Yours faithfully,
    The Ideal Film Renting Co. Ltd.

In *The Cinema* of 10 October the following appeared.

Writ for Libel Issued.
    Constitution of the Company.

In the last issue of *John Bull* a very serious attack, conveying most unpleasant inferences, was made upon the Ideal Film Renting Co. Ltd., in connection with the picture it has under production, depicting the remarkable career of the present Prime Minister of England, Lloyd George. Few films have aroused such general interest, and it might well have been imagined that such a subject, valuable from more than one standpoint, would have been spared even the most veiled criticism, and that for those who had been so enterprising as to prepare it for the screen, there would have been nothing but praise. Having regard to the letter we publish below, we must refrain from further comment. It is sufficient for the present to emphasise the very high reputation Ideal enjoys in the cinema world. Since its foundation the firm has presented to the screen many notable and excellent productions, and its business relations with the Trade generally have always been cordial and honorable.

The attack in the article to which we refer was primarily based upon the constitution of the Company. Adverse comment was made upon the names of certain of the directors, the innuendo conveyed being that they were apparently of German origin. In view of this, it will be of interest to publish the following particulars of the directors and shareholders of the Company:

H. Rowson. Born and educated in England.

Jane Bernstein. Born and educated in England. She has two sons, both in the Army, one of whom has been wounded two or three times, and now holds a Captaincy. Formerly he was Ideal's manager at Leeds, and left there at the outbreak of war to join up.

S. Gilbert. Born in England and educated at University College, London. Graduate B.A., London University.

A. Gardner, wife of T. Gardner, both born in England. T. Gardner, who had previously fought in the Boer War, joined up during the present war, and has since died.

E. Rowson, wife of S. Rowson. Born and educated in England.

Hilda Jacobson. Born and educated in England. Sister of the Rowsons.

S. Rowson. Born and educated in England. Graduate M.Sc. Victoria University, now Manchester University.

J. Wilmot. Born and educated in Glasgow, nephew of S. Rowson.

D. Rowson. Born and educated in England. Fell in action in France October 1916.

A. M. Kay. Born and educated in England. Son in the Army.

Rose Brodson. Born and educated in England. Sister-in-law of S. Rowson.

Nathan Brodson. Born in Russia. Mr. and Mrs. Brodson have four sons, all in the Army. One, who fell in Gallipoli, was mobilised with his

Territorial unit at the outbreak of war, and Mr. and Mrs. Brodson are the successors to his shares.

Leslie Rowson. Born and educated in England. Son of S. Rowson.

Immediately this letter appeared, proceedings were taken against the paper and ourselves by the solicitors for *John Bull* for Contempt of Court, as an action was already taken against them and therefore all *The Cinema's* comments were alleged to be *sub judice*.

So far as we were concerned, the Court decided that, even if *sub judice*, a trading company like ours had every right to reply to libel, and dismissed the application.

So far as our business was concerned, it disappeared completely. But after these preliminary proceedings, it began coming back.

Within a very few days, my brother was asked to see the same 'somebody', who told him that Lloyd George didn't want us to issue the picture, and then that *John Bull* had nothing to do with that!

It was hinted, however, that friends of Lloyd George, who didn't like 'pictures' at any price, had persuaded him that the status of cinemas would be so enhanced if the film were shown that the whole country would be in danger.

Admittedly, even Lloyd George had no legal way of stopping it, but we would be indemnified.

We were now confronted with an entirely new aspect. If Lloyd George, Who Had Just Won the War, merely let it be known publicly that he didn't want the picture to be shown, who would have booked it in this country? From everybody, to nobody.

But, so far as America was concerned, especially after it was banned, its value was doubled.

Lloyd George was the prototype of Abraham Lincoln, each small town lawyers, one becoming the Prime Minister of this country, the other President of the U.S.A.

My Four Years in Germany, first a book, written by U.S.A. Ambassador Gerard, then a play, had proved to be such a big success that everybody in the film trade, there as here, cast envious eyes on our *Life of Lloyd George*, ready to be shown to the public from the very day the armistice was declared – a successful conclusion brought about chiefly by the English-speaking world.

My closest American film friend, Carl Laemmle, who controlled the Universal Film Company, made us promise not to sell the picture for America until he or his representative had had an opportunity to see it.

Like nearly all American film chiefs, he was a first generation immigrant – all of whom wholeheartedly supported their country when it came into the war.

The money prospects dangled before us for this picture were too incredible to set out now. I can only say they were based on the highest figures that had been realised on any picture ever made in America.

After some consideration, we decided that, unless or until we put it out here, we would not let it be put out anywhere else. We knew that if we did, it would be a world scandal – in which Lloyd George and ourselves would be the central figures. Great pressure was brought on us – by our greatest personal friends – to prevent this, at any cost, from becoming a Jewish question – the only way we could look at it.

Immediately the Armistice was declared, I was released from the Ministry of Information – which was tantamount to being discharged from the Army.

I do not know exactly how it happened, but Reginald Poole, member of Lewis & Lewis, the best known company of Solicitors at the time, came on the scene, in order to try and effect a financial settlement.

After seeing my brother and myself on this matter, Poole stuck to his instructions only, to make a financial settlement, refused to discuss anything else. He suggested:

(1) an audited account of cost of film;
(2) report on Ideal losses through concentration on the *Life of Lloyd George*;
(3) estimate of losses through not issuing it.

We immediately ruled out (2) and (3); taking the Quixotic line that our losses could never be measured with money . . .

All attempts to see Lloyd George were futile. We were shaken and helpless against an unseen force . . .

Finally, we agreed to accept £20,000, the actual cost incurred of production of the Life of Lloyd George film.

The day after this was agreed, Reginald Poole came in a taxi to our office at an appointed time, after office hours, took out of his pocket 20

Bank of England notes of one thousand pounds each, which he handed to my brother. We placed the negative and the positive films of the *Life of Lloyd George* in his taxi, and that is the last I saw or knew about it.

I don't know why, but it seems to be expected that the chief of a company should not show his feelings when drama or tragedy hovers over it, that he should suppress or disguise them. Although I had known so well what it was to be hard up, jobless, foodless and homeless, I was more depressed now than ever before and tried, unsuccessfully, not to betray it . . .

For days after the conclusion of this Lloyd George matter, the directors hardly said a word to each other. What shook us all was not the over-riding disappointment but the humiliation . . .

We were not even permitted to lick the wounds of our shattered pride, for very soon, our solicitor, a personal friend of all of us, walked into our office to tell us we must discuss the *John Bull* action further. That woke us up! In litigation, lawyers are like generals – and a good job, too. No matter how confident they are, they only prepare for the worst. In order that our Action should be properly prepared, he demanded from each of the directors full particulars of our past, our parents, where they came from, when they came here, when they were naturalised and what they did. He also wanted to know when and where each of the directors was born, what school, or schools, we went to, what we did on leaving school, and how we came to be in the film business. And although during the war tens of thousands of people changed their names, from the highest to the lowest, he wanted specifically to know why we changed ours. It was also necessary, he pointed out, to prove what damages we had actually suffered, quite apart from what was claimed for special damages. On the subject of actual damages we were rather fortunate: there existed a lot of correspondence from our branch managers, written before the libel appeared; estimates of the amount and value of the bookings they expected to make, which, from our experience, were always below the actual, and therefore some guide of what we would have received in bookings. The reason was that as they received special commission for exceeding their quota, they quite naturally were conservative in their estimates.

He also told us that we (or *John Bull*) might be advised to call Lloyd George to testify whether his desire that the picture should not be shown was influenced by the article in *John Bull* and, of course, if not, why?

The lowest possible damages we could have suffered through not putting the picture out in this country would have been £100,000, besides what we would have received from other countries and particularly from America. But, he reminded us that on the question of damages, it might be urged that there was nothing to stop us, legally, from offering it to cinemas here.

The solicitor then wanted to know what our attitude would be in regard to damages, if *John Bull* decided not to defend the Action. In order to settle the matter I asked my colleagues to meet me at my house, the first real opportunity I had had since marrying, just before 'joining up', of entertaining them. After a long afternoon's discussion covering every point of view, our attitude was determined without voting; though it was not unanimous. A Board of Directors is rather similar to the Cabinet; only what is decided, matters, not what is said in course of reaching the decision. Individual directors' opinions at such a time, are somewhat irrelevant. It is the collective opinion that matters. We decided that if *John Bull* unequivocally withdrew every allegation, innuendo and insinuation in open Court, and furthermore undertook to publish a statement acceptable to us to appear in an agreed position in *John Bull*, and also paid us all our costs, we would not ask for any damages. We only wanted complete vindication, so that no-one should ever be able to taunt us with placing any money value on that.

Now, in order to finish this episode I jump ahead in order to be done with it.

30 January 1919. Page 62. [?]

Ideal Co. v. *John Bull* and Messrs Odhams.
    Action for Libel ends in confession of Regret and apology.
    Defendents withdraw all imputations and Pay all Costs.
    Mr Patrick Hastings and Mr Wallington appeared for the plaintiffs, Sir Edward Marshall Hall, K.C. and Mr Barrington Ward for *John Bull*, and Sir Hugh Frazer for Messrs. Odhams Ltd.
    Withdrawal of Imputation and Apology.
    Sir E. Marshall Hall, K.C., said that 'enquiries were made and the result was to show that the statements made by Mr Patrick Hastings were accurate. There was no honourable course for the defendant's paper to pursue but at once to withdraw the statements they had made.'

The defendants had undertaken to indemnify the plaintiffs against any costs which they may have incurred in these proceedings.

Mr Justice Darling: The record will be withdrawn on the terms arranged between the parties. I must say, what I think I have stated in other cases, that it is a pity the people who write about matters of dangerous public controversy should not ascertain the facts before they write, instead of afterwards.

[The memoir concludes the story with correspondence from 1945.]

The following correspondence with Mr A. J. Sylvester, Private Secretary to Lloyd George for nearly 20 years, speaks for itself, in reference to a proposal to produce a new Life of Lloyd George.

18 Oct. 1945

Dear Mr Sylvester,

As promised in our interview a week ago I am now sending you particulars of the statement which I desire, subject to your approval, to issue to the press in regard to the Life of Lloyd George film.

(1) Copy of letter of 7 February 1945 to the Right Hon. D. Lloyd George, Esq., M.P. By presenting the whole of this letter, it becomes known why the picture made in 1917 never appeared in the Cinemas . . .

Sir,

During the first World War I was joint Managing Director of Ideal Films Ltd., which, among its activities produced a film version of your life story. This Company has since merged in the Gaumont British Corporation which I am not now connected with.

That film was never shown to the public because it was intimated that some members of your family and some of your close friends did not wish to be associated in a project which they regarded as somewhat 'infra-dig'.

This attitude was conveyed by the late Captain Guest as representing the views of your family and friends. The Board of the Company on my recommendation acquiesced in his request and did not proceed with the distribution of the picture, even after unmistakable evidence from the Trade that this decision entailed great financial sacrifice. Although the Company was finally reimbursed the actual costs incurred, it was deprived completely of the certainty of large profits from a picture awaited for by every section of the country and sought after in all parts of the world, including even Germany itself.

Since then new and brilliant chapters have been added to your life story, altogether constituting one of the most outstanding, picturesque and precious possessions of our people during the same period.

The technique of film-making has been considerably advanced during the past thirty years. Speech and sound and colour have been intimately integrated. The grammar of film composition has been developed and weaknesses of earlier films eliminated.

In recent years there have been noteworthy biographies of Zola, Curie, Pitt, Pasteur, and most recently of President Wilson. This Wilson picture which concentrated on his advocacy of the League of Nations was a great factor in the last Presidential Election and is said to have determined the attitude of the people of America in its rejection of the policy of isolation.

I take this opportunity, therefore, of asking you to signify your approval of the preparation of an entirely new production of your life story; as those concerned would like to be able to describe it as 'authoritative'.

With the great advance in technical resources I am satisfied as to the possibility of producing a picture which will be distinguished, dignified, beautiful and dramatic. It will carry on your stand for all those 'freedoms' which are now the whole world's aspirations. A permanent contribution to history!

Before proceeding further I would like to know your present attitude and any personal views on the subject which you may care to put forward.

If you would desire some friend of yours to be associated in the preparation of this 'life' I will be glad to meet him or her, and, if desired, make satisfactory financial arrangements for such assistance.

I may mention that my brother and co-managing director of the company which produced the film of your life referred to – at present film adviser to the Board of Trade – would be associated with me in this production – subject to the consent of the Board.

I am,

Yours faithfully,

(Signed) Harry Rowson.

(2) Towards the end of March you wrote me that Earl Lloyd George was too ill to reply to the above letter, a few days before he died.

(3) Through a friend I was able to obtain a vast number of obituary notices – over 1000 – which make a valuable collection of pictures and incidents for the preparation of this life.

(4) Subsequently I approached you with a view to helping us in gathering the facts on which this film life would be based.

(5) Your acceptance of this proposition.

Hoping you will find all this satisfactory,

I am,

Yours sincerely,

(Signed) H. Rowson.

Appendix

Interestingly, Rowson did not quote the *John Bull* article in full in his memoir. The following details of the Board and shareholders of Ideal with the German and English versions of the names was excluded, although Rowson later quotes Ideal's refutation in *The Cinema* with all the names in English.

The Lloyd George Film

Take this much-advertised film of the life of the Prime Minister. It is being produced by the Ideal Film Renting Company – against which I have nothing to say; I believe it enjoys a first-class reputation. But what is the composition of the Company? I have before me the latest Return filed with the Joint Stock Registry, and this is how the Board is described:

Name	Former Name	Occupation
Harry Rowson	Harry Rosenbaum	Director
Simon Rowson	Simon Rosenbaum	Statistician
Sara Wilmot	Sara Wohlgemuth	Widow
Simon Gilbert	Simon Gelberg	Journalist
A. M. Kay	A. M. Koppel	Secretary

But it is only right to say that they all declare themselves to be British. Then take the present list of shareholders; it is dated 11 January 1918:

H. Rowson (Rosenbaum)	1950
Jane Burnstein	500
S. Gilbert (Gelberg)	515

A. Gardner	285
E. Rowson (Rosenbaum)	315
S. Wilmot (Wohlgemuth)	200
Hilda Jacobsen	150
S. Rowson (Rosenbaum)	100
Jacob Wilmot (Wohlgemuth)	100
D. Rowson (Rosenbaum)	85
A. M. Kay (Koppel)	130
Rose Boodson	30
Nathan Boodson	20
Leslie Rowson	1

[Editors' note: there is a discrepancy between this list and Harry Rowson's memoir which refers to the 'Brodsons' rather than the 'Boodsons', as above.]

Notes

[1] The Rowson memoir and other material is at present being sorted and listed at the British Film Institute Library Services (Special Collections), London.

[2] Northcliffe papers (British Library); Lloyd George papers (National Library of Wales, Aberystwyth); Lloyd George papers and Beaverbrook papers (House of Lords Record Office); Ministry of Information and Home Office papers (Public Record Office); Milner Diaries (Bodleian Library, Oxford).

[3] Archives consulted were the National Film Archive, the Imperial War Museum and the Rank Organization.

[4] Simon Rowson wrote the Jewish section of Booth and Rowntree's *Survey of London Life and Labour* in the late nineteenth century. He was a central figure in Ideal Films and Gaumont British when Ideal was absorbed by that company in the late 1920s. He also worked as a statistician at the Board of Trade and advised on film matters for many years. In the 1930s he published articles on the economics of the cinema industry in the *Journal of the Royal Statistical Society*. He died in the late 1950s.

[5] R. Low (1948) *The History of the British Film, 1914–18* (Allen & Unwin), 92–3. [Editors' note: Elvey directed at least five Ideal films: see Denis Gifford, *The British Film Catalogue 1895–1985* (David and Charles, 1986) and Linda Wood (ed.), *The Commercial Imperative in the British Film Industry: Maurice Elvey, a Case Study* (British Film Institute, 1987).]

[6] *Kinematograph Weekly*, 3 October 1918, p.67.

[7] *Kinematograph Weekly*, 28 February 1918, p.59.

[8] *Kinematograph Weekly*, 12 September 1918, p.72.

[9] *Kinematograph Weekly*, 26 September 1918, p.69.

[10] Later Viscount Southwood. Elias was responsible for Odhams's connection with Bottomley, eventually taking full control of *John Bull* in 1921. See R. J. Minney, *Viscount Southwood* (Odhams Press, 1954).

[11] At the height of its popularity in 1920 *John Bull* had a circulation of 1,700,000. In 1918 *John Bull*'s profits were £113,000 whereas Odhams showed a profit of £35,000. The popularity of the paper meant that Odhams gave Bottomley a relatively free hand in its editorial policy. The paper reflected his passion for political and financial showmanship: 'He had an unerring instinct for detecting the tendencies of popular feeling, and he was assiduous in his search for a popular cry. He was the demagogue "par excellence"', H. J. Houston, *The Real Horatio Bottomley* (Hurst & Blackett, 1923).

[12] Bottomley (1860–1933) edited *John Bull*, 1906–21. He entered the printing business and in 1884 started the *Hackney Hansard* and in 1906 *John Bull*. He was elected Liberal MP for South Hackney in 1906 but in 1911 was declared bankrupt as a result of his many dubious financial ventures and left Parliament in 1912. During the war he gave patriotic war lectures and in 1918 regained his seat at South Hackney as an independent. In 1921 he lost the editorship of *John Bull* and was imprisoned 1922–7 for fraud. In 1928 he made an abortive attempt to start a rival to *John Bull* called *John Blunt*. Bottomley died in 1933 in poverty and obscurity.

[13] *John Bull*, 24, 644, 5 October 1918.

[14] J. Symons, *Horatio Bottomley* (Cresset Press, 1955), 165–7. On one occasion Bottomley suggested suitable treatment for the Germans after the war: 'If by chance you should discover one day in a restaurant that you are being served by a German waiter, you will throw the soup in his foul face; if you find yourself sitting at the side of a German clerk, you will spill the inkpot over his vile head.'

[15] Guest was the government chief whip. In August 1917 he became chairman of the National War Aims Committee, a domestic propaganda organization.

[16] Lloyd George knew that Bottomley's magazine was influential: early in 1918 Bottomley was invited to Downing Street with Sir Edward Carson and Lord Rhondda. Bottomley is reported to have suggested that Lloyd George should appoint a director of war propaganda. Lloyd George was supposed to have replied, 'I thought you were filling that role.' On one occasion Lloyd George was reported to have relied on Bottomley to calm strikers on the Clyde. See Symons, op. cit., 200, 164. Lloyd George was extremely interested in propaganda, especially the press; see M. Saunders and P. Taylor, *British Propaganda during the First World War, 1914–18* (Macmillan, 1982), 77–8.

[17] D. Chapman Huston, *The Lost Historian: Sidney Low* (Murray, 1936), 285–6.

2

The Man who Saved the Empire
– Postscript

SARAH STREET

Ten years have passed since I drew attention to the mystery of the (as I then believed) 'lost' film about the life of David Lloyd George and the intriguing circumstances surrounding its suppression in 1918–19. Imagine my surprise when in 1994 a Channel Four television news journalist telephoned me, asking what I thought about the discovery of the missing film and if I could provide him with details for a news item they were planning to transmit later that week. He told me the story-book tale about Viscount Tenby's attic treasure and the Wales Film and Television Archive's accidental stumble on the notorious reels, produced by Ideal Films in 1918, but never publicly exhibited until John Reed of the Wales Film and Television Archive had pieced together the disparate contents of cans which had been at the centre of a possible scandal all those years ago.

That telephone call prepared me for further involvement when the Archive invited me to comment on the film and advise on the ordering of the unmarked reels, along with Lloyd George historians, including John Grigg, biographer of Lloyd George, and Kevin Brownlow, film historian and restorer of silent classics for public exhibition. We were an extremely privileged audience in Aberystwyth, watching the reels unfold their story of a 'great man in history' some seventy-seven years after the film was whisked off in a taxi, unseen by the audience for whom it was intended. What a different crowd we were with our familiarity with television's *Spitting Image* caricatures of politicians and a generally irreverent attitude towards those who hold positions of political power. The film revealed an uncomplicated view of history, famous 'progressive' achievements attributed to the political genius of one man, Lloyd George, *The Man who Saved the Empire*, a title which interestingly appeared in pre-advertising but not on the completed film.

The title conjures up the very different world of 1918, a national outlook and attitude which assumed British responsibility for a vast empire and a sense of duty as one of the victors in the First World War to prevent subsequent conflict with Germany. Politicians were revered figures, treated with deference in much the same way as royalty. Lloyd George emerges from Ideal's film as a figure for the future with his contribution to welfare economics and semi-socialistic legislation, stealing the thunder from the young Labour party and threatening to unbalance in a charismatic fashion the Conservative domination of the coalition government in 1918. Lloyd George's political position was however unstable: as prime minister of a coalition government he was dependent on the support of its constituent parts, Conservative, Liberal and Labour. The film presents him as a trustworthy 'leader', deserving of adulation and respect. *The Life Story of David Lloyd George* has no place for 'Lloyd George was my father' jokes or for rigorous analysis of the socio-political situation in the early twentieth century. Instead it offers a reassuring portrait of the post-First World War world, carefully establishing the progressive trajectory of a nation worth fighting for, led to victory by Lloyd George, the natural leader who 'won the war'. How mystifying that a film which advanced this thesis with such certainty should never reach the cinema screens at a time when Lloyd George needed all the support he could get: the man who won the war had yet to prove that he could also 'win the peace'.

The discovery of the film prompted many questions. In 1987 I thought I had researched my topic as well as I could, trawling numerous archives and offering a theory about the film's suppression which centred on the involvement of Horatio Bottomley and the *John Bull* hate-campaign which had been unleashed on the Ideal Film Company and its alleged German connections.[1] Bottomley's involvement emerges as fairly clear – the instigator of jingoistic 'smear' tactics and their possible impact on the fragile political position of Lloyd George in 1918, a salutary lesson about the power of the press in a period before the movies became a major medium of persuasion but when a growing perception of the medium's potential was definitely on the official agenda. What was missing was concrete evidence of the £20,000 pay-off – who instigated it and why? As well as detailing the involvement of Horatio Bottomley and the press, my original article outlined other possible theories behind the film's suppression, the most intriguing of which is direct interference by the

Home Office because the film portrayed Lloyd George as the father of semi-socialistic schemes which in the context of the 1917 Russian Revolution and post-war industrial unrest in Britain, could be construed as pro-Bolshevik. Sir Sidney Low (author of the scenario) wrote in his diary that Sir Basil Thomson, assistant commissioner of the Metropolitan Police, had been instrumental in persuading Ideal that it should not be distributed. Further examination of Home Office, Metropolitan Police and Treasury papers at the Public Record Office in Kew Gardens has not, however, provided further evidence for this tantalizing but unproven theory. Whoever's hand was behind the suppression has yet to be ascertained, but it is possible that the sort of propaganda represented by *The Life Story of David Lloyd George* was not deemed suitable for the post-war world by the coalition and/or even by Lloyd George himself, who was anxious to maintain his position as prime minister, an office he kept until October 1922.

Although no documentary evidence has been discovered to reveal who actually instigated the pay-off to Ideal Films, several factors which are relevant to the key years 1918–19 provide a fascinating context which may go some way towards explaining the film's dramatic disappearance. To extend my argument about the power of the press, it is well known that Lloyd George was anxious to maintain the support of major newspapers which had wielded considerable influence over public opinion during the war. Two key propaganda jobs went to press barons in 1918: Lord Beaverbrook became head of the Ministry of Information and Lord Northcliffe took charge of a special Department of Enemy Propaganda. As Ken Morgan has commented: 'The presence of Lloyd George in Downing Street after 1918 ensured in itself that the press would remain a powerful factor in politics . . . He was anxious to have the Coalition reported in the press in an extensive and favourable way, as an essential means of sustaining his personal communion with the people.'[2] While Bottomley was no Beaverbrook or Northcliffe, it is significant that Lloyd George was concerned not to alienate sections of the press at a time when his enemies were keen to exploit any 'dirt' about him which came their way. His recognition of Bottomley's role as a primary propagandist is also relevant here: early in 1918 Bottomley was invited to Downing Street, along with Sir Edward Carson (head of the National War Aims Committee, a propaganda organization) and Lord Rhondda (Minister of Food). Lloyd George is also reported as relying on Bottomley to calm strikers on the Clyde, a fact which supports my argument below about Lloyd George and the fear of Bolshevism.[3] As a severe critic of Lloyd George's appointment of Beaverbrook and Northcliffe, Austen Chamberlain claimed that the 'demarcation lines which previously existed between Fleet Street and Downing Street' had been removed.[4]

The Conservatives wanted to control radical tendencies, particularly the rise and constitutional development of the Labour party (Clause Four was adopted in 1918), industrial unrest and the effect of the Russian Revolution. Although Lloyd George was a Liberal it is not difficult to imagine him extending his popularity by championing Labour's causes, a move which would not have appeared to be inconsistent with the incidents chronicled in Ideal's film *The Life Story of David Lloyd George* (the 'People's Budget', Old Age Pensions and National Insurance etc.). The immediate post-war threat of Bolshevism and fear of the growth of the Labour party on the part of the Liberals as well as the Conservatives, however, firmly impelled Lloyd George to the anti-Labour camp. As Ken Morgan has pointed out: 'Throughout 1920, the fear of Bolshevism, the belief that Labour was the demure front for much more dangerous assaults on the economic and political structure, was Lloyd George's fundamental theme and a major determinant of his strategy.'[5] Immediately after the war many leftist groups wanted to take advantage of industrial militancy and Lloyd George was determined to contain the spread of extremism. In January 1920 Lloyd George told the cabinet that if strike action persisted in the major industries he would authorize the use of ground troops and the air force to attack strikers.[6] Bearing this in mind, it is therefore unlikely that Sir Basil Thomson saw Lloyd George as a socialist – the *film* character perhaps, but not the real man, a view presumably shared by Lloyd George, which made the film's suppression necessary and urgent. It is probable that the Liberal party's weak position in 1918 and its dependence on the Conservatives explains a rather confused response to the production of a major film which virtually canonized Lloyd George as the father of social reform and the main instigator of the extension of state powers during the war. Politically, this image was not an appropriate one for Lloyd George in the post-war context. Lord Riddell wrote in his diary on 27 March 1920 that Lloyd George seemed 'convinced that Socialism is a mistaken policy. I have observed this conviction growing upon him during the past four years. His point of view has entirely changed.'[7] Sure enough, it was Labour rather than the Liberal party which went on to command the 'progressivist' ground after 1918. It is conceivable that Lloyd George did not want to be associated with the Ideal film because it might have threatened his (and the Liberal party's) understanding with the Conservatives concerning their mutual interest in containing the growth of the Labour party which emerged after the war as the natural alternative to conservatism, complete with a new constitution and with increasing support from newly enfranchised voters. Instead of breaking to the left and establishing a centre party with progressivist goals, Lloyd George became more and more a prisoner of his Conservative supporters and was driven steadily to the right.

Rowson's memoir noted that 'friends of Lloyd George, who didn't like pictures at any price, had persuaded him that the status of cinemas would be so enhanced if the film were shown that the whole country would be in danger'.[8] The key word is 'danger': in 'danger' of increasing demands for socialism which *The Man who Saved the Empire* might unwittingly encourage? Lloyd George was no socialist and, in the context of 1918–19, the release of a major film claiming that he might be was too big a risk for the coalition to take. Better to rely on the press, a known quantity whose support could be won by the inclusion of press barons in the 'official' propaganda machine. In support of this argument a minute to the Cabinet by T. L. Gilmour (assistant director of the Department of Information's Cinematograph Branch) in 1917 reveals the extent to which the cinema was feared:

At the cinema theatre Tory, Liberal, Labour man and Socialist must sit side by side and see the same thing presented in the same way, and insensibly their views are affected by what they see. Moreover, at the cinema theatre the spectator must see all that is shown, while he may refuse to read even in his favourite newspaper anything which offends his preconceived ideas. It is true that the spectators may interpret what they see differently, and it is precisely because we can never predict with any certainty what the effect on the minds of the audience will be, that there is great danger in the use of the cinema when it is employed among a population which is either wholly uneducated or only partially educated. The cinema theatre, by bringing the world to the door of the poorest and most ignorant, opens up all sorts of beatific visions, but equally suggests problems to the statesman which are calculated to excite his fears as much as his hopes. The cinema cannot be suppressed, even if the wish to do so existed. It must, therefore, be recognised and controlled'.[9]

Again, note the use of the word 'danger'. If *The Life Story of David Lloyd George* had been released people might have expected 'beatific visions' to be realized in the post-war world, 'visions' which extended welfare provisions and state intervention into peacetime. This was indeed a 'problem' for a politician like Lloyd George who was uncertain of his role in the new party-political arena in 1918, in a mood which was intent on suppressing extremism. In these delicate circumstances he probably preferred to steer clear of film propaganda, the impact of which he could not entirely control. In this case, however, the cinema was suppressed, strike activity was quelled, wartime controls were dismantled and Lloyd George remained prime minister.

Notes

[1] See Sarah Street, 'The Memoir of Harry Rowson: David Lloyd George, M.P. – *The Man who Saved the Empire* (1918)' in *Historical Journal of Film, Radio and Television*, 7, 1 (1987), 55–70, reprinted in this volume.

[2] Kenneth O. Morgan, *Consensus and Disunity* (Oxford University Press, 1979), 169.

[3] J. Symons, *Horatio Bottomley* (Cresset Press, 1955), 200, 164.

[4] Michael Sanders and Philip Taylor, *British Propaganda during the First World War* (Macmillan, 1982), 91.

[5] Morgan, op. cit., 214.

[6] James Hinton, *Labour and Socialism* (Wheatsheaf Books, 1983), 109.

[7] From Lord Riddell's *An Intimate Diary of the Peace Conference and After, 1918–23* (Gollancz, 1933), 27 March 1920. Lord Riddell was chairman of the *News of the World*, 1903–34, and a confidant of Lloyd George. He was liaison officer betwen the British delegation and the press at the Paris Peace Conference, 1919.

[8] Sarah Street, op. cit., 64.

[9] T. L. Gilmour, 'Minute on the Cinema Industry and its relation to the Government', 13 October 1917, Public Record Office papers, CAB 27/17 and INF 4/6.

3

Speculating on the Projections of History

JOHN GRIGG

The Harry Rowson/Maurice Elvey film of the life of David Lloyd George, made in 1918 but suppressed at the time and until recently thought to be lost, is both an imaginative projection of history and a historical event in its own right. The circumstances in which it was made and then mysteriously suppressed, and its discovery last year by Lord Tenby, a grandson of Lloyd George, in his barn, followed by its masterly processing by the Wales Film and Television Archive and its showing to enthusiastic audiences in north and south Wales, all constitute history at its most intriguing.

When I saw the film at an early stage at Aberystwyth, invited with a number of others to advise the dedicated Film Archive team on various aspects of its presentation, I was struck at once by its technical quality and dramatic power. But I came away more puzzled than ever by what exactly happened in 1918, and why. Before seeing the film I vaguely imagined that the reason for its suppression might have been that Lloyd George, as head of a coalition government in which the Conservative party predominated, became uneasy at the thought of his belabouring of the Tories before the war – above all during the controversy provoked by his 1909 budget – being shown on film throughout the country and throughout the world.

As I watched the film, however, this explanation seemed less plausible. Certainly his 'cottage-bred' origins are emphasized, as are his crusading efforts as a social reformer in peace and a leader of the nation at war. But the robustly partisan character of his pre-war career is very noticeably played down. The aim of the film seems to be to present him throughout his early life as a coalition man in the making – which, in an important sense, he was, though under heavy disguise.

Some of Lloyd George's colleagues, in his own as well as the Tory party, might have been expected to resent the glorification of one man, which was hardly consistent with the idea of parliamentary, as distinct from presidential, democracy. Yet most people in 1917 and 1918 accepted Lloyd George's quasi-presidential style of leadership as a practical necessity. It was not really an issue at the time. His status as a national leader had been firmly established since his Queen's Hall speech in September 1914. Tories would, however, have been quick to react against any film that provided a sharp reminder of his hostility to them, and theirs to him, at an earlier period, and this was clearly a point of which Harry Rowson and Maurice Elvey, and the film's scriptwriter, Sir Sidney Low, were acutely conscious. It is obvious that they took great pains to include as little as possible that could touch Tory sensitivities and so impair the spirit of the coalition.

Since, therefore, my tentative theory was not supported by the evidence of the film itself, what of the alternative explanation that it was suppressed because of Horatio Bottomley's attack in *John Bull* on the ethnic background of those who made it? It is worth remembering that when work on the film was started, and for most of the time that it was in production, the struggle on the Western Front was still critically poised and its victorious outcome far from assured. Even when the German spring offensive seemed to be decisively checked, it was by no means immediately apparent that the war would soon be over. Until the early autumn it was generally believed that it would last well into 1919, if not longer.

Nobody could reasonably – or unreasonably – object to the film on patriotic grounds. It was, first and foremost, a contribution to wartime morale and very powerful as such. Ethnic prejudice against those who made it, whether anti-German or anti-Semitic, can hardly have been the decisive factor in its suppression (though Lloyd George had certainly made anti-Semitic remarks in his time of a kind that were normal for the period). More relevant, surely, is the unexpectedly early end of the war which deprived the film of its principal purpose.

In October, when the *John Bull* article appeared, the chance of earlier victory could for the first time be contemplated, and then – on November 11 – it had occurred. Lloyd George decided to go to the country without delay as 'the man who won the war' and as the leader of a coalition for peace.

The situation had manifestly changed from the time when *The Life Story* was first mooted and he had given it his blessing. He was now

9. Young Lloyd George on the bridge at Llanystumdwy – an early scene from the film.

fighting a domestic election rather than a foreign war. In the absence of opinion polls it was hard to read the public mind, but it was a common assumption among politicians that the press both reflected public opinion and influenced it to a formidable degree. Consequently Lloyd George may have judged that the value, to him, of the Rowson film would be more than offset by the damage that Bottomley could do, at any rate in the short term, by involving it and him in negative publicity.

Yet there is one other hypothesis to be considered. On 24 February 1920 Frances Stevenson recorded in her diary: 'Last night went to see a film of D's [Lloyd George's] life which Captain Guest had put on the screen in No 12 [Downing Street] – a perfectly appalling thing. The idea was all right but the man who was supposed to be D. was simply a caricature. I begged D. not to let it be shown. Mrs Ll.G. very angry with D. because she said I had put D. against it because I had objected to the domestic scenes in it!'

This was, of course, long after the Rowson film had been removed from Ideal's offices, but was the film that Frances Stevenson saw in

February 1920 the film that Rowson made and surrendered?[1] It is significant that it was screened by Captain (Freddie) Guest, who was Lloyd George's chief whip, and who, we know, had been actively concerned with the Rowson film from the outset. He may well have had temporary custody of the film – though it was presumably Lloyd George's property, and must in due course have passed from him to his younger son, Gwilym (later Lord Tenby, and father of the present peer).

It is quite credible that Frances Stevenson would have felt upstaged and excluded by the scenes of home life depicted in the film, and that she might, on that account alone, have argued against its being shown publicly. 'I begged David not to let it be shown' may have referred back to 1918.[2] If so, it is equally credible that Dame Margaret Lloyd George would have felt angry about Frances's role in the matter.

We shall probably never know the whole truth. Unfortunately Frances Stevenson did not keep a diary for 1918. Left to speculate, we do not have to make a stark choice between what one might call the Bottomley and Stevenson hypotheses. Both may be partly true. There may also be other factors which will come to light in the future, or of which we shall remain forever ignorant. Apart from the aspects of Lloyd George's pre-war career that are passed over or played down in the film for the reasons suggested, how true is the impression it conveys of his early life?

Despite its undeniably propagandist character, the film does not wholly misrepresent the man or his origins. It vividly portrays the north Wales in which he spent his childhood and in which, after leaving the village school at Llanystumdwy, he trained and practised as a solicitor (the 'little Welsh attorney'). It shows the physical modesty, not to say austerity, of his home background which enabled him, when standing for parliament in 1890, to proclaim that 'the day of the cottage-bred man has at last dawned'.[3] But it does not show that this famous phrase was, to a very significant degree, misleading. To most people the phrase must have implied, and must still imply, that Lloyd George's home was proletarian and totally unprivileged. It was, however, nothing of the sort; in many ways he was a privileged child, despite the physically austere circumstances in which he was brought up.

Lloyd George's father (who died when he was an infant) was not a farm labourer or quarryman or proletarian of any description. He was a schoolmaster, whose library of historical works and literary classics remained, after his death, to stimulate the mind and kindle the imagination of his supremely gifted elder son. The boy's uncle and guardian Richard Lloyd, was a master cobbler employing several hands in his workshop. He was, therefore, a capitalist, if on a very small scale. But what matters far more is that he was a Baptist minister and local sage, deeply respected throughout the whole neighbourhood. By birth and upbringing, therefore, David Lloyd George belonged to the Welsh-speaking Nonconformist elite which, at the time of his birth, was coming into its own. Politically, at that time, he could hardly have hoped for a more advantageous start.

The film is equally misleading about his marriage and personal life as a young politician. Naturally enough, it presents an extremely bland picture, which – again – is by no means entirely false, but which fails to reveal the tensions in his marriage, even before he fell seriously in love with another woman. He was, of course, as egocentric as creative artists of any kind normally are, and his declared priority in life was to 'get on'.[4] Though genuinely devoted to Wales as an idea and as a culture, he never relished for long the climate of Criccieth or the restrictiveness of his life there. He was, therefore, all the more drawn to the excitement of life in London and the pleasures of foreign travel. His wife Margaret was selfish, too, with a strong mind of her own and a love of north Wales which she was not prepared to subordinate even to her love for him. As a result, she would often insist on staying with their children at Criccieth, while he would be pleading for them to join him in London. The consequences were predictable. But it is important to stress that he was, and never ceased to be, very fond of Margaret (and he was also a much better father to his children than many great men have been).

In 1912, during the period covered by the film, he fell in love with Frances Stevenson and she became his mistress. From this time onwards he was, effectively, a bigamist (until Margaret's death in 1941). No hint of this is given in the film, nor should one expect it to be. On the political side, the film exaggerates and over-simplifies, but does not fundamentally mislead. Lloyd George's pioneering work as a social reformer was almost as momentous as the film makes out, and although his motives may not have been purely altruistic – personal ambition also bulked large, as did his desire to humiliate the traditional ruling class – nevertheless his anger at the injustices of society and his compassion for its victims were strong and sincere.

His attitude in 1914 was, similarly, more complicated than the film suggests. He decided, after much head- and heart-searching, in favour of British participation in the war, not simply because he wanted to champion a small nation, Belgium, against a mighty, aggressive neighbour. In reality he regarded the prospect of another German defeat of France, with the probable result of German domination of the whole European continent, as a potentially mortal threat to Britain and its empire. The violation of Belgian neutrality, combined with the spectacle of brave Belgian resistance, made it easier for him – and others – to decide as they did. The David-and-Goliath motif, of which the film makes so much, is inappropriate to the 1914–18 war, which was a struggle between great powers. I happen to think that Britain and France, in defending their own vital interests, were also defending the cause of freedom and democracy. But in British wartime propaganda, of which the film (had it appeared) would have been a prime example, the accent was upon crusading idealism, not upon the defence of national interests.

Yet whatever allowance has to be made for the film's propagandist content, it is an immense boon that it survived. In its own right, it makes a fascinating contribution to history.

Notes

[1] Frances Stevenson (ed. A. J. P. Taylor), *Lloyd George: A Diary* (Hutchinson, 1971), entry for 24 February, 1920, p.203.

[2] Ibid.

[3] Quoted as such in many works on Lloyd George, though a *Daily News* correspondent – covering the by-election at which Lloyd George was returned – reported the phrase on 7 April 1890 as 'hamlet lads' – perhaps an alternative translation of words originally spoken in Welsh.

[4] Letter to his future wife, Margaret Owen, undated but, from its context, written late in 1886, cited in John Grigg, *The Young Lloyd George* (Eyre Methuen, 1973; paperback edn, HarperCollins, 1997), 67.

Fighting the Hun: Lloyd George and British Propaganda Movies, 1914–1918

DAVID BERRY

Watching *The Life Story of David Lloyd George* you might be excused for seeing Britain in 1918 as a classless, essentially homogeneous nation which had buried all social divisions to unite against the 'Hun'. You would not credit from the film that in the summer of 1918, even as its director Maurice Elvey was preparing to move from the set of his 'heroic' biopic *Nelson* to the Lloyd George film, the country was in turmoil – beset by industrial disputes. Even the London policemen struck in August just when Elvey needed them for his *folie de grandeur*, the remarkable reconstructed, technically exhilarating scenes of the suffragette riots outside Queen's Hall – scenes fraught with physical peril to the participants. The only police available to control the crowds in the fierce mêlées spilling through the street were extras in uniform employed by the film-makers, Ideal of Wardour Street. This was taking a chance, especially when the filming of a Birmingham Town Hall fracas in the film led, according to one report, to a 'real riot as the crowd got so much in earnest . . . and the bona fide police contended with their fellows in borrowed plumage'.[1]

It is also salutary to note that the film unit had initially moved with alacrity into London from Wales when they heard of a conductresses' strike paralysing bus services and allowing them easier access to the streets without fear of anachronistic intrusions.[2] Miners, cotton spinners, Clyde shipbuilders, busmen and tramwaymen all came out on strike during 1918; as a noted Lloyd George biographer Frank Owen recalled, 'that steaming summer, there was rising unrest in the factories of Britain against labour conditions, prices, rations'.[3]

The situation was not new. In 1917 there were reports from Commissions of Industrial Unrest, who thought the major causes of grievances were high food prices in relation to wages and the unequal distribution of food. The nine separate commissions agreed generally that 'feelings of a revolutionary character are not entertained by the bulk of men'. Yet the spectre of the 1917 Russian Revolution loomed large especially with more timorous politicians. Lord Beaverbrook – Britain's first Minister of Information, appointed in February 1918 – recalled in his memoirs (written long after the fact) that early that year discontent was again welling up in the factories and shipyards. All Britain's perceived problems and social conditions were 'attributed to a well organized system of German propaganda', he claimed, not altogether facetiously. His tongue may have been firmly in his cheek writing this passage but there is slightly more conviction in his recollections that 'the public clamoured for a propaganda ministry to raise morale at home, convince the Allies and the Dominions of the vast strength of the British effort and persuade the neutrals to believe that the victorious Armies of Europe would bring peace to a war-weary world'.[4]

The Lloyd George film must be seen in the context of Britain's patriotic agitprop of the day. It is a work of hagiography even if – set against the more strident publicity of the day – its castigation of the Germans and their allies was relatively restrained. Its praise for the premier was not cloyingly intemperate, testimony perhaps to the comparative objectivity of the film's scriptwriter, the historian Sir Sidney Low. Low was an admirer of Rhodes, Milner and other Boer War 'heroes' and an unabashed imperialist, but there is, thankfully, little gung-ho swagger in the movie, for all its uncritical view of Lloyd George.

The film (as stated elsewhere in this volume) was originally conceived as a history of the war as related by, or on behalf of, the young Winston Churchill. The film's final (roughcut) version seeks to glorify not merely the prime minister but, by implication, the whole British government. Filming was initially encouraged (whatever Lloyd George might have thought of the film later), and indeed there is internal evidence – for instance Lloyd George's appearance in the movie – that he may have agreed to his own filming.[5] The British government and the industry were certainly by 1918 anxious to create a large-scale propaganda feature, with the war's outcome still desperately uncertain. The government had brought Irish-born director Herbert Brenon from Hollywood to make the so-called 'national film'. The film, known as *The Invasion of Britain* in the trade press during its production, was finally titled *Victory and Peace*, as events overtook it, and never saw the light of day.[6]

Around six minutes of that film survive, now viewable at the National Film Archive in London. Produced for the National War Aims Committee, the released version featured a cast of Britain's leading performers, including Matheson Lang, Sam Livesey (as 'the most Hunnish of Huns') and the stage stars Ellen Terry and Ben Greet. Brenon's film was expected to be released by November 1918 but it had not appeared by the Armistice on 11 November and was summarily shelved for good despite allegedly costing £23,000, compared with the then unusually high individual budgets of £20,000 for two of Britain's leading features, George Loane Tucker's *The Manxman* (1916) and Ideal's *The Second Mrs Tanqueray* (director Fred Paul, 1916), and the £20,000 which Ideal supposedly lavished on the Lloyd George feature.[7] *Victory and Peace* was considered no longer relevant, and it was thought German sensibilities would be offended if the movie was released in peacetime. Brenon, with the extravagant taste for excessive footage which had previously incurred the wrath of producer William Fox, was too slow in shooting the film, said the trade press. Its failure pushed Brenon to the brink of bankruptcy.[8]

The War Office also helped finance D. W. Griffith's trip to Europe to make his 1918 film *Hearts of the World*, a huge undertaking starring Lillian and Dorothy Gish and Bobby Harron, and Griffith later claimed that the picture (shot partly in France) was made as 'a propaganda film for the British government'.[9] Griffith had previously talked to Lloyd George and 'impressed upon the man who has the destinies of civilisations in his hands the tremendous possibilities of a methodical screen campaign. He then set off for the Western Front with the premier's blessing.'[10] 'The entire resources of the British Army were practically put at his service', *The Cinema* magazine noted wryly, reflecting the resentment many home film-makers felt that they were not accorded the same treatment. 'The War in fact might have been staged for his benefit.'

The Lloyd George and Brenon films were merely the climax of an intensive propaganda assault by the British film industry which began with a flourish in 1914 and a rash of fictional war shorts. 'For a while film people, like everybody else in Britain, could think of hardly anything but the war', noted the historian Rachael Low.[11] The leading British director Cecil Hepworth was first out of the blocks, producing *Men of the Moment*, which was advertised nine days after the declaration of war for release two days later. By 1915–16 the enthusiasm of the film producers had subsided a little, but it gathered momentum again from 1917 on.

Today the Lloyd George film should be viewed against the contemporary backdrop, when the home trade sought to consolidate the industry and take advantage of the fall in US-imported footage during the war period. US films already dominated British screens – a trend which increased alarmingly in the 1920s, forcing the British Quota Act of 1927. The US percentage of all films shown in Britain had reputedly reached 85–90 per cent by that year, and British films accounted for only 5 per cent in 1925.[12] The indigenous industry was, throughout the years 1910–20, effectively running scared of the Americans. The national cinema needed heroes and the reassurance provided by heroic icons on screen, and also continued to seek respectability and kudos by handling serious literature. The prolific Maurice Elvey is a pivotal figure in any study of the period. It is significant, in retrospect, that he helped give the British film status in following up Thomas Bentley's Hepworth movie *Oliver Twist* (1912) by reworking more Dickens in the first decade of the British feature, with *Dombey and Son* (1917) and *Bleak House* (1919), both made for the Ideal company. He was also intent on re-creating morale-boosting iconic figures. He followed his 1915 *Florence Nightingale* (for British and Colonial) with *Nelson* for International Exclusives, and then the Ideal company's Lloyd George feature.

The Lloyd George film contains much of the same emblematic imagery Elvey used in his (much inferior) *Nelson*. Despite its shortcomings, *Nelson* was sold quickly (in pre-rental days) for an alleged record sum in a British deal.[13] In the same mould were G. B. Samuelson's *Life of Lord Roberts* (1914), the Windsor Company's *Life of Lord Kitchener* (1918), Percy Nash's feature *Disraeli* (1916) and Percy Moran's film for the small Phoenix company, *Nurse and Martyr*, centring on the betrayal of the English nurse, Edith Cavell.[14]

But the bulk of fictional films were of one to three reels, and there was still a shortage of genuine feature-length war/propaganda dramas or British movies with serious artistic pretensions. 'The criticism levelled at British productions is that they are on a small scale. *Nelson*, as far as numbers is concerned, is on the grand scale', Maurice Elvey said in a revealing 1919 interview.[15] Elsewhere in the trade press Elvey stressed the need for greater investment in British pictures and as late as 1922 even complained that actresses were compelled to bring their own frocks to the set to help out cash-strapped costume departments. He wondered whether Mae Marsh or Lillian Gish in Hollywood 'suffered like this'. The British cinema was 'attempting to create grade one pictures with grade three technical staffs and resources', but he insisted that 'English photography and sets can challenge the world'. Output was small and 'we found it hard to manufacture on strict American commercial factory lines', he admitted. But small was beautiful apparently – 'we weren't compelled to use studios as a form of film cannery'. Eliot Stannard, the screenwriter originally due to help script Ideal's Winston Churchill war film, was convinced that British movie companies were to blame for 'not publicising their own film stars' and not just those who were better known for West End stage roles. 'We do have stars but seem to be in a mighty conspiracy to prevent the public knowing of their existence.'[16]

In the light of Beaverbrook's claims about the British public's paranoia concerning German propaganda, it is interesting to examine the period's trade papers for the insight they provide into domestic film production and the industry's attitudes. Just two months from the end of the First World War, *Bioscope* thundered against the government's perceived inefficiency or apathy in coping with the German propaganda machine.[17] Its criticisms were largely directed at the Department of Information which had preceded Beaverbrook's control of the new Ministry, but it also called for 'radical changes' in that ministry.

The Germans had spent the equivalent of £16 million on propaganda during that year, and the British government a mere £2 million, compared with three-quarters of a million in the first year of the Lloyd George coalition government formed in 1916. German propaganda movies, 'faked though they be', were dominating the cinemas of Switzerland and Russia; the 'Hun' was making big inroads into neutral territory. There was, *Bioscope* warned, 'a considerable danger of Great Britain falling behind its arch-enemy in the utilisation of the motion picture screen as a means of propaganda'. The Ministry of Information, the paper concluded, should involve 'those who understand pictures and producers. When will Rip Van Winkles awake from their slumbers and make good their lack of initiative by condescending to copy others?' *The Cinema and Property Gazette* was even more scathing. An article in June 1918 titled 'Fooled: Can we Stand it any Longer?' pointed out that the Germans during the first two years of the war budgeted to spend

250 million marks annually for propaganda, 'much of it through cinema'.[18]

In Switzerland Nordische Film had bought up thirty to forty cinema houses. No allied propaganda films were shown in Switzerland, the writer stressed. President Wilson had emphasized the value of both the cinema and the aeroplane in war, and the Department of Information 'had been voted to us as a sure antidote to the Machiavellian tactics of the Hun'. The War Aims Committee had been responsible for war propaganda, but this committee was 'a regular salad of conflicting opinions' and resulted in 'every effort at effective propaganda being nullified'. The public would not be fooled any longer and would 'refuse to allow such an important department to be controlled by a body of party hacks who individually and collectively would probably be incompetent to run the smallest retail shop'.

The *Cinema* article demanded that Lloyd George, 'the man of genius . . . to whom the nation looks for guidance and salvation' should act to ensure that Britain's propaganda machine was well oiled. Beaverbrook had already proved himself to Lloyd George as a great propagandist for the Canadian government and Lloyd George willingly accepted Liberal chief whip Frederick Guest's suggestion that 'the Beaver' should head an information and propaganda ministry.[19] The trouble was, as Beaverbrook found, the service ministries had their own propaganda departments, and the Foreign Office in particular was not prepared to surrender its power or its administrative staff to the new ministry. Edward Carson, in charge of war propaganda, had not been a success, and a War Aims Committee set up under John Buchan (author of *The Thirty-Nine Steps* and later Lord Tweedsmuir) was only 'possessed of uncertain authority'[20] (in February 1918 Buchan became director of intelligence in the Information Department).[21] Lloyd George had also asked Hall Caine, the novelist whose work had inspired several films (including *The Manxman*), to direct a cinema propaganda campaign on behalf of the National War Committee (and Caine in fact furnished the script for the aborted Brenon movie).[22]

Lloyd George was convinced that Beaverbrook was the right man to lead the agitprop drive but, in installing Lord Northcliffe as propaganda chief for enemy countries, Beaverbrook faced the wrath of many politicians. One press mogul was enough – but two? Lloyd George, it was pointed out, risked the public and fellow politicians assuming that views expressed in the pair's newspapers were the views of the government. Beaverbrook faced considerable hostility during his spell as minister of information (ending November 1918) but at least he had some appreciation of the power of cinema. Beaverbrook thought he could spread Britain's propaganda message through newspaper proprietors, by pictorial publications 'and especially by the cinema, which at this time was just emerging from the Nickelodeon age'.[23] The troops also needed convincing and 'artists and cameramen must be seen at the front'.

The *Kinematograph Year Book* of 1919 certainly found Beaverbrook's tenure successful, referring to the 'splendid achievements' of the Ministry of Information and applauding the choice of Beaverbrook, formerly chairman of the War Office Cinematograph Committee. Fleets of Kinemotors (government-backed travelling cinemas) had been touring Britain on the government's initiative. As *Cinema* noted, this was inspired by the recent success of Col. A. C. Bromhead (of Gaumont) in showing British agitprop films in Russia. Screen propaganda had been effective in neutral and allied countries, according to the *Kinematograph Year Book*. The War Office topicals and *Topical Budgets* – early newsreels – had both proved successful.[24]

In May 1917 the War Office Cinematograph Committee had officially taken over *Topical Budget*, a newsreel run by the Hulton Press and it became the *War Office Official Topical Budget*. Later *Topical* was bought up for the duration of the war and Harry Rowson, co-director of Ideal when it embarked on the Lloyd George film, became head of sales.[25] But as early as 1915 the War Office had effectively monitored the domestic newsreels or newsfilms, via the Cinematograph Trade Topical Committee dominated by Gaumont. The renamed British Topical Committee for War Films had sent two cameramen to the Western Front, the first official British First World War photographers. A third was sent out later. Censorship and safety restrictions meant that many of the early 1914–18 films were hopelessly unrevealing, containing little more than troop movements. The huge success of the much more ambitious compilation feature film *The Battle of the Somme* (1916) encouraged the War Office Committee to start producing its own films. The government had its pick of the best topicals, and many of these films (actual or reconstructed) gained formidable reputations, as Luke McKernan has pointed out. By the war's end restrictions on photographers visiting the front had been relaxed considerably.[26]

The *Kinematograph Weekly* in August 1919 highlighted a 'War Office Kinematograph [Cinematograph] Committee' report which announced a total profit of £71,975 in the year ending 31 July. The committee's share was £13,324 and the bulk of this money had gone to war charities. 'Valuable pictorial records of certain battles and phases of the war' had been obtained 'free of any charge on the public funds'. The committee's expense for *Hearts of the World* was £2,324 and the film had gained 'immense prestige for the industry'. By October 1918 it was smashing all box office records at that haven for early films, the Palace Theatre, Shaftesbury Avenue.[27]

But the public were probably more susceptible to propaganda through the fiction films of the period. That was hardly surprising, for between August 1914, when the conflict began, and the Armistice around 200 British films of this type flooded the domestic market.[28] These ranged from such quasi-educational films as G. B. Samuelson's *The Causes of the Great European War* (1914) and *Incidents of the Great European War* (1914), both directed by George Pearson, to a string of war comedies featuring the screen and music-hall comedian Fred Evans. *The Causes* was made in the war's first month, with Fred Paul playing both Kitchener and the Kaiser and Norman Stuart as Winston Churchill. Numerous British pictures sought to provide home audiences with a flavour of the battlefields of Europe and the plight of the French and Belgians.

Certain titles left no doubt about the film's tone – *Huns of the North Sea* (1914), *In the Clutches of the Hun* (1915), and *Under the German Yoke* (1915), for instance – though there was almost nothing from Britain billed quite as uncompromisingly as one early American movie entry into the propaganda stakes. *The Beast of Berlin* (1918) was directed by and starred Rupert Julian as the 'Beast' – the Kaiser, of course. One compilation film to emerge with similarly histrionic publicity was *Germany's Mad Crime*, edited by, and with commentary from, the former *Daily Mail* correspondent in Berlin, Frederick Wile (author of *Who's Who in Hunland*, according to *Cinema* magazine). He described the film, 'showing how Germany uses one war to make ready for the next', as 'a warning to the British never again to trust the Hun'. The movie was 'a picture to make your blood boil', said *Motion Picture News*.[29]

Comic shorts were probably a great audience relief after all this. In October 1914, in *Pimple Enlists*, the comic hero – played, as always, by Fred Evans – was merely a territorial sentry dreaming of his capture by the Germans. By November 1914 he was seizing the Kaiser (*How Lieutenant Pimple Captured the Kaiser*). That film was re-released in 1916 and in September of that year Pimple repeated the dose (*Pimple Strafing the Kaiser*). Pimple was unusual in 'regarding hatred of the Germans as a source of pure and legitimate fun', said *Bioscope*.[30] Only film cartoons or comic films 'were able to make current affairs the subject of laughter'.[31] These knockabout comedies were only one strand of the wishful-thinking or wish-fulfilment movies of the period. There were numerous other movies of slumbering central characters performing valorous deeds in the land of nod and a clutch of films of youngsters helping to save the nation. *A Boy Scout's Dream or How Billie Captured the Kaiser* (1917) combined both trends, and in *Girl Boy Scout Shot* (1914) a girl donned her brother's scout uniform to capture a German. In *Two Little Britons* (1914), even the foreign secretary's children 'unmask a teacher as a spy'.

All too typical, apparently, was *The Bridge Destroyer* (1914), described by *Bioscope* as 'a conventional little spy drama telling a conventional story of a conventional German bridge-wrecking spy and plans thief whose machinations are frustrated . . . by a minister's daughter and her lover aided, incidentally, by a troop of enthusiastic boy scouts'. In *Over the Top* (1918), Arthur Empey, a former American soldier, starred as a man who enlists in the British army, then gains a commission in the American army and kills a German spy chief who has abducted and imprisoned a girl in a French chateau.[32]

Young women spies, girls playing their full part in the war industrial effort, or female innocents regularly outwitted spies or bloodthirsty Germans in films such as *A Munition Girl's Romance* (1917) and *If* (1916). The War Ministry's own Cinematograph department released *Mrs John Bull Prepared* (1917), which paid due homage to women's role in the war in a fictional drama and complemented the numerous newsreel items on women workers. Brenon's fated *Victory and Peace* movie centred on a nurse who had saved a captain during the (fictitious) German invasion. In the more romantic escapism, girls on the battlefield wound up nursing their loved ones.

Often cads and thieves gained redemption by heroism in the war, for example in *Your Country Needs You* (1914) and *Jimmy* (1916) and in Bertram Phillips's Holmfirth company film, *A Man the Army Made* (1917). Occasionally a pacifist was won over by events, as with the hero of *An Englishman's Home* (1914), who apparently saw sense only when Germans invaded his house and killed his son, and with the vicar spurred to action by his son's death in *For the Empire* (1914). *An Englishman's Home* was made for British and Colonial by Ernest Batley, who, with his wife Ethyle, shot many patriotic shorts during the war. Those who did not enlist were usually regarded in these films as 'slackers' or 'shirkers' who could only gain respect by entering the fray, in *England's Call* (1914), for instance.

Some film-makers played on the British people's deepest fears with invasion films, notably the Dreadnought company's *The Great North Sea Tunnel* (1914), in which the Germans build a tunnel to enter England.[33] Other shrewd directors took no chances in catering for those with specific genre tastes. Fight movies, sometimes featuring champion boxers in fictional roles, were popular in the period, but when A. E. Coleby starred world flyweight champion Jimmy Wilde in *The Pitboy's Romance* (1917) he took all necessary precautions. After triumphing in a fictional fight (and the film showed round after round in order, presumably, not to tax the acting ability of the 'Ghost with a Hammer in his Hands') the Wilde character appeared in the ring in khaki at the finale.[34]

Some ostensible dramas scarcely bothered to veil their message to any recalcitrants or laggards not yet in uniform, for example the London company's *You* (1916, director Harold Shaw) which featured high-profile British stars Edna Flugrath, Gerald Ames and Douglas Munro and centred on a note passed from hand to hand asking, 'What are you doing for your country?' Profits from this movie went to the Cinema Ambulance Fund.[35] The Red Cross gained the proceeds of Elvey's war film *Comradeship* (made 1918, released January 1919) centring on a pacifist who enlists and is blinded.[36]

Rachael Low's comment that after 1915 'the battlefield seems to have been regarded as box office poison' is not confirmed by a trawl through films catalogued by Denis Gifford, though in the war's later stages the general tenor of the films had become less lurid and there were fewer war comedies. The 1918 feature *Democracy* (directed by Sidney Morgan, who had advocated an exhibition quota to protect British films as early as 1917) and Elvey's *Comradeship* emphasized the way war broke through social barriers, a theme apparently unusual enough at the time to excite comment.[37]

But there were exceptions to the comparative restraint. *The Hidden Hand* (1918), was a truncated version of a 1915 film, *It is for England!*, written and directed by stage playwright Laurence Cowen. A novel

10. Jingoistic anti-naturalization advertisement for *The Hidden Hand*, released in 1918 and sponsored by *John Bull*.

based on the earlier film sold at least 300,000 copies.[38] The release of the
five-reel *Hidden Hand* had implications for the Rowsons (see the
Introduction) but 'the topical stuff was cut out' and this excised material
included a short epilogue showing the Kaiser 'in the hour of his defeat
with the wraiths of his victims' including Nurse Cavell and *Lusitania*
passengers 'gibbering and pointing with avenging, accusing fingers at
him'. It was backed by *John Bull* magazine and its fiercely xenophobic
editor Horatio Bottomley, concurrently the scourge of the Ideal company.
The film was about German spies in Britain, and the advertisement in the
trade press was accompanied by a disturbingly jingoistic drawing of
St George slaying the dragon of 'Naturalisation'.[39] Bottomley, under the
guise of patriotism, was spending most of those weeks calling for the
Kaiser to face trial at the Old Bailey but also demanding that 'pacifists
and people with Teutonic alliances of various kinds do not stand in the
way of a just peace that would punish Germany as she deserves'.[40]

Bottomley, at that time facing the libel action successfully brought
against him by the Ideal company for his slur on the Lloyd George
feature, told an Albert Hall rally on 7 November 1918 – four days before
the Armistice – that he hoped *The Hidden Hand* would go a 'long way
toward helping to get rid of the enemy alien influence in this country'.
Bottomley stated his intentions of running a campaign in *John Bull*
simultaneously 'in an effort to purge our country of the horrible thing
which has spread its tentacles in and around every branch of society'.[41]
These bellicose pronouncements were scarcely designed to appease Ideal
(or in fact help *John Bull* in the Ideal libel case), but Bottomley's speech
reflected an apparent mood in the country. There were 'Huns in our
Midst'-style rallies all over Britain and, in this climate a few weeks earlier,
the government brought in a British Naturalisation and Status of Aliens
Bill which laid down that no alien was to be employed by the
government. An Aliens Advisory Committee was set up as a watchdog,
and apparently an unoffical committee, the Aliens Watch Committee,
was formed under the government's former war propaganda chief,
Sir Edward Carson.[42] In this atmosphere, the president of the Board of
Trade Sir Albert Stanley answered public accusations that he was called
Nuttmeyer and was by implication a foreigner. (In fact, his father was a
Scandinavian originally named Knatriess, and Sir Albert's family had
been settled in Derbyshire for years.) He made his case and his political
adversaries backed off.[43] The secretary of state for war, Viscount Milner,

was also among those who had to answer questions about his family and roots.

More pertinent, perhaps, is the case of *The Life Story of David Lloyd George*'s scriptwriter. The eminently respectable Sir Sidney Low found himself a casualty, just months after the announcement of his knighthood on 1 January 1918. In February he accepted a post from Northcliffe on the Propaganda Committee for Enemy Countries. In May he took charge of the wireless service at the Ministry of Information library and in the summer he was still deeply worried about the war's outcome, fearing that 'the Hun was almost at the gate'.[44] On 22 July Sir Harold Snagge, secretary to the Ministry of Information, questioned Low, born in Blackheath of Hungarian stock, about his parents' nationality. On 23 July Low tendered his resignation from the wireless post, Beaverbrook and Northcliffe apparently stalling on the issue, though Beaverbrook was certainly anxious, fearing questions would be asked in the House. The final straw came when Northcliffe, at the Enemy Propaganda committee, read a letter drawing attention to Low's 'Central European origins'. On 23 August Low wrote to Northcliffe resigning from the committee, ostensibly on the grounds of 'want of time', and his resignation from the wireless job was accepted in September.[45] This sorry episode and the general climate did not augur particularly well for the immediate peacetime atmosphere.

The British film industry, at least, emerged from the war with some optimism. Gaumont spent £30,000 on its Shepherds Bush studio in 1915 and the London Film company, at St Margaret's, Twickenham, claimed to be the biggest indigenous movie company of all, employing a staff of 130 and facing a total wage bill of £750 a week. Other major production companies included Clarendon of Croydon, Neptune at Boreham Wood, British and Colonial in Walthamstow, and Hepworth at Walton-on-Thames. Oswald Stoll's company, building on the theatre entrepreneur's Empire theatre circuit success, opened its studio at Surbiton in 1918 and in 1919 began running Britain's biggest studios in Cricklewood. But the Stoll firm soon lost ground in the 1920s and ceased production late in the decade.

The war years also saw the rise of the Ideal company, starting as renters in 1911 and beginning production in 1915–16 with two Fred Paul features. The third Paul film for Ideal, *The Second Mrs Tanqueray* (1916), helped establish the company's executives Harry and Simon Rowson, and by 1918 Ideal was comfortably among the top ten UK movie producers. The company retained that position for a few years but was absorbed by Gaumont in 1925 after producing more than seventy films, mainly four- to six-reelers. Paul and A. V. Bramble were Ideal's most prolific directors, though Elvey directed five films for the company between 1917 and 1920, including a two-reel war drama *Lest We Forget* which gained huge bookings and contained a scene showing the sinking of the *Lusitania*. Its prospects were helped by useful trade publicity that its French star Rita Jolivet had survived the *Lusitania* tragedy.[46]

Ideal's executives were clearly no slouches in film publicity and originated several gimmicks in the trade press, soliciting reactions from the public and the trade and presenting statistics of exhibitors' responses to their films. Two-page spreads advertising (or 'booming') the firm's latest products were commonplace. In 1918 Ideal also announced plans to cut ten of its earlier films to five reels and re-release one a month from March 1919 onwards if the war continued, to plug the gap created by a fall in US imports. In the first seven months of 1918, US imports dwindled by almost 50 per cent on the same period in the previous year, and the shortage of shipping was likely to continue, warned the trade press.

The *Kinematograph Weekly* opined in 1920 that British producers had shown in the previous year that they were 'now able to hold their own against the best that the world can produce'. That proved to be almost childishly optimistic in view of American film domination and problems which hit studios hard in the 1920s and led to closures. There was no longer a diet of propaganda to sustain them; some companies had almost lost their *raison d'être*.

Elvey's *The Victory Leaders*, a series of thirty-minute films with footage of Lloyd George and other statesmen of the war, came out in 1919. Proceeds went to the blinded soldiers and sailors at St Dunstan's – but long before the Armistice there were signs that many exhibitors had had their fill of the war and were suspicious of propaganda. At the end of 1918 some exhibitors rejected victory slides of the war leaders and, with the December 1918 election looming, A. E. Newbould, later the cinema trade's representative in Parliament, inveighed against those who would use the cinema for propaganda.[47] The 1919 *Kinematograph Year Book* claimed that 'futile attempts to exploit the kinemas for electioneering purposes have somewhat discredited screen propaganda . . . the trade has to face the fact that it is in the film business as a business and that its exploitation as a means of free – and even cheap – publicity can no longer be tolerated'.

Exhibitors certainly had no intention of allowing themselves to be 'used' in the run-up to the 1918 election, and some lost no chance to stress that their film audience was sated with politicians on the screen. Interestingly, the trade press reported in 1920 – when Lloyd George's Tory-dominated coalition government had lost popularity – that 'topical' films of Lloyd George, the 'Man who Saved the Empire', were booed off in Lancashire.[48]

The film industry returned to its normal brand of movies and the unequal battle against the United States whose standards in the last years of the silents could only be envied by British producers operating on short commons. Bottomley himself soon tired of pursuing the Hun through his *John Bull* columns and turned to Bolsheviks instead. Despite all his social reforms in the war years, lovingly recorded in Elvey's triumphalist film, Lloyd George, the Welsh Wizard, had been ousted from power by 1922. That same year Sidney Low, the inveterate imperialist, was complaining to a friend that 'nobody cares or will pay twopence to read about the war heroes or the war. We have forgotten them and it and [are] apparently afraid of both.' 'Patriotism is "off" at the halls', he added. 'Does one ever see a patriotic play now?'[49]

Notes

[1] *Kinematograph and Lantern Weekly*, 12 September 1918. See Frank Owen, *Tempestuous Journey* (Hutchinson, 1954).

[2] *Cinema and Property Gazette*, 29 August 1918.

[3] Owen, op. cit.

[4] Lord Beaverbrook, *Men and Power 1917–1918* (Hutchinson, 1956).

[5] Lloyd George appears in what is clearly meant to be a victory procession, but this does not seem to be library footage. Repeated screenings of the sequence at the Wales Film and Television Archive have shown that the scene is clearly orchestrated and directed, as the movements of the troops lining the procession indicate. If Lloyd George willingly took part in this segment of the film it was obviously shot much earlier, when the government still approved of the project.

[6] *Bioscope*, 12 September 1915; *Kinematograph and Lantern Weekly*, 29 May 1919; Rachael Low, *The History of British Film, 1914–18* (George Allen & Unwin, 1948).

[7] Low, op. cit.; see also Sarah Street, 'The Memoir of Harry Rowson: *David Lloyd George M.P. – The Man who Saved the Empire*', in this volume, and *Kinematograph Weekly*, 29 May 1919.

[8] Low, op. cit. and *Kinematograph Weekly*, 29 May 1919.

[9] *The Cinema and Property Gazette*, 18 July 1918.

[10] Ibid., 4 July 1918.

[11] Low, op. cit.

[12] Low, op. cit. and Margaret Dickinson and Sarah Street, *Cinema and State: The Film Industry and the British Government 1927–84* (British Film Institute, 1985).

[13] *Bioscope*, 27 June 1918 and 30 January 1919; *Cinema and Property Gazette*, 19 December 1918. The Nelson film was extensively re-edited, and Elvey claimed that Apex, who bought the film for £15,000, allowed him to cut it back to 'the state in which I left it a few months ago'. This was a clear hint that the previous owners, International Exclusives, had tampered with it (*Pictures and Picturegoer*, 12–19 April and 8 February 1919). *Nelson* was finally completed in October 1918 (*Pictures and Picturegoer*, 26 October–2 November 1918). The *Nelson* sale deal was clinched at the London trade show. See also Low Warren, *The Film Game* (Werner Laurie, 1937) and Denis Gifford, *The British Film Catalogue 1895–1985* (David and Charles, 1987).

[14] Gifford, op. cit. See also Andrew Higson's article on *Nelson* as a classic British heritage film in *British Cinema and the First World War* (1994).

[15] It was revealing not least because Elvey made no mention of the Lloyd George film, already completed by that date and probably seized by the government before the January 1919 Ideal High Court libel action against *John Bull* and Odhams Press. Indeed the leading actors and people involved, except for Sir Sidney Low, were remarkably silent in public after the film's disappearance. See also *Pictures and Picturegoer*, 12–19 April 1919.

[16] *Cinema and Property Gazette*, 24 October 1918; *Kinematograph Weekly*, August 1922.

[17] *Bioscope*, 8 August 1918.

[18] *Cinema and Property Gazette*, 27 June 1918.

[19] *Bioscope*, 14 March 1918; Beaverbrook, op. cit.; Frank Owen, op. cit. In *War Memoirs of David Lloyd George, II* (Odhams Press, 1936) the former prime minister praises Beaverbrook and Northcliffe for their propaganda work of 'great skill and subtlety', especially 'crossing the frontiers . . .' (p.1873).

[20] Beaverbrook, op. cit.

[21] *Bioscope*, 21 February 1918.

[22] Gifford, op. cit. Letter from Lloyd George to Hall Caine, 23 October 1917, and Caine's reply, 26 October 1917.

[23] Beaverbrook, op. cit.

[24] *Kinematograph Weekly*, 26 September and 3 October ('Germany Fears the Kinemotor') 1918.

[25] Luke McKernan, *Topical Budget* (British Film Institute, 1992) gives a detailed account of this magazine's history and particularly its wartime contribution.

[26] McKernan, op. cit.

[27] *Kinematograph Weekly*, 28 August 1919; *Cinema and Property Gazette*, 29 August 1918.

[28] Gifford, op. cit.

[29] Quoted in *Kinematograph Weekly*, 21 November 1918.

[30] *Bioscope*, 4 April 1918.

[31] Gifford, op. cit.; *Bioscope*, 1 October 1914.

[32] *Bioscope*, 22 August 1918 and *Bioscope Supplement*, 5 November 1914.

[33] David Berry, *Wales and Cinema: The First Hundred Years* (University of Wales Press, 1994); *Bioscope*, 29 March, 31 May and 7 June 1917.

[34] Gifford, op. cit.

[35] Gifford, op. cit.; *Bioscope*, 6 February 1919.

[36] Low, op. cit.

[37] *Bioscope*, 6 February 1919.

[38] *Cinema and Property Gazette*, 14 November 1918.

[39] *Cinema and Property Gazette*, 31 October, 14 and 21 November 1918; *Kinematograph Weekly*, 21 November 1918.

[40] *Richmond Herald*, 16 November 1918.

[41] *Cinema and Property Gazette*, 7 November 1919.

[42] Owen, op. cit.

[43] Ibid.

[44] Desmond Chapman-Huston, *The Lost Historian: Sidney Low 1857–1932* (Murray, 1936).

[45] The source of the letter is not stated in Chapman-Huston's biography.

[46] Memoir of Harry Rowson (unpublished, British Film Institute Library); Gifford, op. cit.; *Kinematograph Weekly*, 8 August and 5 September 1918.

[47] *Kinematograph Weekly*, 12 December 1918; *Cinema and Property Gazette*, 5 December 1918; *Bioscope*, 17 April 1919.

[48] See Sarah Street's 'Postscript' article in this volume tracing Lloyd George's political decline.

[49] Chapman-Huston, op. cit.

PART II
Rediscovery and Restoration

Film archives around the world play a vital role in preserving celluloid for future generations, but theirs is a difficult task at the best of times. Even when the necessary funding is provided by local or national governments – and this is by no means always the case – film archives have to rely as much on good luck as good judgement, a situation which is amply illustrated by the story surrounding the chance rediscovery of *The Life Story of David Lloyd George*. For the Wales Film and Television Archive in Aberystwyth, this was undoubtedly their biggest coup but, as Gwenan Owen and John Reed demonstrate in this section's first article, finding the film was only the beginning of the story.

In a detailed account of the WFTVA's work, Owen and Reed touch on two principal (and often conflicting) aims of film archives: to maintain films as their original producers intended them to be seen while, at the same time, making them accessible to a contemporary audience. A case in point came when decisions had to be made about musical accompaniment which, as Owen and Reed comment, is vital to the experience of silent cinema.[1] Because the material unearthed by the WFTVA contained no instructions regarding music, this was a particular challenge faced by those who were asked to offer musical interpretation when *The Life Story* was finally ready to show in cinemas.

John Hardy's task, to compose a score which would accompany *The Life Story*'s world première in Cardiff, presented him with several problems, not least the need to cater for a 1990s audience. His account is nicely complemented by Neil Brand, who touches on the particular challenge facing a solo pianist asked to interpret a long and provocative movie.

Ultimately, all the articles in this section provide a fascinating insight into the questions – practical and theoretical – faced when preparing *The Life Story of Lloyd George* for the screen some three-quarters of a century after it was made. Silent cinema is currently undergoing something of a renaissance at film festivals and art cinemas, but without the kind of work detailed in the three articles which follow there would be very little to see or hear.

S.H.

Note

[1] For a discussion of how and why silent cinema developed its musical accompaniment, see Claudia Gorbman's *Unheard Melodies: Narrative Film Music* (British Film Institute, 1987), 33–41.

5

Uncanning the Uncanny

GWENAN OWEN with JOHN REED

The coincidental and interlinking events which led to the discovery and identification of *The Life Story of David Lloyd George* point to the unpredictable nature of film archiving and to the need for archives to be constantly alert to the possibility of unexpected discoveries.[1]

Referring to *The Life Story of David Lloyd George*, Kevin Brownlow describes the discovery of the film by the Wales Film and TV Archive as 'the find of the century'. The film, by timely coincidence, was acquired just as plans were being made to celebrate the centenary of cinema in 1996. What better gift could a film archive wish for than the possibility of screening, for the first time ever, and in the centenary year, a film made in 1918 by the well-known British director Maurice Elvey about the celebrated prime minister, David Lloyd George?

A gift indeed, but the arrival of the film at the WFTVA, and its impact on the staff, was disconcerting. Our joy was dampened by the realization of what the next few months or years would entail: much hard work and frustration, constant head-scratching, expensive mistakes but hopefully, success and a sense of achievement when the task was complete.

Inspection and Identification

When a film arrives at the Archive and has been logged as an acquisition it is passed on to the technical department for initial inspection and identification. Each item is individually checked and given an identification number.

Items in the substantial Lloyd George collection deposited with the Archive by Lord Tenby included sixteen square film cans stored in one large wooden metal-clad box. It was found that all sixteen contained several individual rolls of 35 mm nitrate-base, black-and-white, silent, full-gate-format negative film, a total of 137 rolls in all.

Each individual can in this intriguing box was labelled with an Ideal Films Ltd label detailing the title and number of rolls in the can. These included :

10 cans labelled *L.G. Neg Pt 1–Pt 10*
1 can labelled *L.G. Neg Uncut (16 rolls)*
5 cans labelled *L.G. Neg titles*

Label information is not by any means guaranteed to correspond with the contents of the film cans and the preservation officer always needs to check and cross-refer every item with the detailed attention of a detective. In this case, however, all the information was accurate except on can 7, which contained nine rolls instead of the eight indicated. The information contained on and in the cans proved crucial in the work of reassembling this film, as we explain later.

The next stage involved a more thorough physical examination and a listing of the film's condition. The material was inspected for mould, scratches and abrasions, splice condition, damaged perforations, shrinkage, brittleness, rust stains, dirt and, crucially, nitrate decomposition.

Nitrate material is always given priority, as once it has begun to decompose it becomes, because of its chemical composition, potentially explosive. There is, therefore, some urgency to process nitrate, particularly in the case of small film archives whose nitrate storage capacity is severely restricted by fire regulations.

An initial Archive inspection sheet (14 June 1994) reports the general condition of *The Life Story*, as 'very good considering the . . . less than ideal conditions this footage is likely to have been stored in for the last 70 years (an attic and then stables). Of the 8000′ plus [already] examined less than 500′ displays any immediate signs of imminent decomposition . . .' Of greater concern at this stage was the effect of mould on the material which this early report indicates as ranging 'from a light surface mould extending across the base from heavy deposits in the perfs to heavy attacks upon the emulsion apparently endangering image accutance'. In fact the film was remarkably unharmed by mould, but a very small number of images have been permanently and irrevocably damaged. Most of the material was untouched.

Despite the damaged perforations, the dirty splices, the varied intensity of shrinkage, in general, the original nitrate-base negatives were in good condition with outstanding technical image quality. A more surprising defect, from the point of view of modern film practice, was the amount of avoidable physical damage such as fingermarks, emulsion and base scratches, poor processing consistency and what appeared to be a general lack of care in handling what, at the time, were the master negatives of a major film production. Apparently film was treated with far less regard than that given to it by present-day film archivists!

During this inspection a listing of each roll was undertaken giving a brief description of images or wording of titles, tinting and toning details, section identification and intertitle positions found on the tops and tails and spliced inserts at the relevant points in the negative rolls (see appendix for examples).

At this stage although the film was still not formally identified as *The Life Story of David Lloyd George,* our preservation officer John Reed had a good idea that here was a major feature film about the famous Welsh politician.

Coincidence plays a very important role in the work of a film archive. In this particular case, the film historian David Berry was undertaking some last-minute research at the BFI for his book *Wales and Cinema: The First Hundred Years* and had recently come across an article by Sarah Street documenting the 'strange tale of the film that was made, never shown and is now lost'. The article cited extracts from Harry Rowson's unpublished memoir revealing that 'in 1918 Ideal Films produced a picture about the life of Lloyd George that never reached the cinema screens'. The film was referred to as *The Man who Saved the Empire* (1918).[2]

From the Archive's point of view the evidence at this stage was still tenuous. Nevertheless the film's subject matter was obviously the same as that cited in Rowson's memoir, while can-label information identified the production company as Ideal Films Ltd. Moreover the film stock could be dated as being 1916, 1917 and 1918 Eastman Kodak, which corresponded with the dates given by Sarah Street for this production.[3]

Once the tenuous link had been made it became vital to follow up the research in greater detail. This work was undertaken by David Berry with reference to trade publications such as *Kinematograph Weekly, Bioscope,* to the Rowson memoir and a number of other sources, and was also carried out in consultation with other experts in the field. It took relatively little time to establish that the rediscovered film was indeed *The Man who Saved the Empire,* also known as *The Life Story of David Lloyd George.*[4]

Restoration and Preservation

The fundamental role of any film archive is to preserve and then to render accessible the moving images in its collection. In filmic terms, preservation means creating the possibility of extending the life span of any given film, which in most cases is done intially by creating a preservation negative. The preservation negative becomes what is known as master material and is stored in temperature- and humidity-controlled storerooms. The master negative is only made available when the Archive needs to strike a print of the film for access purposes. For reasons of security, master and access material are ideally stored separately.

The route to preservation has several permutations and depends largely on what original material is acquired by the archive. As only the negative of *The Life Story* had been acquired, the route to preservation would inevitably be via an interpositive. Moreover, although the film was apparently complete, it had not been finally edited and remained in its unassembled state. It was clear that the Archive would have to undertake this work based on the technical information provided. This was a major undertaking and a field hitherto not ventured into by this still young and relatively inexperienced archive.

Following initial inspection, the next stage was to evaluate the best technical procedure to ensure full preservation of the original material and to allow for progression to show prints for the widest possible access. The ideal route was described as being:

1   to ensure archival preservation of the material in a format as close as possible to the original (it is common archival practice to transfer all nitrate material to safety stock, i.e. acetate or polyester);
2   to provide working material that could be assembled in a chronological order based on the technical instructions available and any subsequent information uncovered;
3   to work towards the production of one or more show prints that represented as closely as possible the film the Ideal Company had intended for release;
4   to produce one or more show prints using the 'Flash Filter' procedure on colour print film to represent the colours outlined by the tinting and toning information;

5   to establish viable methods of presentation including the addition of
    music, either live or recorded.

The first two steps could be described as the process of restoration and
preservation. The other three relate more specifically to access.

As has been indicated, smaller film archives are not in a position to
process nitrate internally. In the UK the National Film and Television
Archive (NFTVA) offers this service to the smaller archives. The process
tends to be a long one as there is a considerable backlog of nitrate material
waiting for transfer. However, the increasingly evident importance of
this film, and the fact that the film was now known to have been directed
by Maurice Elvey, was sufficient justification for it to be put into the
'nitrate fast track'. The willingness of the NFTVA to collaborate with the
WFTVA and to give this film priority was one of the elements which
made this major preservation undertaking possible.

Another vital element was funding, for although the main function
of a film archive is film preservation, the funding available is
minimal. Preserving *The Life Story* was obviously a priority, but it
could not be done at the sacrifice of other material, nor would the
WFTVA's annual budget stretch to meet the costs of such a major
undertaking. Sponsorship would have to be found urgently. The
National Lottery Unit of Wales provided substantial backing for this
project, while money, or support in kind, was also secured for various
stages of the project, from the Welsh Broadcasting Trust, Morgan Bruce
Solicitors, Film and Photo Design and TK Films. Kodak provided the
appropriate film stock to enable the Archive to generate the following
essential elements:

two fine-grain positives from each of the 137 rolls of original nitrate
    negatives. These high-quality images duped directly from the original
    material would be kept in the order found in the original cans and
    would be classified as master material;
two fine-grain negatives from one of the above – one to be held by the
    WFTVA as a preservation master, the other to be used to produce a cut
    negative for assembly;
one 16 mm black and white reduction print from one of the above
    negatives to enable the Archive to view and perform assembly work.

Reassembly and Restoration: The Jigsaw

The background to the making and subsequent 'suppression' of this film provided some vital evidence which informed the reassembly process. It would be misleading to suggest that the documentation available solved all the problems. Decisions based on informed speculation had inevitably to be made. It is also necessary to remain open to the possibility of new evidence which may change our perspectives and require us to review the work done to date.

The information provided on and in the cans was very useful and was certainly an indication of how the Ideal Company intended the final cut to look. This information was nevertheless incomplete and many questions remained unanswered.

The initial assembly was done using the alphabetical sequence noted from the tops and tails. Upon viewing, this appeared to make very little chronological sense and it was later understood that these alphabetical references were related to the tinting and toning instructions rather than the film's chronology. Having spent hours creating this first assembly, the preservation officer was forced back to the drawing-board to reassess the situation. An alternative approach, using the section numbers as a guide, was attempted. When completed, it was generally agreed that the chronology of most parts was better but that some fine tuning was probably still required (see appendix for details of can information and explanatory notes).

Further reassembly included the insertion of previously unused titles, particularly in parts 9 and 10, which had apparently only reached the roughcut stage and did not include much intertitle information nor the apparently complete definite section information provided for parts 1–8 (see appendix information pertaining to can 9). The absence of information for these final parts can probably be explained by the context of the events which took place towards the end of 1918 when, following the publication of Horatio Bottomley's article in *John Bull*, it became known that Lloyd George no longer wished the film to be released.[5]

It seems likely that the rapid course of events following the publication of the *John Bull* article would have interrupted the editing process and that the missing final cut information was never formally generated. This inevitably made the order of the final parts of the reassembly process far more speculative. Discussion, consultation and further research helped to inform decisions which had inevitably to be made on the basis of very little real evidence.

The speculative aspect of the reassembly was not confined to parts 9 and 10. The information provided for the other parts, although more complete, was nevertheless limited. While an outlined structure is a statement of intent and provides a working tool, it is difficult to assume that such a structure resembles what the final product might have become. During editing, of course, modifications are inevitable due to the organic nature of the creative process.

Serial or Feature?

Other reassembly problems arose from the sometimes conflicting nature of the evidence uncovered through research. A very fundamental issue was the question of whether *The Life Story* had been intended as a serial or as a one-off feature.

For present-day exhibition purposes, it was obvious that the latter option was preferable. Although modern requirements might well have influenced certain decisions, as has already been indicated, the guiding principle throughout was the re-creation of a film which represented as far as possible the intentions of the original production company. The Rowson memoirs and the information released by the trade publications provide conflicting evidence on this matter, as the following quotations indicate.

It seems from the trade papers that Ideal's intention was to release the film in serial form, an approach likely to increase their returns substantially, and, it was claimed, an option which suited the nature of the production. One inconsistency here is the conflicting references suggesting that the film was intended as a ten-, eight- or six-parter. Late into the movie's production, an advertisement in *Kinematograph Weekly* referred to the film as a ten-part serial which corresponds to the information acquired with the film:

> Resolved to issue the picture in ten episodes or chapters, one a week, beginning Dec 2 next . . .
>
> . . . It is imperative that the trade should understand that the film has been built up in such a way as to be easily divisible into separate chapters. The division into separate chapters was projected at the outset, and the plan has been steadily kept in sight in the making of the picture.

> . . . The consequence is that each chapter is clear cut – not beginning
> or ending arbitrarily, but complete in itself . . .[6]

The Rowson memoir gives a rather different story, which, it has to be
pointed out, was told with hindsight. It nevertheless indicates that,
despite the temptation of increased returns and wider distribution, the
view held by the company was that the impact of the film lay in the
cumulative effect of the rags-to-riches story told as a whole. Despite the
conflicting evidence, and aware of the advantage of hindsight which
Rowson had acquired at the time of writing, the Archive opted for the
feature-length version because it was Rowson's stated view. Our
preservation officer is convinced that the way in which the film was
constructed makes both options feasible.

Fine Tuning

Once the second assembly had been completed, a special screening
was organized at the Archive to which a number of experts were
invited to give their opinion on the work in progress. These included the
film historian and silent-film expert Kevin Brownlow, David Berry, Lloyd
George's biographer and historian John Grigg, Sarah Street, John Hefin,
Emyr Price and the Archive staff. Other experts consulted but unable to
attend this screening, were sent VHS tapes of this assembly and asked to
comment on specific issues, some of which were ethical, some technical,
but most represented a combination of both.

In some cases the answers were fairly obvious, although as a novice in
this process the WFTVA was eager to have its decisions validated by
experts in the field. The Archive staff were also well aware that close
involvement can result in the most obvious solution to a problem being
overlooked.

Relatively easy decisions to take were those concerning glitches,
double takes and flash frames. A letter from senior staff consulted at the
NFTVA confirmed our belief that they should be removed, as it would be
'what the film's editor would have done at the final cut stage'. It could be
argued that this is an assumption; but it can be justified in the name of
coherent sense, which after all, is the job of both the effective film editor
and the film restorer.

Other editorial decisions were more delicate and, in some cases, they remain to be satisfactorily resolved. Certain scenes in the film are – by present standards at least – excessively lengthy. Two examples come to mind, namely the scenes depicting Lloyd George's anti-Boer War speech at Birmingham Town Hall, which resulted in riots and in his hasty departure dressed as a policeman, and secondly the factory scenes shot to depict the efforts being made by industry, at Lloyd George's urging, to support the war. In the former, the crowd scenes are impressively filmed, especially given the resources available at the time. They are, however, repeated *ad nauseam*, making this very dramatic moment in Lloyd George's career a rather tedious episode in the film, as testified by modern audience feedback. But can we be sure that 1918 audiences would have reacted in the same way? And more importantly, is it ethical to cut these scenes which, according to the documentation provided, were intended to be included, even if, as some claim, a few of the frames in certain takes appear to be cues rather than actions? To what extent can the film restorer become an editor, and on what basis should those editorial decisions be made, if at all?

The case of the factory scenes is similar except that they have the merit of providing very interesting documentary-style information regarding factory processes and conditions at the time. So realistic is the representation that one can quite easily forget that the striding politician, so obviously interested in the processes being applied to the war effort, and so warmly welcomed by the factory staff in true VIP tradition, is in fact an actor and not the real Lloyd George.

In both these cases opinion is split on whether these scenes should be edited for aesthetic purposes or left, in the absence of any clear indication that Ideal intended removing them. Both viewpoints are valid; but for the moment both scenes remain in the film in their entirety, based on the archival viewpoint that, as no documentation exists to indicate the company's intention to edit these scenes, they should at least be included in all preservation material. This argument need not preclude the creation of an edited version which would be more palatable to modern audiences.

The issue of the length of intertitles was less contentious and there was general agreement that they could be shortened by approximately 0.5 seconds per word. This decision was based on the argument that contemporary audiences have a higher degree of literacy and can therefore read more quickly. Equally important was the added bonus that this would substantially shorten the length of the film.

Read My Lips

As has already been indicated, there was considerably more difficulty with assembling parts 9 and 10 than with the other parts. A graphic example of this occurs at the climactic end of the film. The war over and the army disbanded, Lloyd George is left alone to muse over his achievements and responsibilities, and to face the future. The premier is depicted standing alone, one arm on the fireplace, the other free to express the forcefulness of the Lloyd George fist. As he reflects on the past, he recalls that, despite the recent victory, the country should have been readier for war. The intertitles read: 'Next time we must be better prepared . . . we must have have more and bigger guns – more U-boats, more aeroplanes, more food stores, more ruthlessness . . .' He then warns, 'There must be no next time!' In all the takes related to this scene Lloyd George is seen talking to camera, the framing is close enough to allow the spectator to read his lips and it becomes obvious at this important crescendo that the words he is miming are not the same as those in the intertitles. While this might not have mattered in another scene it was a distraction at this point of dramatic finale. The contradiction can probably be explained by the fact that the action was probably filmed before the end of the war and that a more bellicose conclusion had been intended. By the time of editing, the war had already been won, and it seems likely that the intertitles for the concluding scenes were revised to accommodate this and to meet the public's need for reassurance rather than aggression.

It is difficult to know how Ideal intended dealing with this apparent contradiction between the written word and the miming mouth and whether it would have considered re-shooting some of the final images in order to eradicate this difficulty. The course of events which led to the removal and subsequent disappearance of the film prevented such action. Nevertheless there is no evidence that this is what would have been done. For the Archive these concluding scenes presented a real problem and provoked heated arguments, the outcome of which was to attempt a number of different assemblies. After considering all permutations, and bearing in mind the need for a dramatic conclusion to the film, a decision was made. To reveal the details would be to spoil the film's ending for, once one becomes aware of the irresolvable contradiction, it becomes difficult to ignore. It is in such a situation that the music beomes an extremely important element as it can help to increase the dramatic content of the climax and distract the audience from too close a scrutiny of the image.

The Narrative of Colour

Colour film did not yet exist in 1918 but there were processes which enabled colour to be added to black-and-white stock. The documentation included with this film indicates quite clearly the intention to use the colouring process known as tinting and toning in certain sections of the film. The can information provided in the appendix gives a clear idea of how this was to be done. It appears that each part of the film was prepared individually and that, within each part, the sections which required the same colouring were numbered and spliced together for this process. Once the colouring process had been completed the sections would be separated and re-spliced in numerical order to achieve the narrative logic intended.

The technique of tinting and toning is not at present easily available. A number of film establishments are researching ways of introducing this process into laboratories. Consequently, the option which is currently available is the technique known as 'flash filtering' which is used to simulate as closely as possible the effects of tinting and toning. Upon conclusion of the final 'cut neg assembly' with intertitles; laboratory logs including footage and frame counts, scene description and tint-and-tone information, were produced to enable the laboratory to programme its printing machine for grading and colouring.

11. Elvey's ambitious use of lap dissolves draws an analogy between David's struggle against Goliath and Lloyd George's conflict with the Kaiser.

All the intertitles in *The Life Story* are in black and white but ten different tints and tones are used in the action sequences. They can be described as follows:

Tint	Tone
yellow	
yellow	brown
orange	
orange	brown
pink	
pink	brown
pink	blue
	blue
	red
	light red

An initial colour test was made by the Film and Photo laboratory to aid the evaluation of final printing, while decisions regarding the hue and intensity of colours was made in consultation with the NFTVA who provided samples for comparison. The initial answer print from the laboratory required a number of modifications: several scenes were too dark, the pink and pink/brown tints had failed, while the colour change was incorrect at some points. The process was continued until a satisfactory answer print was achieved.

The colourization process greatly enhanced the film's general impact and the coherence of some of its more obscure scenes. There are many examples of anecdotes within anecdotes, of anecdotes in political speeches and of visual representations of abstract concepts. For a modern audience, unused to the narrative style of silent films, these might be difficult to follow. The colourization of certain scenes provides clarity of meaning in a narrative which can, at times, be long-winded.

The way in which colour is used in the adolescent Lloyd George's reverie as he listens to his uncle relating the story of David and Goliath immediately intensifies the impact of this powerful scene. Later in the film, scenes such as the story of the Girl or the Gun, which is shown as part of Lloyd George's visit to the front, and elements of the Mansion House speech become more effective. The colourization instructions provided by Ideal were followed to the letter, yet although they clearly help, there remain some sections of the film where the logic of colour is less evident.

Credits

Not surprisingly, apart from the title frame, *The Life Story of David Lloyd George,* there were no credits with the film. It was nevertheless decided that credits should be added as they would undoubtedly have been included had the final production reached the screen. Questions of credit content, placing, order, style and script had therefore to be addressed. In addition to the original credits, it was decided that there should also be restoration credits to acknowledge the work undertaken to bring the film to the screen, with an obvious distinction made between the two types of credit.

Research undertaken involved referring to other films produced by the Ideal Company around the same period in order to establish the contents and visual style of presenting production credits. Some facts also needed verifying, for while the main actors had been identified as being Norman Page, Alma Reville and Ernest Thesiger, there was still some uncertainty regarding Douglas Munro, who it was thought played the cameo role of Benjamin Disraeli. Similarly, information regarding the production team was incomplete. It was decided that only credits which could be confirmed as correct would be included. It was known that the film was directed by Maurice Elvey, scripted by Sir Sidney Low and produced by Simon and Harry Rowson. However speculation that the camera work was undertaken by the Italian Frenguelli could not be confirmed and the information was therefore omitted.

Restoration credits were generated on computer by a local publishing firm which was also able to provide a typeface to match that used by Ideal in the intertitles. Frame surrounds, incorporating the Ideal logo which already appeared in the film, were also generated. Both restoration and contemporary credits were generated on computer in the Archive using complementary typefaces to differentiate between them. Restoration credits acknowledged the technical work undertaken by John Reed on behalf of the Wales Film and Television Archive, the collaboration of the National Film and Television Archive, the funders, the help and advice of certain individuals, and finally, the support and co-operation of Lord Tenby and other members of the Lloyd George family.

Both sets of credits were then photographically reversed to produce a white on black text which was then re-photographed on black and white reversal film within the Ideal surround taken from one of the original intertitles. This was then sent away to the laboratory to produce 'held frame' negatives for addition to the cut neg assembly.

The Archive was also responsible for generating a copy of Lloyd George's birth certificate and a photograph of his parents (acquired via a member of the family), both of which were known to be intended for inclusion in the original production. A certain amount of cosmetic attention was necessary to create a more authentic appearance.

From Preservation to Presentation

The completed film was given a preview to an invited audience at Pwllheli on 27 April 1996. This extremely successful screening was accompanied by the silent-film piano accompanist Neil Brand. Eight days later, on 5 May, the world première of *The Life Story of David Lloyd George* was held at the MGM (now ABC Cinemas), Cardiff. For this event, organized to celebrate the centenary of cinema in Wales, a special musical score was produced by the Welsh composer John Hardy and played by the Cardiff Olympia Orchestra. This powerful score provided the film with a totally new dimension.

The print shown at both these screenings is, in 1998, still the only one available for screening purposes.[7] For a number of technical reasons this print cannot be made readily available for every cinema. One problem is that the film was made to be projected at 18 frames per second. This means that any venue wishing to screen the film will be required to adjust its projector. The cost of such an adjustment is estimated at £200–£300, to which can be added another £50–£60 to cover costs of a specially manufactured aperture plate to accommodate the full gate required to screen this film. The use of the incorrect aperture may result in damage to the film and will provide only a partial image on the screen. It is also difficult to imagine screening this lengthy silent film without live music or a synchronous sound-track, a supplementary cost for cinemas on tight budgets.

The WFTVA is seeking to address these difficulties so that the film can be made more generally available. One way round the screening restrictions would be the creation of what is known as a 35 mm stretch print. This is achieved by adding one frame to every three existing frames enabling the film to be screened at the habitual speed of 24 frames per second. At this speed it becomes possible to envisage adding a musical soundtrack, though this will nevertheless inevitably result in a marginal loss of image. One disadvantage of this option is that, when projected, a stretch print may exaggerate certain movements, which can be distracting to more critical spectators.

To produce a stretch print a considerable amount of intermediate laboratory work has to be undertaken. This includes the creation of a new fine-grain positive and negative, the transfer of the sound recording to optical negative and so on. The cost of this stage alone is estimated as around £25,000. This does not include the cost of rehearsing and recording the music or clearing the musical rights. Despite the cost, and the fact that it is far from ideal from a technical and archival viewpoint, this option has not yet been ruled out.

In the meantime the WFTVA is investigating other technical options, including the possibility of creating an edited version of the film which, at its present length of 2 hours 32 minutes, is regarded by some as too long. While technical, ethical, musical, legal and, perhaps more crucially, financial issues remain to be resolved, the WFTVA is fully committed to making this remarkable film more widely available for public screenings. This would seem more than justified by the interest shown both before and after the screenings.

Appendix

Below are examples of contents of the cans containing elements of *The Life Story of David Lloyd George* acquired by the Wales Film and Television Archive.

Can No. 5 Negative (8 rolls)

Item no.	Description	WFTVA no.
68	LlG Pt 5 Roll A Sec 1/3/5/7/ ORANGE 'The General Election of 1900 . . .'	MN/35/94/100
69	LlG Pt 5 Roll B Sec 2/4/6/11 BLUE 'The crowd at the early . . .'	MN/35/94/101
70	LlG Pt 5 Roll C Sec 8 ORANGE	
71	LlG Pt 5 Roll D Sec 10/12/14/16 ORANGE	

72	LlG Pt 5 Roll E Sec 13/19 BLUE	
73	LlG Pt 5 Roll F Sec 15 TONE	
	BROWN TINT YELLOW	
	'Meanwhile he had added . . .'	
74	LlG Pt 5 Roll G Sec 17 YELLOW	
	'After the Railwa . . .'	
75	LlG Pt 5 Roll H Sec 18 PINK	
	'On May 28th . . .'	MN/35/94/107

Explanatory notes

Item no. refers to each individual roll numbered consecutively.

LlG Pt 5 refers to the 5th part of the chronology of the film.

Rolls – alphabetical order refers to colouring instructions. Sections of the same colour and relating to the same scene would be printed up together and then separated into their sections for assembly purposes. The first incorrect assembly of the film was based on this alphabetical order.

Sec – refers to the section numbers which provided the editing chronology of the images within any given part. Once colourized, the individual sections would be cut up numerically to provide the editing chronology.

Colour references refer to Ideal's precise tinting and toning instructions.

Intertitles relating to each section within the part are cited. As the first words of each individual title are, on the whole different, the insertion position was always clear. Insertion was, nevertheless, a lengthy job as the titles were not chronological in the title reels.

NB: for part 9 only limited intertitle information was available. For part 10 no intertitle information was available. In both cases reassembly was consequently more difficult and involved a measure of speculation.

WFTVA no. – master-negative individual reel-numbering system used by the Wales Film and Television Archive

Can No. 9 Titles can (8 rolls)

Item no.	Description	WFTVA no.
102	Ll.G Pt 9 ROLL A Sec 1/3/5/7/9/15 TONE	MN/35/94/134
	BROWN TINT YELLOW	
	'I came into politics . . .'	
103	Ll.G Pt 9 ROLL B Sec 2 B/W	MN/35/94/135
104	Ll.G Pt 9 ROLL C Sec 8/10/24 ORANGE	
105	Ll.G Pt 9 ROLL D Sec 12 B/W	
106	Ll.G Pt 9 ROLL E Sec 13 RED	

107	Ll.G Pt 9 ROLL F Sec 14/20/22/25/27 YELLOW	
108	Ll.G Pt 9 ROLL G Sec 16 TONE	
	BROWN TINT YELLOW	
109	Ll.G Pt 9 [ROLL J] [Sec 19]	
110	Ll.G Pt 9 ROLL I Sec 19 TONE	MN/35/94/142
	BROWN TINT YELLOW	

NB: Absence of title information and some inconsistency relating to alphabetical and sectional details.

Can No. (no number) Titles can (8 rolls)

Item no.	Description	WFTVA no.
30	Lloyd George Titles 3	MN/35/94/62
31	Lloyd George Titles 9	MN/35/94/63
32	Lloyd George Titles	
33	Lloyd George Titles	
34	Lloyd George Titles 3	
35	Lloyd George Titles	
36	Lloyd George Titles 6	
37	Lloyd George Titles 10	MN/35/95/69

Explanatory notes

The significance of the numbers related to titles remains unclear. Titles were inserted according to roll instructions.

Can No. 9* Uncut negative (16 rolls)

Item no.	Description	WFTVA no.
122	LlG Uncut Negative Sec 2 YELLOW	MN/35/94/154
123	LlG Uncut Negative [FISHING]	
124	LlG Uncut Negative 4 YELLOW	
125	LlG Uncut Negative (Slate 69 C/U)	
126	LlG Uncut Negative Pt 9 Roll H Sec 17/24 PINK	
127	LlG Uncut Negative Pt 9 Roll K Sec 28 YELLOW	
128	LlG Uncut Negative Roll 3 TONE	
	BROWN TINT YELLOW	
129	LlG Uncut Negative 5	
130	LlG Uncut Negative	
131	LlG Uncut Negative Sec 10	
	TINT YELLOW [LETTERS]	

132	LlG Uncut Negative	
133	LlG Uncut Negative H YELLOW (Scene 311)	
134	LlG Uncut Negative Roll [42]	
	TONE BROWN TINT YELLOW	
135	LlG Uncut Negative Roll 50	
	TONE BROWN TINT YELLOW	
136	LlG Uncut Negative Roll 43	
	TONE BROWN TINT YELLOW	
137	LlG Uncut Negative Scene 197	MN/35/94/169

Explanatory Notes

* Two cans were numbered 9.

This can contained a selection of negative material. For a number of reasons our preservation officer believes the cutting work on these negatives was unexpectedly and suddenly curtailed when the film was removed from the Ideal premises. The uncut negative can contained sections which had been noted earlier in other parts, but which were missing from these parts. An example is the letter from Richard Lloyd in part 1 which was discovered to be item no 131. The fact that item 131 was assigned to section 10 indicates the pressures under which the company must have been working before the film was removed.

Notes

[1] For more details on how the film came to the Wales Film and TV Archive, see the article in *Viewfinder*, 24 (May 1995).

[2] Sarah Street, 'The Memoir of Harry Rowson: David Lloyd George, M.P. – *The Man who Saved the Empire* (1918)', *Historical Journal of Film, Radio and Television*, 7, 1 (1987), reprinted in this volume.

[3] See Sarah Street's article above. The process of identifying the film would certainly have been far more complicated without the information provided by her.

[4] Although both titles are cited in the Rowson memoir, Ideal appears to have used only the latter.

[5] See reference to Bottomley's article in this volume's Introduction, p.5, and reprint of the article, pp.6–7.

[6] Extracts from a double-page advertisement, 'How the Great Picture Will be Put Out', *Kinematograph Weekly*, 3 October 1918.

[7] The showprint used for the Cardiff and Pwllheli screenings is printed on 35 mm Kodak acetate-base colour film stock and measures 10,390 feet. This silent colourised print is currently the only one in existence apart from the 16 mm black-and-white reduction print created as a cutting copy. The replacement cost of this material is in the region of £10,000.

6

Lots of Notes: A Personal Memory

JOHN HARDY

When the Cardiff Olympia Orchestra's final chord came to an end – at the same moment as the last credit faded to black, the long and arduous journey that brought about the creation of over two and a half hours of new music in response to this extraordinary film felt all too short, the end too sudden, the high point curtailed in a flash.

I was completely exhausted, but I wanted to go back, to see and hear it again. I was in a bubble, but everyone around me was leaving, packing up instruments, clearing the popcorn. It was over.

Not more than a few weeks before, I was at a loss how to meet the deadline. I stared at pages and pages of John Reed's meticulously detailed log-sheets (every single shot in *The Life Story of David Lloyd George* is listed and given a cumulative duration in seconds and feet). I stared at my extensive musical annotations and sketches, many of which would have taken months to realize for full orchestra in the way I had originally heard them in my head. And I wondered what the audience was going to say when I was forced to stand up at the première and apologize for getting only half-way through the composition of the sound-track.

I wondered why I had agreed to undertake such a commitment. Several sensible composers had turned it down. The few composers in the UK who have done this kind of thing before were not available at such short notice (around six months). But I had said yes. What a fool, I thought, in March, as I tried to find a way into the work that did not immediately embarrass as crass, derivative or overly ambitious. I wondered if anyone would notice if I used the same music for each of the three parts, each an average of fifty minutes long. But it was no good – there was no escape, and I could not let down the kind and supportive people at the Wales Film and TV Archive.

Then my son was born. Our first child. I was working on yet more sketches in the morning, while Heledd was under observation in hospital. Nothing will happen today, they said. So I came home. Then the phone call, at lunchtime. Come, immediately. By the time I got there, the 100-minute labour had less than an hour to run. The next day, mother and firstborn were at home. She needed a rest, so I took the baby to the piano. Holding the little bundle in my left arm, I played with my right hand. He seemed to be listening attentively. At least someone seems to like my music, I thought. Then new ideas started to come, influenced by the warm wide-eyed thing on my knee. This sounded much better than the beginning I had planned. And then another idea, and another.

Once I had the opening and a couple of other main themes, other material seemed to flow freely. Suddenly I was producing between three and nine minutes of full score a day. Just in time.

But having ideas is one thing. Working them through, varying the instrumentation, checking key relationships, and connections before and after – this all takes time. Sometimes I would slave away for ten hours over a section that felt quite full and detailed, but which could do with more variation in colour, dynamics and harmony, and I would find it was still only two or three minutes long. Other sections were more thinly scored, and I could be pleasantly surprised to knock out five minutes of finished music in as many hours.

The hardest thing is to be sure the music fits the pictures. There was much discussion in the planning stages of the conductor having a click-track in headphones. As the film was a real print, projected live, there was obviously no chance of timecode being shown visually anywhere. Fortunately Michael Rafferty reckoned that if he had the score in time to learn it properly, he could memorize the tempos precisely enough to fit the music to precise timings, watching the screen while conducting.

In the end the actual detailed composition took about four weeks. The last section (around fifty minutes) was produced in four days.

So, the music had to be composed to very precise timings. Unfortunately, there was no way of recording the film on to videotape with anything like the accuracy that would be achieved on the night by slowing down the cinema's projector to match the eighteen-frames-per-second format of the original film. (Modern films are normally made at 24 or 25 frames per second, which gives a smoother, less flickery picture, and that is the speed at which modern projectors function.) The first

12. Lloyd George in the trenches in Elvey's film. The prime minister never visited the trenches with Clemenceau, the French premier, contrary to the impression given on screen.

working VHS video I had from the Archive ran to nearly three hours. Then John Reed's log-sheets began to arrive, and by adding up the durations of the various original reels, I was able to calculate that the actual running time should be nearer to two and a half hours. Then there was an interim VHS which ran more or less to time, with some strange discrepancies. But it was very flickery and dark, and it was very difficult to see detail, especially some of the text.

In the last month, the final wave of log-sheet amendments arrived, at which my heart sank, plus the VHS of the colour-tinted test print which lifted my spirits again. The film was suddenly transformed from a fascinating but slightly obscure, flickering oddity to a radiant, bright testament to real enduring quality, with strong acting, some stunning photography, and a sense of pace and structure which had seemed strangely missing before.

The big problem with composing to specific timings is that it needs decisions about tempo and time signatures before one can calculate how many bars are needed for any particular section. For example, to take an easy tempo, at 80 beats per minute, at four beats per bar, one bar is three seconds long. So a sequence of, say, $39\frac{1}{2}$ seconds, comes out at a nice round 13.16666 bars long. To make it even simpler, you can make the thirteenth bar into a five-beat bar, which comes almost exactly to $39\frac{1}{2}$ seconds, and so on for 152 minutes of film. Even though you begin to feel like a human calculator, you are actually supposed to be making a personal and emotional response to an extraordinary work of art about the life of a remarkable man.

That is what I tried to do. I knew that, armed with hindsight both about the conventions of film, of documentary realism and of acting styles, and about Lloyd George's own life, his misdeeds, the disastrous results of the First World War and, even worse, the Treaty of Versailles, it would be impossible for a modern audience to take this film entirely at face value, and I felt morally and artistically obliged to adopt a modern view in setting some of the key sequences to music. At Versailles, Lloyd George's election slogan, 'Make the Germans pay', won the field against the gentler approach of the ailing President Wilson, and this decision led directly to the collapse of the German economy, hyperinflation, the Wall Street crash, the Depression, and the rise of Hitler. You could also take into account Lloyd George's hypocritical philandering, his sale of titles and honours for financial and political gain.

During the interminable, and to our eyes sombre, tour of shell factories at the end of the second part, I felt that the only response it was possible to make was one of melancholy and of foreboding. I am sure that the intention of the film at this point is to convey a sense of Lloyd George's mastery of logistics, organizational skills, determination to defeat the enemy whatever the cost, and his ability to inspire others to follow his example. But now, those shells, in their impersonal tens of thousands, how they give me the shivers. Each is (to me) symbolic of a life lost and the point when the British Empire slipped from the front rank of world powers and Britain's economy fell behind the USA's.

Each day of the four-plus years of the First World War the Empire is said to have spent over £1 million on artillery shells – a phenomenal sum eighty years ago. During and shortly after the war, especially in the influenza epidemic that swept through America and a malnourished central Europe in 1918–19, more civilians died of disease and starvation than soldiers had died in action. Grim preparation indeed for the ravages of the Spanish Civil War and all that followed. We know these things now. At the time that this film was made such things were neither known nor understood, and even had they been, it would have been treason to discuss or publicize them. So when I see those brave, thin, wiry women and men hammering fuses into shrapnel shells, and think of the cost, the damage they inflicted and the noise of the hammering, the image is of sadness, and the creative response is muted, dark, almost despairing.

By contrast there are moments in the film where my response is to be swept off my feet by the exuberance and optimism which the personal history of Lloyd George and his public achievements engender. A powerful example is the last few minutes of part I. Lloyd George has won an audacious and risky court action on appeal, then he has stood for Parliament and upset the Caernarfonshire *status quo* by winning. The section finishes with some staggering night scenes shot, I believe, in Caernarfon town centre, with large crowds of enthusiastic supporters carrying banners, and illuminated only by the flickering light of flaming torches. Briefly, Lloyd George and his family pause in their conveyance to acknowledge the cheering throng, before moving on into history and disappearing from view. This sequence is among the most magical in the whole film. It seems at once highly modern – it could have been staged by Fellini or Coppola – and very ancient. Here I was unable to resist the feeling of elation, of achievement in the face of impossible odds, and the triumph of the successful individual as symbol of all good people striving to aspire above their station. The music accordingly has to be optimistic, hopeful, confirmatory and triumphant (I wished the sequence had been much, much longer).

I had been anxious but happy throughout the screening. As each section of the film unfolded, with the music fitting the pictures without major mishaps, my pleasure increased. There was a hiccup at the beginning of part III. The blip on the screen, five seconds before the first frame of the pictures, which gives the orchestra time to prepare and begin on time, did not appear. There were no pictures, as the lamp on the projector had failed to fire correctly. Then, suddenly, there were the pictures, some way into the first sequence. Michael Rafferty realized what was happening, and immediately sprang into action. The orchestra followed him, and the next two minutes were a dash to catch up without the music sounding too rushed. But they were unruffled; for the rest of the section, they were spot-on, and, even though the first run-through of the final section – the projector having been adjusted – had only taken place that morning, they completed the film with perfect timing and great spirit.

What a wonderful experience for a composer to have such a rewarding focus for one's work, with a captive audience, a relatively free hand, and no competition from dialogue and sound effects. In many ways it was more like a ballet score than a conventional film assignment.

Factfile

The original orchestral score is split into three roughly equal sections, and at my suggestion the divisions fall at the point when Lloyd George has been elected to Parliament for the first time, and after a long sequence of tours of the battlefront, munitions factories and their workforce canteens.

Part I lasts 50 minutes 40 seconds, 976 bars and 174 pages of full score.
Part II lasts 55 minutes 46 seconds, 958 bars and 144 pages of score.
Part III lasts 45 minutes 8 seconds, 859 bars and 132 pages.
Total duration is 2 hours 32 minutes. Total 2,793 bars, 450 pages.

The Orchestration

2 flutes, doubling piccolo and alto; oboe, doubling cor anglais;
2 clarinets, doubling E♭ clarinet and bass clarinet;
bassoon, doubling contrabassoon;
2 horns; 2 trumpets; 2 trombones; tuba;
2 percussionists, playing: 3 timpani, side drum, large bass drum, 3 large tom-toms, tambourine, woodblocks, clash cymbals, suspended sizzle-cymbal, 2 triangles, tam-tam, a single octave of chromatic crotales, often bowed, 2 steel brake drums, a single octave of tubular bells, marimba, glockenspiel, and vibraphone;
harp; piano; normal string section: violin 1, violin 2, viola, cello, and five-string double bass.

After lengthy debates with the Archive, with Peter Harrap, who contracted the musicians, and with the stage management team, it was decided that we could just fit twenty-two musicians into the restricted space at the MGM Cinema. I wanted the full range of colours available from a conventional medium-size orchestra, and a possible solution was to have the string parts played by single musicians, rather than the normal group of players to each part. I was afraid this might mean we would need to amplify the five solo string players, but after several visits to the cinema and careful consideration, we thought we could manage without microphones.

The players had approximately twenty-three hours of rehearsal, on the weekend before and the performance weekend. Rehearsals were mainly at the Welsh National Opera, and they had a total of about $2\frac{1}{2}$ hours play-through in the cinema with the film running. As the film had been sent back to the laboratories for corrections only days before the première, this was also a last chance to check the final print.

Most of the musicians were members of the two professional Cardiff orchestras – the Welsh National Opera Orchestra and the BBC National Orchestra of Wales, but there were a few freelance players, and the leader, violinist Madeleine Mitchell, is based in London, although she has long-standing associations with Music Theatre Wales and the Vale of Glamorgan Festival, as well as other Welsh connections.

There were a few difficulties in avoiding obstruction of the screen by some of the larger instruments, especially the double bass, the contrabassoon and some of the larger percussion instruments. The first rehearsal at the cinema was our only chance to test the acoustics, and it worked surprisingly well, the sound balance and quality improving markedly the further up and back into the auditorium you went. Only the upright piano, which had been hired in preference to a grand in order to save space, sounded woolly, and for the performance we had a medium grand, with its lid slightly open.

If only we could have gone back eighty years, to when the ABC Olympia Music Hall, later the MGM Cinema, was a huge, resonant and well-attended auditorium. Oh to have filled it with a full orchestra, a full house of two or three thousand, and an enormous screen. Now that would be something.

7

An Audience with Lloyd George

NEIL BRAND

My first glimpse of *The Life Story of David Lloyd George* was in 1995, when the Wales Film and TV Archive invited me to see the footage they had so far restored. The quality of the images was mesmerizing – indisputably this would be a film of power, a real discovery. How on earth would a piano be able to do justice to it?

My job is that of playing improvised accompaniments to silent films. I make up the music as I go along. I have learnt the trade over fifteen years, since I was asked to play for the Eastbourne Film Society's performance of Buster Keaton's *Steamboat Bill Junior* (USA, 1928) in 1982.

I was very lucky, having always been able to play by ear, adored the movies and had a training in drama. I took on *Steamboat Bill* and revelled in it. More than anything else I was awestruck by the effect the combination of film and music had on a modern audience. The film was the main element – that was a given, immutable. My music was a secondary element, flexible, changeable from moment to moment. The audience was the third element – its presence was palpable, even with my back to the stalls. I could feel the effect Buster was having – not just the laughs, but also the sympathy, the sadness, the joy. I was along for the ride, with a tiny amount of control which I would soon learn to shape, harness, possibly even understand. All these things came back to me as we approached Pwllheli, 27 April 1996.

In late March I went with WFTVA administrator Jane Davies to visit the Lloyd George museum in Llanystumdwy to look at Lloyd George's piano and meet the curator, Emrys Williams. I had seen the completed film, realized that it was a magnificent and unalloyed paean of praise throughout, and so best approached as an 'Attenborough-style' biopic but I was otherwise still at a loss to know how to encompass this huge film musically. Welsh harp? Mars, the Bringer of War? On a piano? Cliché piled on top of cliché until Jane said: 'You should get to know som

Welsh hymns. Lloyd George grew up in that tradition.' An enquiry to Emrys sent him scurrying to the hollow piano stool to return with a book. Lloyd George's hymn-book. I began to play through the hymns, here in the politician's home village, with Emrys and Jane breaking in from time to time with 'Oh, that's a baptist hymn' or 'Oh, that's beautiful, you must use that', feeling that I was some part of an ancient ceremony. The personality of the man was palpable, as it had been in the film through the extraordinary performance of Norman Page. For almost the first time since my first film in Eastbourne I was aware that I was part of something special. This film was not just about a long-dead politician. It was about a spirit.

We found four hymns that we knew would help to add depth to the score: J. A. Lloyd's 'Brynteg' (the baptist hymn), 'Gwahoddiad' (a traditional Welsh tune and the tune I was to use most), R. H. Prichard's 'Hyfrydol' (which I knew, although with English words) and J. Richards's 'Sanctus'. Thus armed, I waited for the day.

At Pwllheli I was amazed at the buzz in the audience – I knew when I sat down at the piano that I was going to enjoy this experience. The audience was happy, expectant, prepared to meet the film half-way, or more if necessary. The third element was in place, the lights went down. I grabbed Lloyd George's coat-tails and prepared to fly on the back of them.

Playing an improvised score to a film requires really only one thing – total immersion in the images. The musical reaction to a change in story-line or character has to be immediate and instinctive, otherwise the moment will have gone. It is an emotional rather than an intellectual process in which the pianist is controlling the music with fine adjustments, like controlling the flow of water over a dam. The film is doing so much work, all that is required of the music is to support that work. Through the childhood scenes, poignantly realized in that village that I had seen myself only that morning, the hymn tunes sprang to life to dance cheekily beside the running children, lend dignity to the scenes of baptism and prayer and thunder magnificently as David slew Goliath. There was warm laughter in the audience as an impudent young Lloyd George bit an unfortunate adult in the leg, a response to the beautiful shots of 1918 Criccieth and, at last, what every pianist hopes to hear, the silence, heavy with expectation, of an audience that is incontrovertibly hooked. With Norman Page's first scenes we were no longer looking at

13. Exploiting the north Wales landscape; the youthful Lloyd George's screen arrival at Cricc

an actor – that was the man himself up there. The first interval came almost before I knew it, as Lloyd George, re-elected MP for Caernarfon, was cheered in torchlight procession beneath the castle walls. The applause was tremendous, heartfelt.

With bad films or films you do not (as a pianist) understand, you become an 'ivory coaster'. You play musical wallpaper until the next climax comes along. Not once in this astonishing film did I need to coast. The images and narrative fell into place as we went, demanding a continuous sense of urgency, of great issues being discussed and shaped. The scenes of the mob outside Birmingham Town Hall had the effect we knew they would. These scenes were unlike anything I had seen in a film of the 1910s, with the exception of D. W. Griffith's work. The music was violent, uncontrolled, shifting like a great sea with the ocean of faces and bodies that crammed on to the screen before us. A huge laugh, partly release of tension, as Norman Page revealed the pinstripe trousers beneath his policeman's disguise showed that the audience was with us. Into government – the music still contained snippets of the hymns but these were part of a larger picture, heavy with the *gravitas* of a mature personality. Lloyd George's political life, complex though it was, seemed to become a series of bridges crossed, each bridge a boon to the poor, each bridge bringing him closer to the real test – the war.

I was worried about the war scenes. There were two huge, documentary-style set pieces coming up that I had to cover, the munitions factory visit and the battle scenes. Battle scenes are tough on the piano anyway – you can only do so much with impressionism, and I am certainly not of the school that keeps 'It's a long way to Tipperary' going round and round for ever. Lloyd George's visit to a munitions factory came at the end of the film's second part and lasted (as I remember) some eight minutes. I went into it with as much dash and commitment as I could, dragging with me the ghosts of Walton, Elgar, Vaughan Williams, even John Williams. Amazingly, from the welter of ideas a tune began to form.

This does not often happen, and when it does it is a sign of a successful accompaniment and, usually, a delighted and rewarded pianist. The ambition of a silent-film accompanist is to reach the heart of the film, and find the single thread from which its disparate scenes and ideas can be drawn, compared and mapped. If you are lucky it is an insight you reach just ahead of the audience. If you are very lucky the linking thread comes out as a tune.

This is what happened with *The Life Story*: a march, full of muscular determination, began to form in the midst of these factory scenes. I was terrified for a while, convinced that it was deeply inappropriate, something that would have to be speedily killed off before the audience recognized it. It seemed familiar, yet I did not entirely recognize it. Through the second interval I struggled to keep it in my head and to my relief it reappeared, quiet, resolute, determined, in the opening of the third sequence. I went into the battle scenes. And now I knew I could trust this tune. I watched with a lump in my throat the final roll call, made all the more poignant for me by the remembrance of my grandfather's death at Saint-Quentin in 1917. I usually avoid playing pieces that people recognize, because these pieces tend to bring associations with them that are nothing to do with the film, but I now make an exception. Whenever I accompany that scene from *The Life*

Story of David Lloyd George I play 'Sunset', the beautiful bugle tune associated with Remembrance Day. When the grieving widow is comforted by the young wife with a baby, it breaks your heart. Every time.

My tune held up through the battle scenes, through Lloyd George's speeches to the French and Canadians, and then we were at his fireside. I think the end of this film causes a shiver like no other ending. In *JFK* (USA, 1991) Oliver Stone had Kevin Costner look directly at the camera and deliver the line 'The future is in your hands.' To my mind it did not work. When Norman Page says, silently and in intertitle, 'There must never be a next time', holding the audience's gaze, unblinking and with the full force of his carefully drawn character, I have to remember to breathe. I held back the music under this final scene, then used his magnificent line to catapult my theme up and through the credit sequence, and that was it. I was blown away by the response, the audience seemed to love the film, and the beaming Welsh politician Dafydd Wigley and his wife were first through the dressing-room door.

Another politician came to the film six months later. At the National Film Theatre Tony Benn remarked to David Berry that Lloyd George would today be considered well to the left of Tony Blair. There have been tantalizing suggestions of playing the film at the House of Lords or the Liberal party conference.

I have played *Lloyd George* nine times now, most of those performances in Wales. Audiences have been large and small, for and against, but most, I suspect, have not come to a silent film before and have had their preconceptions shattered. I now know the sequences of Elvey's film virtually by heart, and my feelings, as I settle into place at the start of a new performance, are the same as at Pwllheli. I am going to enjoy this experience. The markers go by: the easy familiarity of the early scenes (I still use the hymn tunes); the armaments factory, complete with the Lloyd George march; the shots that seem to be Lloyd George himself in a car procession; Clemenceau as he bangs his head leaving a trench; the easy jingoism of the parade of American presidents and the real power of the workhouse liberation scene, and of Verdun. Overall, the spirit is always there. Despite this being a film of 1918 with the tastes, mores and attitudes of its time, it works for me precisely because it is a survivor, a message in a bottle discarded by whoever it may have been, for whatever reasons, and discovered and presented to the next millennium against all odds by the Archive and the Lloyd George family to inform and delight on its own terms.

In October 1997 it was seen by the international silent-film community at the Pordenone festival in Italy. It joined the ranks of other 'lost' films which have survived to receive audience acclaim. As a celebration of *people*, in the 1910s and 1990s, *The Life Story of David Lloyd George* richly deserves its place, and I am proud to be a part of it.

PART III

Screening Lloyd George

The cinema has always been fascinated by history and historical figures, so it is somewhat surprising that many academics have only recently turned their attention to the profound impact film has made on the way we imagine the past.[1] Film-makers themselves have, of course, long been aware of the problems posed by re-creating the lives of real people, especially when the subject of a movie is still alive to complain of misrepresentation.[2]

In the case of *The Life Story of David Lloyd George*, the process of cinematic reconstruction was made all the more interesting by the fact that the film's central character was, at the time of production, not only very much alive but still at the heart of the British political scene. Suitably, Nicholas Hiley's article places *The Life Story* in the context of contemporary newsreels (which heavily featured Lloyd George), suggesting that Maurice Elvey was profoundly influenced by both their style and their content. Peter Stead, meanwhile, locates Elvey's film in the long tradition of features based on the lives of famous political figures.

This section is completed by two articles which address some of the theoretical implications of this early, monumental, attempt at cinematic biography. In their own ways, both John O. Thompson and Roberta E. Pearson demonstrate that recounting historical events via the cinema is a far from straightforward process. Thompson's concern is principally with the filmic methods employed to convey 'a real life', and he offers a convincing argument for the validity of French theorist André Bazin's work on the ways cinema is able to construct notions of reality. Pearson, on the other hand, places *The Life Story* in the context of other silent films, suggesting that its narrative devices can only be understood by thinking of the intended audience of 1919.

From varying perspectives, then, the articles in this section connect to show how *The Life Story of David Lloyd George* attempts to live up to its title. As earlier parts of this book have demonstrated, the history of this amazing film is quite a saga in itself but the way *The Life Story* presents history is no less intriguing.

S.H.

Notes

[1] See, for instance, Mark C. Carnes (ed.), *Past Imperfect: History according to the Movies* (Cassell, 1996).

[2] The furore which accompanied *Bandit Queen* (UK/India, 1994), a portrayal of the life of the notorious Indian outlaw Phoolan Devi, provides a notable recent example.

8

Lloyd George on the Newsreels

NICHOLAS HILEY

In August 1918, during the early stages of filming *The Life Story of David Lloyd George*, Maurice Elvey took two or three cameramen to the National Eisteddfod at Neath, which Lloyd George was attending. Here, according to Simon Rowson, they filmed the prime minister and his daughter Megan 'amid scenes of enthusiasm such as even the Eisteddfod had never seen or heard before'. This is an interesting insight into Elvey's preparations for re-creating Lloyd George's life on screen, but what exactly was he hoping to discover by this expedition? Norman Page, the actor who was to play Lloyd George, is known to have studied him in the House of Commons in an effort to reproduce his mannerisms, but what was Maurice Elvey hoping to reproduce by following the prime minister to Neath?[1]

Elvey's cameramen were not the only ones to film Lloyd George at the Eisteddfod. Newsreel cameramen from the *War Office Official Topical Budget* and the *Gaumont Graphic* were also present, and their edited reports reached cinemas a few days later. The item in *War Office Official Topical Budget*, no.363-2 was rather more prosaic than Rowson's account suggests. The first subtitle read 'NATIONAL EISTEDDFOD: Freedom of Neath for Lloyd George during the great Welsh Festival', and it introduced shots of druids and women in Welsh costume. The second subtitle read "KEEP STEADY, AYE, KEEP STEADY, AND ALL WILL BE WELL": Mr Lloyd George's message from Neath', and led into shots of the prime minister inspecting troops with various civic dignitaries, filmed by a camera in the middle of the crowd. The item in *Gaumont Graphic*, no.772 was similar, subtitled 'PREMIER AT NEATH RECEIVES FREEDOM OF CITY' and showing the same parade of troops and war workers, with Lloyd George getting into his car and leaving.[2]

It is not known whether Elvey filmed Lloyd George's next public engagement, but if, like the newsreel cameramen, he followed the prime minister to Manchester in September 1918, he would have recorded a very similar ceremony. *War Office Official Topical Budget*, no.368-2 introduced its film with the subtitle 'THE PREMIER IN MANCHESTER: Enthusiastic reception', and showed Lloyd George descending the steps of the council chamber with various civic dignitaries, before again getting into his car. He was then seen speaking to war workers and reviewing troops, all in the pouring rain. *Gaumont Graphic*, no.782 had similar shots of the prime minister getting out of his car and being greeted by the mayor before he is shown reviewing troops and meeting women war workers. The subtitle gave the aftermath to this bleak event, explaining 'PREMIER HAS COLD AND HAD TO CANCEL PART OF LANCASHIRE TOUR'.

This was the public routine of being prime minister, and a study of these films would have taught Elvey a great deal about the cinema presentation of fact and fiction. For one thing, there was a distinct difference in physical location between the two genres. Fiction was largely set indoors but factual events took place almost exclusively in the open air. The predominant mode of factual filming was the newsreel, supplied twice weekly by *Pathé's Animated Gazette*, the *Gaumont Graphic*, and the *War Office Official Topical Budget*. The low sensitivity of their film stock meant that the newsreel cameramen could not work indoors without intrusive banks of arc lights, and as a result factual events in the cinema were largely in streets, squares and parks; in courtyards and on the steps of public buildings; on football pitches, racecourses and similar open spaces. Here public figures moved through public space, and although this may have enhanced the official dignity of politicians like Lloyd George, it was strangely out of place in a medium dominated by the fictional representation of private life behind closed doors.

These distinctions were of vital importance to Elvey's project, for the central character in *The Life Story* had constantly to cross and recross the boundary between public and private life. It might have been possible to produce an entirely fictional presentation of Lloyd George's career, based in the studio and treating public events as part of the drama, had it not been for the fact that the prime minister possessed his own strong media presence. By August and September 1918 Lloyd George had already featured in more than fifty newsreel stories, and, with the newsreels reaching an estimated audience of 12,000,000 people a week, this meant that millions of cinema-goers already knew how he looked and acted on

he real Lloyd George in a scene purporting to depict war victory celebrations.

screen.[3] Lloyd George was indeed the first prime minister whose newsreel image was a significant part of his political identity, and this meant that to represent him on screen it was necessary for Elvey to re-create not only how he looked and behaved in private, but also how he looked and behaved in the newsreels.

This may have been why Elvey took his cameramen to Neath, and *The Life Story* certainly contains a sequence in which Norman Page as Lloyd George receives the freedom of a town. This was a significant part of the prime minister's newsreel image, for a surprising number of stories were devoted to these repetitive public ceremonies, whose details must have been familiar to cinema audiences. In September 1917 the ceremony at Birkenhead had been filmed both for *Topical Budget*, no.316-1 as 'HONOUR FOR MR LLOYD GEORGE', and as 'PREMIER GETS FREEDOM OF BOROUGH' for *Gaumont Graphic*, no.676. In June 1918 Lloyd George had been shown receiving the freedom of Edinburgh in

'THE PRIME MINISTER IN SCOTLAND' in *Pictorial News (Official)*, no.353-2. Elvey himself had apparently filmed the ceremony at Neath, and it is not surprising that although these events formed a very small part of the prime minister's public life, they should have been recreated for *The Life Story* with the note that 'Mr Lloyd George has been presented with the freedom of London, Cardiff, Swansea, Newport, Glasgow and Edinburgh'.

Indeed, when Elvey staged shots of Lloyd George in public for *The Life Story of David Lloyd George*, it seems that he was attempting not so much to reconstruct the actual events, but principally to reproduce their newsreel coverage. A characteristic element in this was distance from the camera, which was much greater in newsreel than in fiction. In Elvey's re-creations of public events the camera indeed approaches no closer than 15 or 20 ft from its subject, and, just as in the newsreel, invites the audience to observe rather than to participate. This technique has been criticized as alienating to modern viewers, but for contemporary cinema-goers it would undoubtedly have added an air of authenticity. Reconstructed sequences, such as those of Lloyd George leaving 11 Downing Street to introduce his 'People's Budget', are pure newsreel, with the camera carefully placed at the back of the crowd, filming Lloyd George as he hurries from the doorway to the car. These images were not derived from fiction filming, but their context would have been instantly recognizable to contemporary cinema audiences, for, as we have seen, the dash across the pavement was often all the cameras could catch of a public figure.

Equally significant as careful reconstructions are the wartime shots of Lloyd George at the Front, where it is apparent that Elvey has taken great care to re-create the look of official films such as the *Battle of Arras*, released in June 1917. It is important to realize once again that these scenes are not reconstructions of events, but re-creations of the screen images already familiar to contemporary audiences. In the front-line sequences Elvey's camera goes only where the actual newsreel cameras went, and does not advance with the troops, or take up a position in no man's land to film Lloyd George in the trenches, or use any of the devices of fiction filming. Even more significantly, in a generic sequence depicting how 'While Secretary for War, Mr. Lloyd George paid several visits to the Western Front', Norman Page is even allowed to acknowledge the camera, just as Lloyd George might have done in a

utside Birmingham Town Hall – Elvey's attempt to reproduce the chaos.

newsreel. This casual gesture, given as he emerges from a dug-out, demonstrates how closely Elvey was using the conventions of factual filming to support his fiction. To a contemporary audience this simple gesture would have indicated that the cameraman was an actual participant in the scene, and thus that the image had to be read as fact and not as fiction.

Even when Elvey re-creates public events that were not accessible to the newsreel cameras, it is noticeable that he adopts the conventions of the newsreel in preference to those of studio-based fiction films. This is evident in the sequence from 1911, where, as the subtitle announces, 'Mr. Lloyd George in a speech at the Mansion House makes a grave and emphatic statement of British policy.' This studio reconstruction was of course entirely accessible to Elvey's cameras, but although he filmed it from four different locations within the set, none of these placed viewers in a privileged position, as they would if he had used the conventions of fiction. The camera indeed remained an onlooker, filming the public Lloyd George from a respectful distance, across the tables and over the heads of those who have a greater right to be close to the prime minister. Even when working in the studio it seems that Elvey still acknowledged the newsreels as the dominant mode of representation for public figures on public occasions, and only when Lloyd George is shown behind the scenes at public meetings, or at work in his study, can fictional modes of representation be substituted. Elvey certainly understood the different modes of representation that were available to him, and it is apparent that *The Life Story* only reproduces the visual style of the newsreels when he deems this appropriate. This can be seen by comparing Elvey's representations of Lloyd George with those of Kaiser Wilhelm II. The mode of representation of the Kaiser is not that of the newsreel, but that of the melodrama and the political cartoon, and he is deliberately manipulated by the camera, being seen from below glaring down out of crimson clouds, or from above with his gloved hand poised over the map of Europe. These shots do not in any way resemble newsreel images, and they demonstrate the care that Elvey took in finding an appropriate mode of representation for the prime minister.

However, it should not be thought that Lloyd George's media image was entirely a creation of the film industry, for he worked on it closely himself, and was indeed the first British politician prepared to co-operate with journalists and cameramen as well as editors and proprietors. A characteristic indication of this came in 1907, when, as president of the Board of Trade, Lloyd George was involved in delicate negotiations to avert a railway strike, and was anxious to have the press on his side. The method he chose was highly unorthodox, for, according to one journalist, he worked through the reporters in the street outside his office, and not only expressed sympathy with them in their long vigil, but 'invited them in, put a room at their disposal, saw that they were provided with tea, and sent up some cigarettes to pass away the time'. The *Central News* representative recalled that Lloyd George took tea and cake with them every day, and passed them carefully selected titbits of information on how his negotiations were progressing.[4]

Lloyd George was also prepared to co-operate with the growing army of Fleet Street press photographers. A handful of British politicians realized the value of co-operating with the illustrated newspapers, but the problems involved were considerable. In 1911 *Punch* satirized the dilemma they faced by describing an imaginary school of 'pose-culture', where the famous could be taught how to behave in public so as to photograph well at all times. Yet even if such a school had existed there would have been few students, for Lloyd George was the only major British politician ready at all times to pose for a press photographer. As one *Daily Mirror* cameraman observed, Lloyd George understood that 'an art editor wants something distinctive in a picture, something that will make the reader look at it twice', and he usually managed to provide it. His ability to photograph well was a distinct advantage in gaining coverage in newspapers of many different political complexions.[5]

The ability to provide a good picture was also important to the newsreels, which began in Britain with the launch of *Pathé's Animated Gazette* in June 1910. This was followed by the *Warwick Bioscope Chronicle* in July 1910, the *Gaumont Graphic* in October 1910, and the *Topical Budget* in August 1911. The question of politics was always difficult for the newsreels, for whereas a London newspaper could appeal to only a section of the newspaper-reading public, the newsreels were obliged to address the whole cinema audience, and could not risk alienating any part of it by appearing to be partisan. Politicians were thus obliged to co-operate with the newsreels on quite a different level from their co-operation with the press, but Lloyd George was equal to the new medium, and in June 1914 he was featured in the *Pathé Gazette* story 'PARLIAMENTARY PIGEON RACE: Mr. Lloyd George at start of Parliamentary London–Pontefract pigeon race.'

After the outbreak of war in August 1914 Lloyd George's duties made him increasingly visible to the newsreel cameras. In March 1915 the *Pathé Gazette* featured him in 'MR. LLOYD GEORGE REVIEWS THE MEN OF KITCHENER'S ARMY AT LLANDUDNO', and in June 1915, after becoming minister of munitions, he appeared in two items in *Topical Budget*, no.199-1, meeting more civic dignitaries for 'MR. LLOYD GEORGE AT BRISTOL', and arriving by car for 'MR. LLOYD GEORGE, MINISTER OF MUNITIONS ARRIVING AT THE CENTRAL HALL TO ATTEND THE MEETING OF THE MUNITIONS COMMITTEE'. Patriotism had now replaced politics as the distinguishing mark of public life, to such a extent that by September 1915 the newsreels' interest in party issues was so slight that only one issue in three contained any political matter, and newsreel editors were happy to ignore the political implications of a march or parade if it could be run for its pictorial value alone.[6]

In some respects this was an advantage, for when public figures like Lloyd George or Winston Churchill supplied the newsreels with visually interesting, non-political events to film, they were guaranteed good coverage. On Friday 17 September 1915, for example, Winston Churchill made a speech to munitions workers at Enfield Lock in north London, whilst on the following day Lloyd George mixed with the crowds at a military sports day in Tadworth, south of the capital. Both men made themselves available to the press photographers and newsreel cameramen covering the events, and *Gaumont*, which normally had little interest in politics, decided to film both of them. The footage arrived too late for inclusion in the *Gaumont Graphic* of Monday 20 September 1915, but both stories were run in the following issue. *Pathé* also decided to film Churchill, and *Topical* to film Lloyd George. All three companies obtained usable footage which they circulated to first-run cinemas within a few days of the events:

Pathé Gazette, Sunday 19 September 1915:
    LATEST PARIS FASHIONS (PATHÉCOLOR).
    THE LONDON SCOTTISH ON A ROUTE MARCH.
    THE LONDON IRISH SPORTS.
    MR. WINSTON CHURCHILL AT ENFIELD.

Topical Budget, no.213-1, Wednesday 22 September 1915:
    LLOYD GEORGE AT SPORTS: Watches Soldiers Eat 'Bobbing Apples' at Tadworth – Minister of Munitions distributes Prizes to Successful Competitors at the Brigade Sports.
    ELGIN MOTOR RACES: Earl Cooper wins the Chicago Auto Trophy.
    LORD MAYOR AT HIGHGATE: Opens the new War Hospital Supply Depot.
    POINCARE DECORATES HEROES: The President Decorates Disabled Frenchmen at the Invalides.

Gaumont Graphic, no.470, Thursday 23 September 1915:
    MR WINSTON CHURCHILL ADDRESSES THE MUNITION WORKERS AT ENFIELD.
    THE FIREMAN HERO: The Funeral of Fireman J. S. Green.

STRAIGHT TALKING: Boxing and Kinema Favourites Recruiting.
THE GAEKWAR OF BARODA ATTENDS THE MARRIAGE
FESTIVITIES OF HIS SON.
THE KINEMA GIFT: Ambulance presented by Members of the
Industry.
THE CHIEF MUNITIONER: Mr. Lloyd George at Tadworth Military
Sports.[7]

The result of this co-operation between politicians and newsreel
companies was impressive. By this date the *Pathé Gazette* was leading the
British newsreel market, and releasing around 180 copies of each bi-
weekly reel, with the *Gaumont Graphic* coming second with around 130
copies, and the *Topical Budget* following up with some 70 copies. These
went directly to 'first-run' cinemas, but three days later, when the next
new release appeared, they would pass to smaller 'second-run' cinemas,
which would keep them for three days before again passing them on.
This process would continue for four or five weeks, and the cumulative
newsreel audience was very large. By September 1915 around 4,700
British cinemas were selling 20 million tickets every week, and the figures
suggest that, simply by speaking at a YMCA canteen and being filmed by
the *Pathé Gazette* and *Gaumont Graphic*, Churchill had managed to reach
an audience of some 5 million people in 2,500 cinemas. In a similar
fashion Lloyd George's informal visit to a military sports day, covered by
the *Topical Budget* and *Gaumont Graphic*, would eventually have reached
some 3.5 million people in 1,600 cinemas.[8]

These levels of exposure were of considerable significance in a month
when Churchill and Lloyd George were the only cabinet ministers to be
filmed for the newsreels.[9] Millions of people paid careful attention to
these bi-weekly bulletins, and those politicians who were prepared to
pose for the newsreel cameras were guaranteed access to a huge
audience. However, to modern audiences a surprising number of stories
featuring Lloyd George still show him at a distance – on platforms,
balconies, and in groups of other politicians, or on his way somewhere –
climbing in and out of cars, or entering and leaving buildings. The
minister of munitions was more accessible, and certainly more colourful,
than his political rivals, but even his collaboration with the newsreels had
very definite limits. Public figures remained at a distance, and even when
Lloyd George was featured in the newsreels he might simply be watching

a parade from a balcony, as in 'WOMEN WORKERS' PROCESSION' in *Gaumont Graphic*, no.558 of July 1916, or arriving at a meeting by car, seen over the heads of the crowd, as in 'MR LLOYD GEORGE AT ABERYSTWYTH' in *Topical Budget*, no.261-1 of August 1916. This was the characteristic style which Elvey would copy so carefully two years later.

Unfortunately by the time that Lloyd George became prime minister in December 1916 relations between the government and the film industry were rather strained, and there was little understanding of the importance of the cinema in national life. Looked at dispassionately, this seems rather peculiar, for cinema attendance had never been greater, and by January 1917 ticket sales stood at some 21 million a week in perhaps 5,000 venues. Equally significantly, the cinema audience was more representative of the British population than the audience for any other medium of news or information – one prominent London exhibitor estimating in July 1917 that '75 per cent of the patrons of the picture theatre belong to the working classes'. Yet there was still a great deal of prejudice against the cinema, and, beyond the sponsorship of a number of official documentaries about the war, the principal intervention of the British government in the film industry was to cripple it with a wartime entertainments tax which fell most heavily on the cheapest tickets.[10]

Despite this official myopia the new prime minister continued to make himself available to the newsreel cameras, and he was helped considerably in gaining non-political coverage by members of his family. Lloyd George was indeed the first prime minister whose fame extended to his relatives in the same manner as royalty. His wife and daughter proved especially popular, and *Topical Budget*, no.288-2 from March 1917 carried the story 'ST. DAVID'S DAY: Mr Lloyd George accepts gift for the Fund at No.10 Downing St and Miss Lloyd George visits the Stock Exchange to sell flags.' In April 1917 *Gaumont Graphic*, no.631 carried a similar item: 'MRS LLOYD GEORGE OPENS HIGHLAND BAZAAR AT EDINBURGH', whilst no.632 ran the story 'PREMIER AT HIS SON'S WEDDING'. *Topical Budget*, no.294-1 of April 1917 also ran this as 'LLOYD GEORGE WEDDING', and it was not long before the prime minister's new daughter-in-law was shown doing war work in 'EMPRESS CLUB HUT' in *Gaumont Graphic*, no.654 of June 1917.

Lloyd George also received valuable newsreel coverage from his Welsh associations. In September 1917 the prime minister's attendance at the Eisteddfod and his reception of the freedom of Birkenhead, were covered both in *Gaumont Graphic*, nos.675 and 676, and *War Office Official Topical Budget*, no.316-1. As we have seen, the following year's Eisteddfod also generated coverage for Lloyd George, but by that time there was greater concern about his personal style of publicity. As the Kinematograph Weekly pointed out in August 1918, 'war conditions give an opportunity for personal publicity to certain politicians', adding that 'when Governmental publicity is conducted on the lines which find favour at present it is sometimes difficult to tell whether the circulated material is designed to advance war aims or extol the existing Government, and the dividing line between Mr. Lloyd George the war Premier and Mr. Lloyd George the politician becomes a very fine one'.[11]

This debate was intensified by the advance publicity for Elvey's project, by the ending of the war and by the certainty that a general election was only months away. It was now unthinkable that any film of Lloyd George's life could neglect his screen presence, but increasingly unlikely that a screen biography could be made. In November 1918 it was announced that Captain James Barber, who had organized cinema propaganda for the National War Aims Committee, would be 'cinema expert' for the coalition whips during the election campaign. The *Kinematograph Weekly* scented danger, and advised cinema managers that 'the wise man keeps politics out of his business'.[12] Given these dire warnings the actual newsreel coverage of the prime minister during the election campaign is something of a disappointment. *Gaumont Graphic*, no.802 of November 1918 had shots of him alighting from a car for 'OPENS COALITION ELECTION CAMPAIGN AT WOLVERHAMPTON', and only in December 1918 could the *Pathé Gazette* run more impressive close-ups in its reporting of 'THE TRIUMPH OF THE COALITION: The Rt. Hon. David Lloyd George and his able Lieutenant the Rt. Hon. Bonar Law'.

Although Elvey's production was quietly suppressed, the newsreels kept Lloyd George on the cinema screens, covering both his public and his family life. In 1919 the chief leader-writer of the *Evening Standard* could still assert that it was 'not very material to this or any other generation that Mr. Lloyd George has been "filmed" ', but the prime minister himself clearly felt the value of such coverage.[13] In June 1921 the marriage of his younger son Gwilym was featured in all the leading newsreels – appearing in *Gaumont Graphic*, no.1069, *Pathé Gazette*, no.782, and *Topical Budget*, no.512-2, where it was subtitled 'PREMIER ATTENDS

WEDDING OF HIS SECOND SON.' It seemed as though Lloyd George could not even go on holiday without taking the newsreel cameras with him, and in March 1922 he was filmed hoeing potatoes both by the *Pathé Gazette*, for 'PRIME MINISTER ON HOLIDAY AT CRICCIETH' in no.859, and by the *Topical Budget*, for 'AWAY BUT BY NO MEANS RESTING' in no.551-1. A few days later both newsreels showed Lloyd George contentedly fishing on the same holiday. Lloyd George was always ready to co-operate with newsreel cameramen, and according to Frank Bassill of the *Pathé Gazette* he was 'the least camera conscious' of all contemporary public figures.[14]

We can see the effect of this co-operation in the work of two experienced *Topical Budget* cameramen, John 'Bunny' Hutchins, who joined the newsreel in 1917, and Fred Wilson, who joined in 1920. By the time that Bunny Hutchins filmed Lloyd George's departure from Dover for the League of Nations negotiations in January 1920, he had undoubtedly encountered the prime minister before. It is thus not surprising that the resulting item in *Topical Budget*, no.437-2, headed 'BACK TO PARIS', carries the subtitle 'Mr Lloyd George laughingly agrees to a special picture for the Topical Budget.' Such openness was valuable to both sides, and over the next three years Hutchins filmed Lloyd George and his wife on at least seven different occasions. He filmed Lloyd George making a pro-coalition speech in 'LLANDUDNO' in no.476-2 of October 1920, and meeting the French premier for 'GERMAN PROPOSALS SENT TO ALLIES VIA USA' in no.505-1 of April 1921. He filmed further political speeches for 'IN THE WILDERNESS – IN SCOTLAND' for *Daily Sketch Topical Budget*, no.584-1 of November 1922, and 'LLOYD GEORGE AT WREXHAM' in no.625-1 of August 1923. He also filmed 'MRS LLOYD GEORGE' in *Topical Budget*, no.476-2 of October 1920, and 'MRS LLOYD GEORGE TO THE RESCUE AGAIN' in no.502-2 of April 1921. Finally he filmed the two of them together for 'MR LLOYD GEORGE EN ROUTE FOR USA' in no.632-1 of October 1923.

The benefits of such familiarity can also be seen in the work of Fred Wilson, another experienced newsreel cameraman. In June 1920 Wilson filmed Lloyd George in conference with the French premier for 'FOLKESTONE – GERMANY MUST DISARM' in *Topical Budget*, no.461-1, and in November 1920 he filmed a portrait shot of the prime minister for 'LLOYD GEORGE' in no.480-2. However, in January 1921 Wilson achieved a notable coup with film of Lloyd George accepting the gift of a country residence for the prime minister. *Topical Budget* was not the only newsreel represented, and *Gaumont Graphic*, no.1024 carried the same story as 'PREMIER'S NEW HOME'. However, Wilson obtained a series of relaxed portraits of Lloyd George and his daughter which indicate their familiarity with the cameraman, and the resulting story, 'DOWNING STREET IN BUCKINGHAMSHIRE', in *Topical Budget*, no.490-1, shows the prime minister walking in the grounds of Chequers, a visually dramatic figure with his stick, felt hat, and cape slung over his shoulder. After a number of relaxed shots, the film closes with the subtitle 'Miss Megan Lloyd George thinks it nicer than Downing Street', and an endearing portrait shot of Lloyd George and his daughter together. Wilson filmed Lloyd George on several other occasions before he left the *Topical Budget*, his last recorded assignment being to film his return from holiday in Spain for 'FROM SUNSHINE TO SHADOW' in no.598-1 of February 1923.

When Lloyd George resigned in October 1922, Norton Gardner of the *Topical Budget* was one of many press photographers and newsreel cameramen who covered his departure from Downing Street. The resulting film appeared in 'LLOYD GEORGE RESIGNS: MR BONAR LAW, NEW PREMIER', in no.582-2, with the subtitle "I AM NO LONGER PRIME MINISTER": Mr Lloyd George stepping out of No.10'. It showed a relaxed and confident Lloyd George with stick and top hat, pausing on the doorstep of No.10 Downing Street, and running his eyes slowly along the line of photographers so that each could obtain a full-face shot. The contrast with Bonar Law, who then appeared looking startled and uncertain in front of the camera, was striking. Lloyd George knew what the cameras needed, and the *Topical Budget* coverage of his resignation ended with the subtitle 'STILL SMILIN' THRO: "In the Wilderness" – but with one faithful friend at least'. Here, library footage showed Lloyd George beside a farm gate, patting a large dog before opening the gate and passing through.

Even when no longer prime minister, Lloyd George retained his newsreel presence, and in the autumn of 1923 his tour of the United States and Canada was reported in at least sixteen newsreel items, from shots of his departure in 'LOOK AFTER THE OLD COUNTRY' in *Pathé Gazette*, no.1021 of September 1923, to 'RETURN HOME: Southampton after American Tour' in *Gaumont Graphic*, no.1319 of November 1923. Moreover he continued to make himself newsworthy, providing a series of photo opportunities on his farm at Churt. 'BACK TO THE LAND!' in *Topical Budget*, no.878-1 of June 1928, showed him with a new motor tractor, and an exhibition of potatoes in September 1932 was reported both in *British Movietone News*, no.172 as 'LLOYD GEORGE TALKS TO SURREY FARMERS', and in *British Paramount News*, no.163 as 'LLOYD GEORGE – FARMER'. An open day in October 1934 produced 'FELLOW FARMERS VISIT LLOYD GEORGE' in *British Paramount News*, no.378, whilst in July 1935 the same newsreel ran 'LLOYD GEORGE SHOWS "NEW DEAL" PUT INTO PRACTICE ON OWN FARM' in no.459. Even the sale of poultry produced 'MR. LLOYD GEORGE IS SELLING HIS CHICKENS' in *British Movietone News*, no.345 of January 1936.

Lloyd George continued to use his farm to great advantage, and enjoyed such a good relationship with the sound newsreels that in May 1938 the visit of a water diviner was covered in detail by *Pathé's Super Sound Gazette, British Paramount News*, no.755, *Universal News*, no.821, and *British Movietone News*, no.468, the latter using the title 'THE WELSH WIZARD FINDS WATER.' In October 1938 the cameras were back at Churt to film a new mechanical plough, a minor story that was nevertheless covered in *Universal News*, no.864, *British Movietone News*, no.489A, *British Paramount News*, no.798, and *Gaumont-British News*, no.502, where it was headed 'FARMER LLOYD GEORGE AND HIS ROBOT'.

The image of Lloyd George as a family man continued to be reinforced by the newsreels, and in January 1938 reports of his golden wedding were carried in *British Movietone News*, no.451A, *British Paramount News*, no.722, and *Pathé's Super Sound Gazette*. The civic celebration held in March 1938 was covered by *Gaumont British News*, no.436 as 'LLOYD GEORGE RECEIVES GOLDEN WEDDING PRESENTS AT CARDIFF', by *Pathé's Super Sound Gazette* as 'MR LLOYD GEORGE RECEIVES GOLD VASE FROM PEOPLE OF WALES', and by *British Paramount News*, no.732 as 'LLOYD GEORGE HONOURED.' If this reputation was at all tarnished by the report in *British Movietone News*, no.751A, from October 1943, of 'LLOYD GEORGE MARRIED', it was not because of any remark by the commentator. The newsreel's story card simply records that 'Former Prime Minister Lloyd George has married his private secretary Miss Frances Stephenson.'

Lloyd George's newsreel presence endured until his death, and his funeral in April 1945 was reported in *British Paramount News*, no.1471,

British Movietone News, no.826A, and *Pathé Gazette*, no.45/28. As the *Pathé Gazette* story card demonstrates, their item was a visual summary of the popular image of Lloyd George the Welshman, farmer, patriarch, and man of the people:

> FUNERAL OF LLOYD GEORGE – Birthplace in Manchester of Lloyd George. Cottage in Criccieth, Wales. House where he lived and died – crowd at gate. Welsh scenic. Bridge over Dwyfor River. Pall bearers – carrying coffin from house. Placing coffin on farm cart (hearse). Hearse leaving house with mourners following on foot. Hearse passing down lane. Hearse passing through crowds of mourners – showing four grandsons in uniform. John Roberts (boyhood friend) sits and watches bearers carry coffin past. C[lose]U[p] Coffin being lowered by pall bearers. Pan shot of mourners around grave. O[ver]/H[ead] shot of grave. CU Mourners. Grandsons saluting grave. Welsh scenic.

By the time of his death Lloyd George had featured in the newsreels for more than thirty years, and his screen presence had only recently been eclipsed by that of Winston Churchill. In the silent newsreels he had been unrivalled. Details of some 25,000 newsreel stories survive from *Pathé's Animated Gazette*, the *Gaumont Graphic*, and *Topical Budget* during the silent period, and of these Lloyd George features in 212 items, and Winston Churchill in just forty-five. Herbert Asquith, Lloyd George's predecessor as prime minister, features in only thirty stories, a number that accurately reflects his dislike of personal publicity.[15] This high level of newsreel coverage was not accidental, for Lloyd George's screen presence was a careful fabrication, designed to ensure maximum coverage. As we have seen, it became so significant to Lloyd George's public image that by August and September 1918 Maurice Elvey was forced to accept it as part of the prime minister's political life, and to reproduce it in his drama.

The problem for Elvey was that Lloyd George's factual screen image had to be incorporated in a fictional drama with quite different conventions. The routine dullness of filmable public life, and the impersonal distance maintained by the newsreel cameras, gave his reconstructed newsreels a different flavour from the rest of the film, and these outdoor, public scenes contrast sharply with the indoor, private scenes that he staged in the studio. For modern viewers melodrama and allegory do not sit easily beside documentary realism, but to contemporary audiences this contrast would undoubtedly have heightened the impact of the film. Modern viewers may not pick up the subtle references, but contemporary audiences would certainly have responded to the visual clues, would have spotted the changes of context and of genre, and would have been drawn even further into *The Life Story of David Lloyd George* by Elvey's striking re-creation of Lloyd George on the newsreels.

Notes

[1] See Sarah Street's article in this volume.

[2] The newsreel coverage of Lloyd George has been identified from the newsreel database being compiled by the British Universities Film and Video Council. This currently contains details of 130,000 newsreel stories released in Britain between 1910 and 1979, including some 350 stories relating to Lloyd George that were released between 1912 and 1945.

[3] Hansard, House of Lords, 8 May 1918, col.1028 (Lord Beaverbrook).

[4] F. Dilnot, *The Adventures of a Newspaper Man* (Smith-Elder, 1913), 251–2; F. D. Bone, 'One Scoop after Another,' *World's Press News*, 17 October 1929, p.11.

[5] E. Jenkins, 'Pose-Culture,' *Punch*, 9 August 1911, p.97; B. Grant *To the Four Corners: The Memoirs of a News Photographer* (Hutchinson, 1933), 236.

[6] The political content of the *Gaumont Graphic*, *Pathé Gazette*, *Topical Budget*, and *Eclair Journal* was examined for September and October 1915, using 349 separate newsreel items identified from surviving footage in the National Film Archive, the *Gaumont Graphic* issue sheets and listings in *Kinematograph Weekly*, *Pictures and the Picturegoer* and *Screen*.

[7] *Kinematograph Weekly*, 23 September 1915, p.28, 'The Latest News Films'.

[8] Cinema attendance was estimated by the *Kinematograph Weekly*, 4 November 1915, p.2. The total number of cinemas was taken from H. Bolce, 'Crowding Cinemas in War Time', *System* (April 1915), 260, and the market share of each newsreel was calculated from 122 sample programmes printed in the *Bioscope* between January and June 1915. The number of first-run copies was estimated from these figures on the basis of eight bookings for each copy. There is some confirmation for these estimates: we know for instance that in 1917 the *Topical Budget* circulated some seventy-five first-run copies and that each copy of the *Pathé Gazette* reached 1,500 cinemas. By 1919 the *Pathé Gazette* is known to have increased its circulation to over 200 copies; House of Lords Record Office, Beaverbrook Papers, BBK/E/2/14, 'Report of Sales Department' (October 1917); *Times*, 12 March 1919, p.4, col.2; J. Ballantyne (ed.), *Researcher's Guide to British Newsreels* (1983), 101; *Kinematograph Weekly*, 10 April 1919, p.64.

[9] Newsreel content for September 1915 was listed by the *Kinematograph Weekly* in its issues for 2–30 September 1915.

[10] *Kinematograph Weekly*, 5 July 1917, p.77, 'News From the Kinema Organisations'; N. Hiley, 'The British Cinema Auditorium', in Karel Dibbets and Bert Hogenkamp (eds.), *Film and the First World War* (Amsterdam University Press, 1995), 160–70.

[11] *Kinematograph Weekly*, 15 August 1918, p.55, 'Keep the Kinema Out of Politics'.

[12] *Kinematograph Weekly*, 28 November 1918, p.53, 'Exploiting the Exhibitor?'

[13] 'E. T. Raymond' (E. R. Thompson), *Uncensored Celebrities* (T. Fisher Unwin, 1919), 9.

[14] M. Seton, 'War', *Sight and Sound* (Winter 1937–8), 184.

[15] These figures come from the newsreel database at the British Universities Film and Video Council.

9

Writing History with Lightning

PETER STEAD

Maurice Elvey's bold ambition to make what would be in effect a blockbusting film portraying the career of the man who was at that time the nation's wartime leader must be seen as a clear reminder of just how confident and uninhibited the best of the pioneering film directors were. In a later era the tag 'biopic' was associated with unremarkable, unambitious and over-cautious films made either as programme-fillers or as an attempt to bring in respectable film-goers. Initially, however, visionary directors had seen the lives of great men as ideal material for films that would go straight to the heart of a culture, combining as they did a sense of history with a clear indication of moral imperatives. Elvey's feature *Lloyd George* has an honourable place in a tradition that was to culminate in France with Abel Gance's masterpiece *Napoleon* (1926). Both directors however were in the debt of D. W. Griffith.

The most memorable and challenging comment ever made by a statesman about the movies was that of President Woodrow Wilson, by all accounts a lover of his country's great new art form, who said of one of the earliest films that he had seen, D. W. Griffith's *Birth of a Nation* (1915), that it was 'like writing history with lightning'. It was clever and entirely appropriate that the president had paraphrased Coleridge's famous judgement on Edmund Kean's acting as he successfully attempted to convey the essence of film at its best. How satisfying it is that the director who created the visual grammar of American cinema, and who first gave it some sense of the cultural space it could claim, should have his work so neatly summed up for posterity by so distinguished a critic. Wilson's apposite judgement, however, remains a challenge, and very definitely an embarrassing one, for how many subsequent directors have been capable of using lightning to illustrate that distant and very different country called the past?[1] Has it not rather been the case that directors have turned rather dutifully to history, and to political biography in particular, when in need of comforting audiences?

What was unique about Griffith was that he combined technical brilliance with a vision of America as a civilization, a vision that was idiosyncratic, utterly romantic and dangerous, but one that was as broadly conceived, coherent, mythic and truly popular as that of the great nineteenth-century novelists in whose work he was steeped.[2] Everything was grist for his mill, every detail could be accommodated in his thesis, and it was therefore wholly legitimate for him to use the story of a couple of families to tell the story of the Civil War and in particular of that disastrous process of reconstruction in which the modern mentality of Griffith's South was determined. The director's true aim was to explain and justify that southern set of values. In the process we see the assassinations of President Lincoln (played by Joseph Henabery) who, like Griffith, was a Kentuckian, and presumably not thought capable of the disastrous policies of his predecessors towards the South. Here was a director, who like his heroes Shakespeare and Dickens regarded every aspect of human nature and activity as his subject. This was all too dangerous and open-ended for Hollywood and for American politicians, and the movies were reined in and encouraged to settle for stereotypes and to be a little more minimalist. Few subsequent directors had Griffith's ambition, but at least he had created Lincoln as a movie icon.

Lincoln is the key movie politician: perhaps not surprisingly George Washington has never really been tackled, a founding father too remote and too sacred. Lincoln had much to recommend him: he was a classic 'log cabin to White House' president, a self-made, homespun, witty, independent man of the people who graduated to statesmanship and a rhetoric that was accessible and historic. He had led the victorious side in the bloodiest of wars, but every aspect of his early career, humility, humanity and sense of democratic nationhood, made him suitable as a symbol of what twentieth-century America aspired to be. In 1930, inspired by Carl Sandburg's biography, Griffith made *Abraham Lincoln*, in which he employed Walter Huston to embody all of the president's best qualities. The notion had been born of using down-to-earth, distinguished-looking, rather reserved American actors to play iconic presidents. Two other actors soon had a chance to do Lincoln, and to ensure that he remained a symbol of natural unity. In 1939 Raymond Massey, ironically like Huston a Canadian, starred in John Cromwell's *Abe Lincoln in Illinois*, and achieved a remarkable physical resemblance to the great man which very much helped to clinch the eventually tragic dimension of the career. In that same year Henry Fonda played the lead in John Ford's *Young Mr Lincoln* (1939), the best known and loved of these films. Ford is the one American director since Griffith who has had a novelist's and historian's sense of a civilization and the poet's vision to deliver it cinematically. Fonda's Lincoln is a saint, but he is one perfectly cast in the popular American idiom: he represents democratic justice but is at the same time a regular and funny guy. His voice is that of the common man, yet it resounds across the plains and the centuries.

Lincoln is the president against whom all others had to be judged. It is not easy to turn career politicians, especially those made familiar by the electronic media, into saints and symbols. However, great crises occasion specific needs, and heroes have to be found. *Wilson*, a movie depicting the presidency of Woodrow Wilson was produced in 1944 by Darryl Zanuck, the Hollywood studio boss who more than any other was aware and approving of the global implications of the country's involvement in the Second World War. He chose another distinguished-looking Canadian actor, Alexander Knox to play the refined, scholarly Presbyterian president who made the decision to take America into the First World War, who persuaded cynical European politicians to set up a League of Nations, but whose health then broke as he failed to secure American involvement in that League. Zanuck wanted a serious warning against the dangers of isolationism and that is what he produced. This was precisely the message that Franklin D. Roosevelt, president since 1933 wanted understood as another great war came to a close.

Roosevelt himself was an inspirational figure, first in the Depression and then in war. He was a tremendous communicator whose disability was disguised from the American people. His great asset was his voice which boomed out of radios and newsreels. Meanwhile Hollywood was fully recruited into the war effort and movies contributed substantially to the nation's understanding and acceptance of the war. Numerous scholars have shown how dangerous it was, however, for film to be too political, and *Mission to Moscow* (1943), the story of Ambassador Davies (played by Walter Huston) and his attempts to charm Stalin, is always cited as the classic example of how history lessons can go badly wrong. Nevertheless in time America's enormous curiosity about its greatest president since Lincoln had to be satisfied and a number of films depicted the heroic aspects of F.D.R.'s private life. The actor Ralph Bellamy developed a second half to his own career playing F.D.R. notably in *Sunrise at Campobello* (1960), having earlier starred in the same character on Broadway and in the mini-series *Winds of War* (1983).

These were worthy films but it was noticeable that, as far as the post-war era was concerned, directors were less inhibited when dealing with soldiers rather than statesmen. Franklin Schaffner's *Patton* (1970) is the best biopic of modern times, notable both for George C. Scott's bravura performance and its sheer military excitement. *MacArthur* (1977) was a lesser film in which the two actors depicting presidents were eclipsed by Gregory Peck in the title role. Clearly Peck was born to play a president rather than a general, and interestingly it was his ambition to play his hero Lincoln.

At this time another actor was generally thought to be the first choice to play presidents. By the 1970s Jason Robards had established himself as America's most distinguished stage actor, and in particular as the definitive O'Neill player. An era opened in which he played the role of any distinguished real person who was to be depicted in a movie or on television. Of course he was F.D.R. in *F.D.R. The Last Year* (1980) and also Ben Bradlee in the Watergate film *All the President's Men* (1976) and Dashiell Hammett in *Julia* (1977). Most memorably he was a brilliantly saturnine President Nixon in the 1977 mini-series *Washington behind Closed Doors*. A new era has opened: clearly television audiences had an insatiable appetite for dramatized history with a human- or family-interest angle, but in the meantime something was happening to the presidency itself. The handsome Prince of the American Dream was bloodily assassinated at Dallas, the Texas Cowboy was broken by the war in Vietnam, and the president who wanted so much to be a world statesman seemingly broke all the rules at home. On television Martin Sheen starred in *Kennedy*, a mini-series which faithfully told the story of that presidency. Elsewhere, however, the indications were that the office of the president had passed into the hands of the authors of fiction. Oliver Stone's *J.F.K.* (1992) firmly established the right of works of art to confront puzzles which historians and politicians seemed unable to solve. Emile De Antonio's *Millhouse: A White Comedy* (1971) and Stone's *Nixon* (1996), with Anthony Hopkins in the title role, clinch the argument that the presidency is now fair game and that the culture is free to interpret the pressures that operate on that office as it will. That in essence has always been the viewpoint of the writer Gore Vidal, who has written a novel sequence that provides an alternative history of the United States and in particular of the presidency. His novel *Lincoln* cuts through the mythology and depicts a president daily faced with huge political and military decisions, who all the time had a clear and realistic sense of what was at stake.[3] What was at stake of course was nothing less than the creation of what was becoming an American imperial state. Vidal's rewriting of history and subsequent television adaptations have infuriated historians and political commentators but have given evidence of a culture in which writers and film-makers feel free to ask the big questions and offer sophisticated and challenging answers.

In Great Britain things are different, and yet it could have been otherwise if Maurice Elvey had succeeded in releasing *The Life Story of David Lloyd George*. Clearly he had been inspired by Griffith, and in Lloyd George he had at hand the perfect politician to serve as the basis for a film that would give British cinema new dimensions and new prestige. Here indeed was a 'log-cabin' premier, a man with rural roots amidst an almost biblical people, but who nevertheless had a rapport with the urban masses and the intellectual ability to outwit the establishment. Here too was a natural war leader who additionally had a vision of a post-war era of peace and security. But if Griffith had been too much for America it is not difficult to see what forces in Britain would want to conspire against an epic cinema in which lightning would be used to relate real people, dead or alive, to the great issues of the culture. This was not the British way. Politics was a matter of sober reflection by interested parties: popular entertainment of all kinds had to be carefully controlled.

Nicholas Pronay, Jeffrey Richards and others have often outlined the rigorous system of British censorship which prevented film studios from tackling political issues and from dealing with real people and the dignified institutions of state.[4] The United Kingdom was a country where politicians were confident that consensus could be managed without the cinematic beatification of party politicians, either dead or alive. The United States had already shown what could be done in 1929, when George Arliss had played in *Disraeli* for Warner (a role he had played in the silents), but it was only the mood of crisis in 1942 which finally prompted a comparable British effort. In that year Robert Donat, who was of Polish extraction but was regarded as the one home-grown star to rival the Americans, played *The Young Mr Pitt* – the story of how an

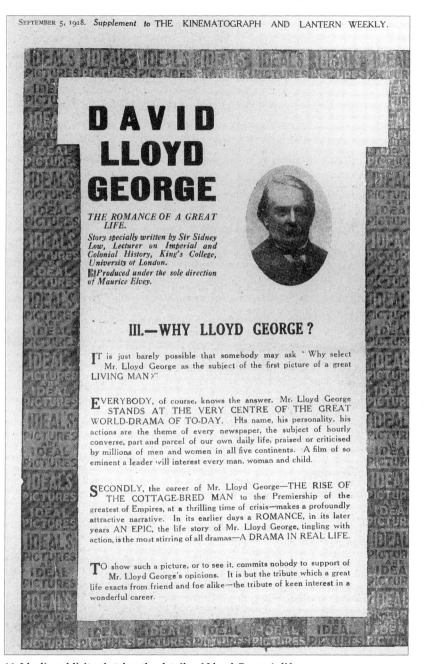

DAVID LLOYD GEORGE

THE ROMANCE OF A GREAT LIFE.

Story specially written by Sir Sidney Low, Lecturer on Imperial and Colonial History, King's College, University of London.

Produced under the sole direction of Maurice Elvey.

III.—WHY LLOYD GEORGE?

IT is just barely possible that somebody may ask "Why select Mr. Lloyd George as the subject of the first picture of a great LIVING MAN?"

EVERYBODY, of course, knows the answer. Mr. Lloyd George STANDS AT THE VERY CENTRE OF THE GREAT WORLD-DRAMA OF TO-DAY. His name, his personality, his actions are the theme of every newspaper, the subject of hourly converse, part and parcel of our own daily life, praised or criticised by millions of men and women in all five continents. A film of so eminent a leader will interest every man, woman and child.

SECONDLY, the career of Mr. Lloyd George—THE RISE OF THE COTTAGE-BRED MAN to the Premiership of the greatest of Empires, at a thrilling time of crisis—makes a profoundly attractive narrative. In its earlier days a ROMANCE, in its later years AN EPIC, the life story of Mr. Lloyd George, tingling with action, is the most stirring of all dramas—A DRAMA IN REAL LIFE.

TO show such a picture, or to see it, commits nobody to support of Mr. Lloyd George's opinions. It is but the tribute which a great life exacts from friend and foe alike—the tribute of keen interest in a wonderful career.

16. Ideal's publicity sketches the details of Lloyd George's life.

earlier British statesman had withstood a military threat from Europe. This was an inspired choice of subject and perfect casting, but director Carol Reed was not to inaugurate a new era of films set in Parliament. As both Churchill and Laurence Olivier realized, Shakespeare was a far better bet for stiffening the national sinews.

Churchill was undoubtedly a figure of Lincoln-like pre-eminence but his legacy was a difficult one for a culture unused to dramatizing politics. *Young Winston* (1972) was a pleasant enough reminder of the statesman's early colonial adventures, but one was left to reflect on why so many other stirring careers had been ignored. In the age of occasional television adaptations of historical events Shakespeare remained the most potent historical resource, as Ian McKellen indicated when he used *Richard III* to explore the notion of a Fascist regime in Britain. Perhaps McKellen's film did at least inspire a television mini-series on Oswald Mosley, but of more significance was the BBC Wales film *Food for Ravens* (1997) in which Brian Cox played the dying Aneurin Bevan. As the National Health Service approached its fiftieth anniversary, here was a reminder of how our most recent past could be illuminated by lightning. From Lloyd George to Nye Bevan and beyond there is much political drama that could be written. The legacy of Elvey could be just beginning.

Surely Gore Vidal and Oliver Stone are in the right. History is not dead, and the day-to-day machinations of politicians should concern us all, not least novelists, dramatists and film-makers. There are lessons to be learnt from the lives of the great and truths to be revealed. These lessons and truths will not always be pleasant and they will often be controversial. Nevertheless the lives of great men constitute a drama at the centre of our culture, and what we need are latter-day Elveys with the nerve to claim that territory.

Notes

[1] Peter C. Rollins (ed.), *Hollywood as Historian* (University of Kentucky Press, 1983), is essential reading, especially the essays by Everett Carter on *The Birth of a Nation* and Thomas J. Knock on *Wilson*. Also useful is Bruce Crowther, *Hollywood Faction* (Columbus Books, 1984). Robert Brent Toplin casts a scholar's critical eye at recent American films in *History by Hollywood: The Use and Abuse of the American Past* (1996) and in the review pages he regularly edits for the *Journal of American History*. An entertaining introduction is George MacDonald Fraser, *The Hollywood History of the World* (Michael Joseph, 1988).

[2] For Griffith see Kevin Brownlow, *The Parade's Gone By* (Alfred A. Knopf, 1968) and Richard Schikel, *D. W. Griffith and the Birth of Film* (Pavilion Books, 1984). David Culbert illustrates all the dangers of movies attempting to portray instant history in his essay on *Mission to Moscow*, in John E. O'Connor and Martin A. Jackson, *American History/American Film* (Ungar Film Library, 1979).

[3] The whole subject of the novelist's and film-maker's right, and indeed imperative, to fictionalize great lives is discussed – with special reference to his 1984 novel *Lincoln* (Heinemann) and the subsequent mini-series – by Gore Vidal in *A View from the Diners' Club* (Random House, 1991) and *Screening History* (Harvard University Press, 1992). A spirited riposte is provided by Mark Steyn in an article 'Hollywood versus History', *Spectator*, 26 March 1998, which is particularly concerned with Oliver Stone's *Nixon*.

[4] The severe and all too often underestimated constraints affecting film production in the United Kingdom are best explained by Nicholas Pronay in 'The First Reality: Film Censorship in Liberal England', published in a very useful volume, K. R. M. Short (ed.), *Feature Films as History* (CroomHelm, 1981), and by Jeffrey Richards in two articles on the British Board of Film Censors, *Historical Journal of Film, Radio and Television*, 1, 2 (October 1981) and 2, 1 (March 1982). The wartime significance of Robert Donat and the importance of *The Young Mr. Pitt* are discussed by Jeffrey Richards in *The Age of the Dream Palace* (Routledge, 1984).

10

A Film of Thought

JOHN O. THOMPSON

Of all the curious features of *The Life Story of David Lloyd George*, not the least curious is that it is a silent film about a great speaker. In what follows I want to draw out some of the implications of this.

1

The first, basic challenge facing the makers of *The Life Story* back in 1918–19 was simply the challenge that faces anyone making a biopic, early or late. The genre is problematic, from a Bazinian perspective[1] (and part of what commends the Bazinian perspective to me is that it always seems to raise the *right* problems), because the photographic image on the screen has to do two things. It gives us some sort of indexical access to people and things that really exist or existed. As time passes, the value of this access grows: we find ourselves looking at things that we could no longer look at were it not for their mechanical capture, earlier, by the camera. Where 'things' are concerned, one of the joys of *The Life Story* is how it presents us with the surface of the world of 1918 as a 1918 newsreel would do. Biopic photography, however, where people are concerned – and here is the problem – can only present us with the persons portrayed via actors impersonating them. So, in a 1918 newsreel, we would see Lloyd George, while in *The Life Story* we see the actor Norman Page and younger figures representing Lloyd George. (Actually, the same goes for things, to the extent that a film needs to use sets or accessible locations to stand in for the real places lived in by the subject of the biography.)

André Bazin clearly, as a critic, had no problems with fiction; he may never have spelled out in precise terms the film-maker/audience compact regarding the photography of fictional characters that our culture has evolved, but his criticism presupposes such a compact

Lloyd George's pithy put-down of a drunken heckler during a key political campaign.

(he is very unlike Grierson in this respect). And if you accept the fiction compact, you might as well accept the 'faction' compact, to use the recent verbal coinage: *The Life Story* is not supposed to be fictional, but the condition under which it, or any biopic, can give us the facts about its subject is that we allow that subject and those around him to be represented by actors. The downside of this is that we do not 'really' get to see Lloyd George; the upside is that we get a whole life (as opposed to the bits-of-a-life that newsreels or their equivalents can give), and in the form of a story (with the cognitive advantages that narrative form bestows on the chaotic and long-drawn-out contents of life-as-such).

Indeed, following the spirit if not the letter of Bazin, we might say that what is photographically caught in the biopic is threefold rather than twofold. We really see Norman Page (no longer available otherwise: this is the overcoming-of-mortality aspect of Bazin's line on photography); we see, via the acting compact, Lloyd George; and we see *what in 1918 would have struck the makers of the film as a viable solution to the problem of linking the actor to the role*. Compare the situation if a film of the life of Lloyd George was to be made today – starring, say, Daniel Day-Lewis. We can prospectively anticipate the pathos which such a film will achieve in a hundred years, with Day-Lewis only encounterable through photographic means; we can, just as in *The Life Story*, learn about Lloyd George through the story-telling applied to the life; but we will necessarily also be looking at a late 1990s approach to 'Day-Lewis playing Lloyd George' (and to X directing Day-Lewis playing Lloyd George, Y writing the script for . . ., and so on). Prospectively, again, this would constitute a photographic 1997 triumph over time, just as Abel Gance's *Napoleon* is as much, or more, a triumph for Gance and Albert Dieudonné and 1927 over time as for Napoleon and the early Napoleonic period over time.

The fact that *The Life Story*, dated 1918, closes with the end of the First World War brings its own third 'photographic capture' into line with the first most intriguingly. (Had Hammer Films specialized in biopics as well as horror, a 'lost' Hammer treatment of the Lloyd George life dated 1956, fascinating though it would be, would not be fascinating in quite the same way.)

2

A late 1990s version of the life of Lloyd George: actually, infinitely many are imaginable. The Merchant/Ivory life, the Ken Loach life, the Oliver Stone life, the Terence Davies life, the Jim Jarmusch life . . . Similarly, *The Life Story* of 1918 ought not to be thought of as just *the* way, the one way, they would (inevitably and primitively) have done it in 1918.

But any non-specialist audience now will indeed experience *The Life Story* as at least 'early', and more likely as 'early and primitive'. Why? No doubt there are a range of reasons, with indeed the film's black-and-white (or tinted monochrome) photography up there among them.[2]

The film's silence is another reason, banally enough – or is this so banal? The viewer of *The Life Story* is necessarily brought up against silence rather a lot, given that this is the life story of an orator.

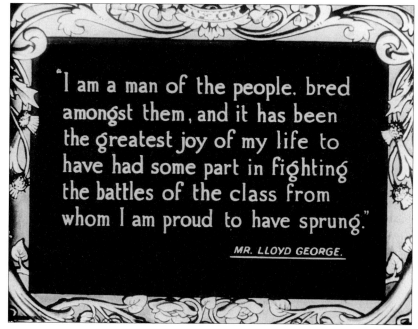

"I am a man of the people. bred amongst them, and it has been the greatest joy of my life to have had some part in fighting the battles of the class from whom I am proud to have sprung."

MR. LLOYD GEORGE.

18. A speech intertitle emphasizes the supposed proletarian credentials of the 'cottage-bred' man.

One of the fascinations for us, now in 1998, receiving this unexpected message in a bottle, so to speak, is to be told the story of an orator at all. What late 1990s screenwriter would dare to concentrate so relentlessly on the 'great speeches' made by the hero – *even with the benefit of sound*? Lloyd George's great lifetime deeds are represented as 'things done with words'. As a young lawyer, he speaks, winning the 'burial case' in the end. As a politician he speaks, to win his seat in the House of Commons and to keep it, then to argue for pieces of legislation. These bills ('Are you busy making another bill, Daddy?') themselves are, of course, written; but their 'silence' poses just as awkward a problem for the representational resources of a silent film as do the orator's speeches, as we shall see. And Lloyd George's accomplishments in the First World War are rendered, to a surprising extent, through citation of a number of key wartime speeches. In all this, Sir Sidney Low, himself clearly a man of the word in his Whitehall professional life, sets Maurice Elvey an interesting filmic challenge, to put it mildly.[3]

An interesting challenge, or an impossible one?

3

In speaking of a 'third photographic capture', over and above the capture of what and who were materially there in front of the camera, one material under two descriptions (role/actor, place/sets), we might want to extend the sense of what is further captured beyond just a 'period' understanding of how to connect the two. Negotiating 'how to play Lloyd George' is only one element within a larger field, one which is overall less tangible, not so material – a field of the conceptual, the ideal, the ideological as we might once have put it.[4] Bazin speaks of photography as answering to the same human desire as did mummification in ancient Egypt; but when we are in the presence of mummies, of preserved Pharoahs, are we not also in the presence of a preserved version of the belief system which led to the production of mummies?

In this light, it seems worth pausing over what the stakes are in the telling of the story of Lloyd George, then *and* now, if the rediscovery of *The Life Story* is not to be an event of merely antiquarian interest.

Maybe I am unusual in my ignorance, but I do not really think so: some of what *The Life Story* tells me about the establishment of key elements of social provision in the British state and beyond (these administrative ideas were to travel – possibly they had already travelled from elsewhere to be available to Lloyd George, but the film says nothing about this), has the weight of *news*. It is amazing, when you think about it – but you do not, until the message in the bottle turns up on the beach – how *forgotten* such a moment of history as 'the first Friday of Old Age Pensions' is. The People's Budget, the National Insurance Bill: every member of the contemporary audience for *The Life Story*, had it had a contemporary audience, would have remembered these well, but how unremembered they are now! The film 'saves against death', in a Bazinian fashion, the moment of their everyday remembrance, but equally for us it has the possibility of straightforwardly conveying new information.

If anyone was to read my essay eighty years on, she or he might in turn welcome a statement here about what we, in the 1990s, remember in this field instead. The answer, of course ('of course' for us), is: we remember Attlee. There is a general sense around that the 'welfare state' came into being as a result of the British people's admirable refusal simply to 'go with Churchill' in 1945, after the end of the Second World War, and instead to elect a Labour government. Such a memory is right and proper, certainly, but it does have the effect of overlaying any sense of what Attlee and his colleagues had inherited. Party-political considerations are not irrelevant here: the eclipse of the Liberal party as a major player in national politics (note that the reasonable showing currently of the Liberal Democrats is not really relevant: the Liberals' near-total mid-century eclipse is what set up the conditions for forgetting) has meant that *The Life Story of David Lloyd George* (and of his colleagues)[5] has turned out to be a story not widely told.

But, insofar as the British moving-image industry does not seem currently to be exactly lining up to produce *The Life Story of Clement Attlee* (not to speak of *The Life Story* of the next seriously reformist British prime minister, Margaret Thatcher), it is possible to wonder whether there is more to the problem than a merely political forgetfulness. Are there not, perhaps, ingrained difficulties with the political biopic which the team which made *The Life Story* faced, and faced up to, in terms of the film technology and film language of their time, but which have not been straightforwardly overcome for our own time, despite all advances? Is what is ideologically captured in the film not something early but something late – the last moment when it would seem feasible to try to tell a popular cinema audience the story of someone making history legislatively and on the basis of a popular mandate won from the platform?

What will turn out to be a problem for the cinema with this story is that the legislator and the orator both deal in ideas, while photography requires objects in front of the camera.

4

Recently, David MacDougall has provided us with a valuable discussion of 'Films of Memory'. Two aspects of his article feed productively into a discussion of *The Life Story*. First, MacDougall offers a workable typology of filmic *signs of memory*, which he divides into four species:

Signs of survival, 'images of objects which have a physical link with the remembered past.' As it happens, *The Life Story* opens with two such signs, a photograph of the real Lloyd George birth certificate and a shot of the real house in Manchester in which Lloyd George was born.

2 *Signs of replacement*, which are the stand-ins required by the fictional contract 'if objects do not survive to be filmed' (and if people do not; or if objects and people, while extant, are not available for filming). Norman Page is a sign of replacement for Lloyd George.

3 *Signs of resemblance:* 'At one remove from replacements in kind are replacements in form . . . These offer a looser, iconic link with their objects, filling in the missing pattern of the past by analogy . . .' MacDougall instances how, in a 1989 film by Renata and Hannes Lintrop (*Cogito, Ergo Sum*), 'an elderly Estonian's daily physical struggle becomes a metaphor for his long resistance to Soviet rule'; and he emphasizes how, 'among signs of resemblance, music is the analogue par excellence for emotion'.

4 *Signs of absence:* 'These signs define memory by its true opposite, an embodied absence. An empty factory thus represents a fully operating one. A market square teems not with peasants and bullocks but with youths on motorbikes.' Perhaps the most famous current example of a film working in this mode – and thus in a position of tension with respect to the 'positive' docudrama ambitions of a film like *Schindler's List* (USA, 1993) – is Claude Lanzmann's *Shoah* (France, 1985).

Second, MacDougall argues for a *film–mind equation*. Here are two key passages:

> If memory forms an aspect of thought, it is possible to regard films of memory as efforts to approximate the process by which the mind represents experience to itself. (p.264)

> Memory is often apparently incoherent, and a strange mixture of the sensory and the verbal. It offers us the past in flashes and fragments, and in what seems a hotchpotch of mental 'media'. We seem to glimpse images, hear sounds, use unspoken words and reexperience such physical sensations as pressure and movement. It is in this multidimensionality that memory perhaps finds its closest counterpart in the varied and intersecting representational systems of film. (p.261)

This is fair enough to a point, but it leaves me feeling uneasy. 'Varied and intersecting representational systems of film' seems a reasonable phrase and certainly the 'flashes and fragments' characterization of memory i unproblematic. But if we are to think of the former as providing a 'counterpart' to the latter, it must be with a full recognition that something in the former's photographic nature seems to pull in the opposite direction from the 'mixed media incoherence' of memory or of thought more generally. Film *can* be pulled in that direction, but something resists.[6]

The Life Story is a wonderful document of that resistance, precisely because its makers – perhaps especially, one might conjecture, Sir Sidney Low as its writer – did try to produce a film which would be memory's counterpart, and thought's counterpart.

5

Throughout *The Life Story* we encounter photography being required to 'tell the life story' against photography's grain, at least against its Bazinian grain. This is because of the nature of the achievements of the hero. But before outlining how our hero's actions prove hard to film, it is worth dwelling in detail on an early stretch of the film where these actions are not presented but prefigured.

It would seem reasonable enough to want to say the following about David Lloyd George: 'Some of his experiences when a child both prepared him for and (in a slightly eerie or magical manner) "anticipated" the achievements of his maturity.' Let us assume that Sir Sidney Low, wishing to make this point, had at his disposal at least two veridical examples. First: Lloyd George and his contemporaries played 'French and Germans' at school, as elsewhere they might have played 'cowboys and Indians': Lloyd George led the 'French' side to juvenile triumph, beating the 'Germans'. Second: Lloyd George was much struck by the biblical account of David and Goliath as read to him by his uncle. How are these facts, as anticipations of the First World War, to be conveyed to the viewer of *The Life Story*?

In the first case, the photographic challenge is to film a play battle amongst little boys, a battle in which Lloyd George leads his side to victory. And the film delivers this well enough. It is not quite the battle in the snow at the beginning of Gance's *Napoleon*, but could it have been at the time? What Elvey provides is an efficient, perhaps more-than-efficient, delivery of the content photographically, within the terms of the great necessary convention: 'See our actors as the real X's (here, the real

19. Lloyd George, in tam o'shanter, replays incidents from the Franco-Prussian War, as Elvey draws parallels with the Great War.

children) whom they must stand in for: since no one was photographing the scene as it really happened, only thus can you access it' (a 'sign of replacement', in MacDougall's terminology).

The footage was, however, felt to require verbal elucidation. The play battle is to be *thought of* by the audience as a near-contemporary remembrance of the Franco-Prussian war, and this needs conveying verbally via not one but two titles: 'David and his school-fellows play at French and Germans fighting . . .' / 'The Franco-German War of this period (1870) suggested the game to the children.' But the real point, of course, is prospective rather than retrospective, as the next title makes clear: 'The German arms sustain a crushing defeat.' If the children's battle is a sign of replacement of a real childhood event remembered by Lloyd George, it is more importantly a sign of resemblance prefiguring the First World War: the play battle is a metaphor for the real one to come.

Nothing, so far in the sequence, goes beyond the usual dialectic between image and written word in the silent cinema (with the words of the titles charged to supply the 'thought' necessary for the image to be fully understood). It is in the sequence immediately following that the status of the photographic as such becomes perplexing.

The sequence is introduced with the simple title 'The story of David and Goliath', and proceeds non-verbally thereafter through the biblical narrative. The young Lloyd George is at home; his uncle is reading the David and Goliath story to the family group. The battle between David and Goliath is photographically rendered. (Low-angle shot of an overbearing, heavily armoured Goliath; shot of the young, lightly clad David; intercutting thereafter of a rather static Goliath with sword and David, more mobile, with sling-shot, running over to a ditch to find a stone; after the stone has been slung and has felled Goliath, the two figures are put in long shot together for the first time, as David runs to Goliath, takes up his sword and poises it for the decapitation; in the midst of this, we return to the parlour in Wales once, to see the young Lloyd George listening with rapt attention to his uncle reading. At the end, we see David triumphant, arms raised to the sky.) Then something very curious happens. Shot of the face of Goliath (which we have not really seen earlier because of the armour). Shot of the face of David – which dissolves to a shot of the face of the mature Lloyd George. Shot of the face of Goliath which similarly dissolves to a shot of the face of the Kaiser (or rather, in both cases, to the face of the actors playing Lloyd George and Kaiser). Shot of Lloyd George. Shot of Kaiser. Shot of Lloyd George dissolving back into shot of David. Shot of the Kaiser dissolving back into shot of Goliath. Now another title: 'Knowing his cause was just David faced tyrannic violence and overcame it.'

While there is more to come in the sequence, this is a good place to pause to assess the strains being put upon photography here.

Clearly the core or spine of *The Life Story* consists of the representation of the deeds of Lloyd George – that is, of things that Lloyd George did over the course of his life. These deeds unfolded in a continuous, homogeneous space and time. To render them via signs of replacement is to create within the film a simulacrum of that continuity and homogeneity. Lloyd George leading the 'French' in the play battle and Lloyd George listening to his uncle reading the Bible story are events which can coexist unproblematically within that simulated continuum.

But the story of David and Goliath unfolds in a space and time other than that of the Lloyd George life story. Just how other depends, technically, on your estimation of the factual status of the biblical narrative. If David and Goliath were historical figures, then they have indeed occupied a space and time which is the same space and time as that of Lloyd George and indeed of ourselves. If they are mythical or fictional figures, then they never did exist in the space and time of our world. The difference, however, does not amount to much so far as the viewer is concerned: even a historical David and Goliath are of such a radically other time and another place from that of Lloyd George that the effect of their presentation 'within' the Lloyd George life story is to fracture the continuum.

The style in which the David and Goliath story is rendered accentuates rather than minimizes the sense of disruption, or irruption. Whereas D. W. Griffith in *Intolerance* (USA, 1916) juxtaposes different times and places but keeps to a uniform detailedness of rendering which lends them all equivalent 'reality', the Elvey David and Goliath are presented as figures with minimal realistic detail: the action unfolds against bare ground and sky, totally unlike the natural world in which the play battle has just taken place, or the detailed domestic interior of the Lloyd George household. (Photography's revenge: there is something eerily striking about the real physical flatness of the landscape, about the particular patterning of the clouds.) The shot-of-Goliath, shot-of-David rhythm of the sequence minimizes spatial realism in the conflict itself, which indeed makes little spatial sense, since Goliath's movements imply that he is close to David (or, at best, is rehearsing what he will do to David with his sword once he gets close to him), while the sling-shot victory *requires* David to be at some distance from his antagonist: how far they have been apart is rendered in the more 'Bazinian' two-shot of them, with David covering considerable ground in approaching the fallen man, which comes as something of a spatial shock to the viewer.

Why make such a distinction between the Lloyd George-childhood world and the David-and-Goliath world? Because, of course, Low and Elvey have no interest in the *independent* reality (or reality-effect, if fiction is in question) of the David and Goliath story: it is the story as it impresses the young Lloyd George that is to be conveyed. The photography of actors playing David and Goliath is not so much standing in for the real David or Goliath as it is standing in for images of

David and Goliath in the heads of those listening to the story, notably Lloyd George. Taken in this spirit, the space-time of the life story of Lloyd George could be felt to be maintained in its spatio-temporal integrity: admittedly, it is impossible to film somebody's mental imagery, but then it is impossible to film the long-departed young Lloyd George too. We can and do compact with the film-makers that the impossible is possible to get on with the delivery of the material. Why not take the shots of David and Goliath as unfolding in the space and time of the young Lloyd George's mental operations as he listens to his uncle reading?

Low and Elvey do not make it easy for the viewer to settle into such a compact, given the shots that follow immediately on from the David and Goliath narration.

The thought to be put across, of course, is simple enough as a thought, indeed it is much the same as the thought conveyed by the play-battle sequence: just as the battle anticipates (is a metaphor for) World War I, so Lloyd George will turn out to be 'like' David in facing up to and vanquishing the Goliath-like Kaiser. But conveying this thought photographically adds another level of complexity, or two, to the 'ontology' of *these* photographic images.

If the photographs of David and Goliath are to be taken as 'photographs' of the young Lloyd George's mental images of these (that is, they are photographs of actors, but these photographs are signs-of-replacement not for David and Goliath as concrete physical beings but for 'David and Goliath in the mind'), what status do the photographs of Lloyd George and the Kaiser have? Again, they are, in reality, photographs of actors, but are they signs-of-replacement for the real historical figures or for these figures in thought? They occupy no space and no time, or rather their space and time is wholly a matter of conditions of concrete presentation (their space is their space on the screen, their time is their time on the screen): by comparison, David and Goliath are spatio-temporally richly specified. Furthermore, they exist primarily as images for the David and Goliath images to dissolve into and dissolve back to: the dissolve undermines 'trust in the image', or more precisely undermines any sense that the point of the image is how it is referentially, indexically imprinted by something real via the mechanical photographic process. The point is the metaphor, 'Lloyd George against the Kaiser is David and Goliath all over again.' (Visually, such a

metaphor might be much more directly and idiomatically delivered via
the political cartoon, where the cartoonist can draw a Lloyd George-as-
David and a Kaiser-as-Goliath very easily: no doubt this actually was a
popular World War I visual trope.) And in what space-time is this
metaphorical mental process taking place? Or *whose*? Certainly not that of
the young Lloyd George. Little is he to know, yet, of the challenges and
the horrors of 1914–18. Nor can he yet know, and this is crucial, how he
will look as an adult statesman. Clearly the thought being filmed is not a
thought that the young Lloyd George has had, but a thought that the
film-makers have had, a thought they wish the viewers to be left with. To
recapitulate the varieties of photography intermixed in the two sequences
described so far:

- Signs of survival: none.[7]
- Core signs-of-replacement level: the parlour in the Lloyd George house,
  with the uncle reading to the rest of the family.
- Same level, but with something more going on: the play battle. This is
  homogeneous with the parlour scene in being part of the continuous
  space-time of the Lloyd George life story, but the titles enhance its
  significance: we not only see the battle, we are led verbally to 'see it as'
  echoing the Franco-Prussian War and as prefiguring the First World War.
  We move into the realm of signs of analogy.
- David and Goliath: signs of analogy in terms of the overall point (the
  biblical story prefigures the First World War and Lloyd George's leading
  role in it); signs of replacement insofar as actors stand in for the
  historical/mythical protagonists. What is being 'replaced' is not David-
  and-Goliath *per se* but David-and-Goliath as a subjective mental
  experience of Lloyd George's – at least, the semi-abstract rendering of
  space would suggest this.
- Statesman Lloyd George and the Kaiser: making explicit the analogy.
  These images are so linked to David and Goliath images (themselves now
  severed from what space and time they had as the story itself was
  represented) as to lose virtually all 'ontological force' photographically.
  The dissolves undermine each image's independent weight in insisting on
  cross-image conceptual equivalence, the images have no space or time
  they can call their own. However, the sequence still requires (since this *is*
  photography) its signs of replacement, with the odd result that Lloyd
  George is replaced successively by a young and a mature actor within the
  space of a few seconds.

It is time now to look briefly at how the sequence concludes.

We have already quoted 'Knowing his cause was just David faced tyrannic violence and overcame it.' Are these the uncle's words, or the film's? Close-up of the rapt face of the young Lloyd George. Then an astonishing shot, participating in the ethos of all the 'glorious leader' shots of the twentieth century, of Lloyd George the statesman: photographic (the wind blows his clothes) but with the monumental gravitas of a statue. Then a crucial title:

> "I am a man of the people, bred amongst them, and it has been the greatest joy of my life to have had some part in fighting the battles of the class from whom I am proud to have sprung."
>
> MR. LLOYD GEORGE

Then the heroic mature Lloyd George again (statue-like, outside particularized space and time), then the boy Lloyd George again (space and time: that of the core 'life story' presumably – but the shot is a close-up, so we never return to the parlour, to the scene of the reading). Finally, before this section of the film concludes and we move on from childhood to youth, one more title: 'He has been the champion of democracy, the champion of nationality, the champion of liberty, and the champion of humanity.'

If there is something tub-thumping about this last formulation, the quotation from Lloyd George himself registers as a simple, powerful expression of value. But how will *The Life Story* render the fight – given that this is a fight conducted in thought, in language, in that binding of practice to language which we call legislation and administration?

6

The answer to this question must be given more quickly and schematically, failing a shot-by-shot exploration of the whole film. But the sequences we have been scrutinizing prefigure the film's later strategies. The accomplishments of Lloyd George turn out to be great speeches, important legislation and inspired administration under pre-war and wartime conditions. Much screen time is spent, in terms of the core life story, watching Lloyd George speak (the oratorical body, with the hand gestures of the 'big delivery' tradition, facing an audience registering reaction in a generalized way: not, especially given the general fixity of camera position, inherently very 'visual');[8] or operate in his office (Lloyd George's head bent over papers, entry and exit of subordinate figures); or, having decreed that something should be done, visiting the site of its accomplishment (Lloyd George in factories, Lloyd George at the Front). All this cries out for sound, one may feel. But even with sound, is this not better material for a radio play than for a film?

The pre-Bazinian intuitions of Low and Elvey suggest to them various ways to open up visually this life-in-words. To mention a few:

- In a core 'life-story' way, making a speech can be shown to be, at times, a physically risky business. This is the point of the Birmingham riot scenes, with their impressive crowds surging threateningly.
- A sense of 'another life' can be given. This is the point of the charming scene in which Lloyd George and his daughter wander off to encounter the ducks and the pelicans.
- Legislative achievements can be conveyed through exemplary scenes: because Parliament did this, certain photographable things will, or will no longer, happen.
- Oratorical achievements can be conveyed by 'photographing the tropes', or providing screen pictures which can stand in for what the listener or reader might imagine under the spell of the speech.
- The silence and privacy of the office itself (where 'office' should be heard as meaning both a role and a place) can be made to speak.

The last three of these turn out to involve anti-Bazinian strategies cognate with those we have just been examining in detail.

Thus, the 'theft of the bread' scene, which is rendered with realist detail in high silent-screen melodrama style, nevertheless is ontologically detached from the space and time of the Lloyd George life: this poor household is not 'out there', available to be visited by Lloyd George, say, as he will later visit factories. It is an example of a state of affairs which the implementation of the People's Budget of 1909 will correct. The 'sick husband' scene has a similar status, which is made all the clearer by existing as two contrasting possibilities: 'here is what happens before the enactment of the National Insurance Bill (1911), and here is the "same" scene but with the legislation in place.' Neither version of the sick husband passes the visitability test: what is being photographed is a sign of substitution for the contrasting *typical cases* being used by Lloyd George in speech to argue for early social-security provision. The wartime speeches tend to get their tropes embodied for photography, as when the advantages of a united Allied command are figured by a tug-of-war, or when the American contribution to the war is figured by a montage of the most distinguished American war presidents, Washington, Lincoln, Woodrow Wilson (a complex sequence, itself heterogeneous in that Lloyd George's contemporary Wilson does pass the visitability test in a way that Washington and Lincoln do not, and is photographed accordingly). And just as it is the thought of Washington that is photographically rendered rather than Washington, so it is the thought of previous prime ministers that is made to materialize (fittingly, out of the array of books on the wall) in a ghostly, ectoplasmic way in Lloyd George's study as he reflects on the mighty dead, his predecessors.

Jean-Louis Comolli once discussed the problems of cinematic historical fiction in a fine essay called 'A Body Too Much' ('Un corps en trop') which ends up as a celebration of Jean Renoir's *La Marseillaise* (France, 1938).[9] The 'too-muchness' in question is a matter of the body of the actor and the body of the historical figure both having to be rendered by the same photographic sign, leading to an at least potential unease for the spectator; the achievement of Renoir's film is seen to lie in its making thematic use of this unease where the figure of Louis XVI (as embodied by Pierre Renoir) is concerned: the king is represented as uneasy himself in his role. What happens in *The Life Story* is almost the reverse of this: the effect of all the irruptions of 'ontologically thin' material, of attempts to photograph thought and speech, the general and conceptual rather than the existent, is to dematerialize Lloyd George himself somewhat, to put him before us as 'the thought of the statesman hero' rather than as a man.

This may sound like a criticism of the film; I would prefer it to be taken as descriptive, and as an invitation to the spectator to feel, and to savour, all the different ontological 'weights' of what is put before our eyes by Low and Elvey. In a way, what *The Life Story* anticipates is not so much the conventional historical fiction or faction film but rock video, where 'thoughts' (in the lyrics, or suggested by the lyrics, or in contradiction to the lyrics) are freely filmed, anchored Bazinianly only in the photographed figure of the performer.

Or there is another, frankly evaluative, way to conclude: might it be that it is really only in its final sequences that *The Life Story* finds itself, finds cinema, 'comes alive'? The penultimate sequence, 'The Last Roll-Call', moves away from everything discussed so far in its visual rendering in (very convincing) signs-of-replacement mode of the moment of demobilization at the end of the First World War: thought here arises from the image rather than constituting the basis for the image, in classically realist fashion. The ultimate sequence, however, with Lloyd George in his office alone again, brings us back to the rendition of thought, though now without any ectoplasmic images. The titles do the work: Lloyd George ponders how to make Britain ready for the next war, how to maintain and enhance armaments and mobilization in readiness for 'the next time', and then, amazingly (how rarely is this rendered on film), *changes his mind:* 'There must be no "next time" !'

Notes

[1] For readers new to these matters, the thought of André Bazin is most directly approachable in the two volumes translated as *What Is Cinema?* (University of California Press: I, 1967; II, 1971). The essay on still photography, 'The Ontology of the Photographic Image' (I, 9–16), written in the immediate aftermath of the Second World War, underpins Bazin's critical engagement on behalf of the 'realist' moving image while underdetermining it, in that Bazin's extraordinarily generous and flexible critical position is the result of other components interacting with his views on photography *per se* (notably, his sense of the quality criteria legitimately importable from the non-photographic arts). 'The Ontology', a dense, infinitely rewarding, but at the same time exploratory and playful essay, is a handy resource for reconstructing something one can call 'Bazinianism' for purposes of particular investigations, such as this essay; but the health warning that needs to be given is that such reconstructions amount to something a great deal less than 'the real Bazin'. The key thought of 'The Ontology' is that it matters that photography mechanically captures something really out there, that there is something more to the photograph than its resemblance to something. A photograph gives us not only the object's *picture* (as might a painting), it gives us something like its *fingerprint*. (In a terminology derived from the philosopher C. S. Peirce, its weight is not only iconic but, crucially, *indexical*.) Of course, problems then arise about photographing fiction, about choice and manipulation within the field of photography, and so forth. But addressing these problems *starting* from the insights of 'The Ontology' has come to seem to me essential.

[2] Ramsey Campbell's fine recent horror novel *The House on Nazareth Hill* (Headline, 1996) includes a striking phrase about the effects, for us (or for us on a bad day), of monochrome. The heroine Amy and her boyfriend Rob are at his place:

They finished their meal, and were at the sink, admiring the rainbow bubbles while they washed up, when he glanced at the flat square clock. 'Back in a moment, have to record *It's a Wonderful Life* for my mother . . .'
 'Leave it on. I used to like it when I was little', she said.
 At first she couldn't see why she had. She sat on the couch and moved over for Rob, which reminded her of cuddling up to her mother the last time she'd watched the film. Now she seemed to be watching people so dead they couldn't even make themselves be in colour. (pp.129–30)

[3] My phrasing here is a shorthand, given that I am not clear about the precise collaborative regime governing the production of *The Life Story*. The film certainly feels as if the script came first and was 'kept to' pretty faithfully, but that is only an impression.

[4] A 'weak' notion of ideology as sets of assumptions (political, social, etc.) about facts and values which underlie what the film explicitly presents is intended here, rather than the full-blown Marxist notions of ideology so influential in the 1970s. The latter, with their interest in exploring why the revolution fails to take place, would be especially inappropriate to bring to bear on a film about a politician working, it would now (post-1989) seem correctly, outside that particular view of what constitutes a progressive politics.

[5] A problem with *The Life Story* which would surely have been registered at the time had the film been released is its almost complete failure to represent Lloyd George as operating in a collaborative context.

[6] David MacDougall, 'Films of Memory', in Lucien Taylor (ed.), *Visualising Theory: Selected Essays from V.A.R., 1990–1994* (Routledge, 1994), pp.260–70. MacDougall is, of course, writing about a range of films including documentary, with voice-over, as well as narrative forms (the biopic, historical fiction), and in the former photography seems to be able to 'follow thought' much more freely than in the latter; even so, the particular strategies of *The Life Story* would, I claim, look curious even if it were recast in a documentary frame.

[7] Immediately preceding the play battle, however, there is a shot of a tree with initials carved in it which, I take it, is a shot of a real tree really bearing the marks of the young Lloyd George's knife.

[8] The film scarcely ever tries to present a point of view from which the oratorical gestures of Lloyd George would register as visually effective in their own right; we get surprisingly little sense of how they might have held an audience.

[9] Jean-Louis Comolli, 'Historical Fiction: A Body Too Much', *Screen* 19, 2 (1978), 41–53; originally in *Cahiers du Cinéma* (July 1977).

11

Lloyd-Janus: Looking Backward and Forward at Film History

ROBERTA E. PEARSON

On 15 May 1996, I entered the Cardiff MGM Cinema in a state of excited anticipation, about to see *The Life Story of David Lloyd George* as a silent film should be seen: projected on a large screen, with live accompaniment in a theatre filled with a favourably disposed audience. Both a devoted fan and a historian of the silent cinema, I relished this opportunity to view a film that had been miraculously rescued after decades in a barn and had never before been projected in a cinema. Intriguing rumours had preceded the Cardiff première: the film would revolutionize our idea of British cinema history, said some of my colleagues.

While I responded less than enthusiastically to the specially commissioned score, the film itself contained sequences that seemed astonishing in the context of a war-weakened British film industry already coming under the domination of Hollywood. Like the Griffith epics, *The Birth of A Nation* (1915) and *Intolerance* (1916), from which director Maurice Elvey undoubtedly drew inspiration, the film does history on a grand, spectacle-intensive scale: vast crowds of extras, amazing location work and 'realistic' war footage. Even more amazing, all this was in aid of a living politician about to run for office again. On the other hand, compared with such films as the Griffith epics, or even more modest features, *The Life Story* is formally somewhat retrograde. This is especially noticeable in the editing: long shots dominate the film, relieved by relatively few of the cut-ins, shot-reverse shots, match cuts or parallel edits that were becoming standard Hollywood conventions even in this period.

I left the MGM cinema that day thinking that *The Life Story of David Lloyd George* was more of an intensely interesting historical curiosity than a revolutionary film. As I sought to compare this film to its contemporary counterparts, repeated viewings left me thoroughly baffled: the film defied neat categorization within the cinematic genres and narrative styles that existed in 1918. Then it struck me that *The Life Story* does not really make sense in 1918 terms: this Janus-faced film looks forward to a genre not yet invented, and looks backward to genres already outdated. It is in another sense trans-temporal, sharing many characteristics with the historical films that had been popular practically from the beginnings of the cinema in the late 1890s, that continued to be popular throughout the silent period and that still remain popular in the late 1990s.

In *Reframing Culture*,[1] my co-author and I identified the primary strategies of historical representation that were established by 1908 and from which history films even today rarely deviate: iconographic consistency; correct period detail; and key events/images, those incidents most popularly associated with particular historical periods or lives presented in a manner consistent with well-known paintings or other visual sources. Iconographic consistency is the easiest to achieve: actors must look like the historical personages they purport to portray. Norman Page's walrus moustache and bushy white hair instantly identify him as the prime minister, while the various walk-on famous personages are all made up and costumed to resemble their historical counterparts; for example, the Kaiser is identified by his Prussian helmet, his withered arm and his menacing demeanour. Correct period detail, in addition to costume and décor, often involves shooting on location at the scene of famous events or on sets built to resemble the original sites. *The Life Story* shows us the exteriors of many buildings associated with the great man's career, from his birthplace to Westminster, as well as recreating locations where filming might have been prohibited, such as the elaborately detailed Commons set used throughout much of the film.

Iconographic consistency and correct period detail add to the realist effect, but key events/images provide the story-line. The incidents deemed to be most familiar to a contemporary audience serve as the narrative jewels, with other less familiar events merely the pearls that string them together: a film about Napoleon, for example, must include his coronation, Waterloo and St Helena, among other events. *The Life Story* employs this strategy to a fault. The film encompasses every event of any significance in the great man's life, to the point of showing the prime minister on the golf course hitting his apparently well-known hole-in-one. But, as befits a film about a politician, the most important key events are political: Lloyd George's election to Parliament; his appointment as Chancellor of the Exchequer; his rise to prime minister and his actions in each office. The film marks each of the key events with a key speech, presented in lengthy intertitles, while key images, other than Lloyd George standing in the House of Commons speaking, seem hard to come by. Key events/speeches, rather than key events/images, serve as the narrative crown jewels, the dependence upon verbal communication creating a problem for this silent film to which we shall return below.[2]

The film makes few attempts to balance its focus on the key events of Lloyd George's public life by including key events in his personal life. *The Life Story of David Lloyd George* is a historical biography, but it is most definitely not a biopic. Biopics, afraid of boring the audience through an exclusive focus on the public sphere, draw upon the narrative strategies common to other films, often, for example, including a romantic sub-plot that rivals the main plot in importance. Even though the biopic did not come to full fruition until the sound era, many historical biographies of the silent era included elements from the main protagonist's private life: films about Napoleon detailed the emperor's relationship with Josephine as often as they did his military and political triumphs. Sound biopics also routinely engaged in what some film theorists refer to as a psychologization, a process by which various cinematic devices (voice-overs, point-of-view shots, dialogue) make the audience privy to the central protagonist's thoughts and feelings, enhancing the film's emotional register.

In *The Life Story* there is an almost total absence of psychologization: the audience sees the hero act and speak, but rarely sees him think or feel. The scenes dealing with the hero's private life – from his childhood right through his ascendancy as a senior statesman – almost perversely eschew opportunities for heightening emotional intensity or dramatic resonance. Deaths and romances provide film-makers with perfect occasions for psychologization but not in *The Life Story of David Lloyd George*. An intertitle tells us that Lloyd George's father died when he was very young. The next shot is not the deathbed scene we might have expected but rather Mrs Lloyd George writing a letter to her brother. In long shot, she hugs the young boy and his sister, but no cut-ins permit us to see the children's reactions to this devastating event. Later the film introduces

20. Early rebellion – Lloyd George resists the sale of his family's possessions.

Maggie Owen, the hero's future wife, but she remains a peripheral character and their relationship a peripheral aspect of the plot. When the two meet in a romantic setting in the woods, the film remains in long shot and the couple do not even embrace.[3] Rare moments of psychologization do occur, mostly during the childhood sequences, but the film immediately links them to the hero's future public-sphere activities. In an extended sequence showing the widow selling her household goods before journeying to her brother's, a Dickensian group of buyers clears the house of furniture. Young David engages in a lengthy struggle with one of them, an intertitle telling us that this is 'the first revolt against authority'. Throughout David's youth and adolescence, each such incident is presented as foreshadowing the glorious future.

The film's narrative structure resembles that of the cinematic Passion Plays that were extremely popular during the 1890s and were still occasionally produced in the 1910s. The film banks on the audience's intertextual frame; it is the audience's knowledge of Lloyd George's career, and thus of the film's future, that fills each key event with meaning and ties it to the hero's pre-ordained destiny. We cannot today fully understand this film without reference to the intertextual frames of the film's intended audience, the audience that never saw the film. The elucidation of this intertextual frame remains beyond the scope of this relatively short article, but I can point to moments that strongly mark the discrepancies between the intertextual frame of the intended audience and that of the audience that eventually saw the film. For example, at the age of twenty-one, Lloyd George visits the House of Commons and witnesses a debate between Gladstone and Lord Randolph Churchill. Later, an MP himself, he debates with that same Churchill. A 1990s audience may be dimly aware that *Randolph* was a key government minister during several Tory administrations but it is *Winston* that the name Churchill immediately evokes. By contrast, a 1918 audience would undoubtedly have known of *Winston* through his involvement in the wartime coalition government, but would most readily have associated the name Churchill with *Randolph*. Significantly, Randolph appears twice in the film and Winston not at all.

Even had we fully reconstructed the original audience's intertextual frame, understanding their probable responses to the film would require accounting for the very different mediasphere they inhabited. Satellite telecommunications may have accustomed a modern audience to the great and the good from around the world speaking in their living rooms, but in 1918 public personages could be seen and heard only at a live event. For reasons other than a necessary acknowledgement of the cinema's technical limitations, then, an original audience may have been far more tolerant of the film's lack of sound. Short of sitting in the Strangers' Gallery or attending a political rally, this was as close as most viewers could get to seeing, if not hearing, the famous Lloyd George. Short of having fought in France or travelled to the front, this was as close as they could get to the 'realities' of the First World War. Contemporary rhetoric surrounding the cinema would have reinforced this impression of 'reality', for since its inception the medium's capacity for a kind of 'liveness' and 'simultaneity' had been celebrated. Yet this 'simultaneity' inevitably happened at one remove – not until the coming of radio was true simultaneity possible. For a 1918 audience, the events in *The Life Story* would have occurred recently, but none the less in the past. In this respect the film resembles a docudrama and looks forward to a genre that would not be invented for several decades, perhaps because docudramas, at least those dealing with public events, required sound.

Given the 1918 mediasphere, the film's original audience, had it had one, might have appreciated the docudramatization of recent events, even in silent form. On the other hand, this hypothetical audience might have judged the film intertitle-intensive compared with others they had seen. Silent films had well-developed strategies for conveying narrative information through images but in *The Life Story* numerous lengthy titles, sometimes even two or three in quick succession, contain great swatches of various speeches. Internal evidence indicates that the film-makers realized the need to compensate for these titles and the lack of sound that necessitated them. The film continually strives to match images to the numerous and lengthy sequences involving speeches, parliamentary debates and bills.

The film's efforts at visualization draw upon a metaphorical/ allegorical style peculiar to the cinema of the 1910s; in this regard, if not many others, *The Life Story* seems very much a film of its time. Take, for example, Lloyd George's introduction of the Old Age Pensions Bill. A mini-narrative of a young girl reading the news of the bill to her grandmother is followed by the title 'The workhouse doors opened', which is in turn followed by a shot of an empty street flanked by a long, curving wall. Suddenly ghostly figures materialize out of the wall and walk off down the street. In another instance of allegorical visualization, after 'The great Somme battles and the immortal defence of Verdun by the French', Lloyd George gives a speech praising his allies' courage. In shots interpolated among the intertitles, an allegorical figure in flowing robes holding laurel wreaths in one hand and the tricolour in the other appears on the battlefield, the lighting and tinting adding to its obvious rhetorical function.

Both these examples seem to work quite well, even for a 1990s audience, but some of the attempts at visualization now appear slightly ludicrous. For example, in his 'famous Paris speech,' Lloyd George insists that the Allies must act on 'one front with many flanks'. In the first metaphorical shot, the Germans and the Allies, all in full-dress uniform, play tug-of-war. The Allies, pulling in several different directions, are losing. In the next metaphorical shot, the Allies all pull in one direction and begin to win. In this instance a figure of speech works much better than the figurative image, which reminded this viewer of a *Monty Python* sketch.

This allegorical/metaphorical style may make *The Life Story* seem of its time, but, in its efforts at visualization the film replicates practically every

21. Liberation for the workhouse denizens – Elvey pulls out the stops to convey the effects of Lloyd George's legislation.

genre of the preceding twenty-plus years of cinema history, including some which seem rather old-fashioned by 1918 standards. At many points, the film draws upon the most popular form of the pre-1907 cinema, actualities, or non-fiction films. These were not documentaries as we know them today, a narrative of sorts structured around a particular topic, but were rather film-makers' attempts to transfer to celluloid the world around them – cities, mountains, oceans, jungles – and bring them before the gaze of the cinema audience. Landscapes, both those close to home and far away, were popular topics. Lloyd George's 'beloved hills of Wales' feature prominently in the cinematic story of his life; the film includes numerous shots of the Welsh landscape that, in the tradition of the early actualities, serve no direct narrative function but permit the audience to contemplate the natural beauty of the hero's homeland.

Static landscape shots such as these formed an important component of the very early cinema, but audiences seemed particularly to have relished subjects exploiting the cinema's capacity to capture movement. An entire genre of train films flourished: trains entering stations; trains leaving stations; trains travelling through tunnels and so forth. Moving water also attracted film-makers: waves crashing on large rocks; waterfalls; rapids and so forth. *The Life Story* draws upon this 'rocks-and-waves'[4] genre, as the politician himself drew upon a rocks-and-waves metaphor when speaking of the war. In an intertitle, Lloyd George says, 'The name of Verdun will arouse imperishable memories in the centuries to come. The evil working force of the enemy has broken itself against this old citadel [the vault at Verdun] as a wave breaks against the rocks.' Here the film interpolates a 'rocks-and-waves' shot that could date from twenty years earlier.

The Life Story also incorporates mini-versions of didactic fiction films which, though less numerous than their non-fiction counterparts, were also extremely popular during the cinema's first decade. Above I argued that *The Life Story* is in one sense trans-temporal, conforming as it does to strategies of historical representation that developed during the cinema's infancy and continue to be deployed even today. This is certainly true of the representation of the recent past that constitutes the film's own present, but *The Life Story* looks more old-fashioned when representing historical personages from the more distant past.

Upon his appointment to the premiership, Lloyd George walks into the Cabinet room at 10 Downing Street to receive 'the welcome of the mighty dead'. Gathered to greet him are the shades of past prime ministers – Disraeli, Pitt, Gladstone and others less iconographically distinct – all superimposed in ghostly fashion around the Cabinet table. Here *The Life Story* resembles the patriotic excesses of the very early cinema, as in the American *Martyred Presidents* (Edison, 1902), a film that shows superimposed heads of assassinated presidents – Lincoln, Garfield, McKinley – over a flag-draped altar. In fact, in his first speech in the Commons, Lloyd George directly invokes one of these dead icons, and the film virtually quotes *Martyred Presidents*; as Lloyd George refers to Lincoln, the film shows the head of an actor made up to resemble 'Old Abe' superimposed over the Stars and Stripes. When Lloyd George invokes another American president, Geroge Washington, the film again superimposes the head over the flag, but also includes a shot of Washington bidding farewell to his Revolutionary War officers that conforms well enough in terms of iconographic consistency and key event/image to be seamlessly edited into the 1909 Vitagraph film *Washington under the American Flag.*

Didactic fiction films dealt with religious as well as historical topics, and the pre-Hollywood-era studios in the United States and Europe cranked out many a biblical film during the cinema's first years. As well as films on Washington, Napoleon and other historical figures, for example, the Vitagraph Company produced a lavish (by period standards) five-reel *Life of Moses* (1909). Moses also appears in *The Life Story*, the film illustrating one of the schoolmaster's 'vivid scripture lessons' about the Israelites in the land of Egypt with footage that could have been taken from the earlier Vitagraph film. Later, David's uncle reads the story of David and Goliath and the film shows the Hebrew lad defeating the Philistine giant. In both instances, intertitles draw a strong parallel between the biblical heroes and the man that the boy David will grow up to be – a defender of the weak and innocent, a resister of tyranny.

The Life Story incorporates actualities and didactic fiction but also borrows from the domestic melodramas turned out in the hundreds by film companies across the United States and Europe. In a scene reminiscent of both stage and film temperance melodramas, Lloyd George visits a 'village in South Wales notorious as a resort for Sunday drinkers'. In front of the Prince of Wales pub, a drunk manhandles two boys. The drunk is knocked down by adult bystanders, then pummelled by the boys. Lloyd George tries to intervene, the boys seem to yell abuse at him, and then one of them thumbs his nose and drinks from the pint glass he holds.

Lloyd George is directly involved in the action of this mini-melodrama, but in two other instances the melodramas illustrate parliamentary speeches. During a five-hour speech advocating a 'People's Budget' that will wage war on poverty and squalor, he explains how new taxes will help the poor. The film cuts to a slum street scene, complete with gambling street urchins and unemployed men lounging around the corner lamppost. Cut to a squalid interior set of a single room inhabited by mother with babe in arms and four small children. The father enters bearing a stolen loaf of bread that he gives to his children. In the street a baker looks for the thief, then finds a policeman. The baker and the policeman enter the room and, after suitable melodramatic business, take the father away. The sets, acting and subject matter of this sequence strongly resemble those of D. W. Griffith's 'plight of the poor' Biograph films, for instance *The Song of the Shirt* (1908) or *A Corner in Wheat* (1909). The same is true of the other mini-melodrama that shows a couple before and after the introduction of the National Insurance Bill.

The final sequences of Lloyd George simultaneously illustrate the power of silent cinema to construct meaning imagistically and reveal the limited impact of the written intertitles. After the intertitle, 'The Last Roll-Call', the film shows soldiers assembling in a vast square, ready for demobilization. Around the sides wait women and children, their arms extended towards the soldiers. The soldiers are dismissed, walk towards the camera cheering, and as they join their families, the magic of superimposition garbs them in their civilian clothes. We then see several reunion vignettes and a shot of one weeping woman whose man is obviously not coming home. For a 1918 audience, these would have been emotion-laden scenes, and the film requires no intertitles to enhance their impact. But the emotional impact of the final shot depends entirely upon an intertitle. For the first time in the film, Lloyd George directly addresses the camera. The first intertitle says, 'Next time we must be better prepared.' After another shot of Lloyd George the next intertitle states, 'There must be no next time.' The direct address emphasizes the crucial importance of this final message, but might even a 1918 audience have longed to have heard Lloyd George actually deliver the lines?

Notes

[1] Roberta Pearson and William Uricchio, *Reframing Culture: The Case of the Vitagraph Quality Films* (Princeton University Press, 1993).

[2] See the previous chapter in which my colleague, John O. Thompson, also discusses the problem of a silent film heavily dependent upon speech, yet does so from the perspective of a film theorist while I do so from the perspective of a film historian.

[3] Given what I have heard about Lloyd George's private life, however, this omission may have been strategic.

[4] I am indebted to my friend and regular co-author William Uricchio for this term.

CONCLUSION

A Truly International Discovery

KEVIN BROWNLOW

In 1997, Trevor Griffiths wrote and directed a television play about Aneurin Bevan for the BBC in Wales. In an angry article in the *Independent*, Brian Cox, who played the lead, accused the BBC in London of scheduling the play belatedly in a late-night network slot as if embarrassed by it.[1] Their attitude seemed to be: 'Who gives a monkey about a dead Welsh politician?'

The same attitude prevailed in 1996, the year celebrated as the centenary of British cinema, when the Wales Film and Television Archive presented their astounding discovery – a great film about the Welsh politician David Lloyd George, produced during the First World War on a vast scale – and never shown. This was the find of the century as far as British cinema was concerned and received extensive press coverage, even attracting an item on the national BBC news (achieved, it should be noted, against strong opposition). But the element that would have made all the difference – a full-length documentary of the sort made about the Tudor ship the *Mary Rose* – apparently did not appeal to the TV companies. Instead, they exercised the 'Oblomov option': they expressed interest and did nothing.

Is there such snobbery, I wonder, that programmes about early film are still regarded with disdain? Snobbery plays an important role in this story, so it should not be discounted, but the inertia can probably be put down to the predominant disease of our time: ignorance. I do not exempt myself. Had I been asked, before I saw this film, to fill a sheet of paper with the achievements of David Lloyd George, the page would have remained almost pristine. But isn't half the point of television to introduce its audiences to what they do not know? I hesitate to use the word 'educate' in these post-Thatcher years, but television has been known to do it rather well. And this story is so unusual, so exciting, so visual – so televisual!

Evaluating Elvey

Without doubt a certain snobbery surrounds the director of *The Life Story of David Lloyd George*; Maurice Elvey was looked upon with affectionate derision in the movie industry because he was so prolific, and made a number of worthless films. We now know, thanks to the 1997 Pordenone Film Festival's retro-spective, that they were not all bad, and some of his silents were in fact among the best pictures made in this country at the time. I had encountered most of Elvey's extant work when I was researching my book on David Lean – Lean worked with Elvey in the late 1920s as assistant director and assistant editor – but I was particularly astonished by the one film I had not seen before Pordenone, *The Flag Lieutenant* (1926).

The Flag Lieutenant is full of action and, more importantly, full of character. Elvey makes you fall for Henry Edwards – showing how skittish he is, how delightful are his impressions of superior officers – and builds up his relationship with a middle-aged officer (Fred Raynham) who will, unwittingly, prove his downfall. The picture is full of *Boys' Own Paper* imperialist propaganda, showing British ships shelling rebellious Arabs to provide exciting action sequences. (Odd how the socialist Elvey was a jingoist at heart.) For once, these sequences are done on a scale to match the Americans – but, while Elvey can stage sweeping spectacle, he seems to forget the detail, so that it is not as convincing as its Hollywood counterparts. It remains, though, one of the most entertaining British silents I have seen.

The Hound of the Baskervilles (1921) should have been equally entertaining. But this is the Elvey one has been led to expect: static, lifeless and boring. The Conan Doyle story is practically impossible to film badly, but Elvey is ably assisted by art director Walter Murton. The latter's idea of Dartmoor is Chobham Common with property rocks, and his interiors are an affront to the eye. Character and action, so strong in *The Flag Lieutenant*, are notably missing; this is the sort of film that helped give Britain such a bad reputation.

Many of those at Pordenone in 1997 felt the same about *The Rocks of Valpre* (1919), but I thought that, given the lurid material – by Ethel M. Dell – Elvey had made a picturesque and impressive job of it. And I thought his direction of *At the Villa Rose* (1920) was even better. Everyone encountered was most impressed with *Hindle Wakes* (1927), which Elvey co-directed with Victor Saville. Much of the film's quality was inherited from the play – some subtitles contain direct quotations. But the playing is of a very high standard, especially Estelle Brody as Fanny Hawthorne. The scene in which Fanny returns after a night of passion with the son of the mill-owner and tells her girl-friend what happened – largely without titles – is a *tour de force*. Elvey and Saville both loved this play; Elvey made an earlier version and Saville would make the talkie – and they depict the characters with affection. The more spectacular sequences stick in the memory: the wild ride at Blackpool (with the camera aboard the roller-coaster) is as inventive as anything in American pictures, and the scenes inside the mill are both impressive and authentic.

22. Maurice Elvey, the most prolific (and among the most critically neglected) of all British film-makers.

Elvey and Saville also worked together on a war film, *Mademoiselle from Armentières* (1926), and two reels were discovered recently by the National Film Archive. They showed the French girl of the title (Estelle Brody) clinging to the lorry which is carrying her lover away – embarrassingly close to that scene in *The Big Parade* (USA, 1925). Victor Saville records in his unpublished memoirs (preserved by BFI Special Collections) that he was accused of plagiarism by Louis B. Mayer, but he insisted that neither he nor Elvey had seen *The Big Parade* when they shot the sequence – it was pure coincidence.

Much more rewarding a film was *Roses of Picardy* (1927), a sentimental title for what was evidently an unsentimental treatment. The *Spanish Farm* trilogy, on which it was based, was a novel, but it took a documentary tone in depicting the minutiae of war. Elvey later said that the quality which distinguished British cinema was that of documentary, so one can be sure that he did not betray this element in this long-lost film. David Lean saw *Roses of Picardy* and was deeply impressed, and years later he wrote its star, John Stuart, a fan letter.

I met Maurice Elvey once, and it is to my eternal shame that I did not sit him down and interview him in depth about his career. But I was full of bitterness about British cinema in those days, having been deeply disappointed in most of the British silents I saw. Luckily, I had seen

Elvey's *Balaclava* (1930), with its excellent Charge of the Light Brigade, and we spoke about that. He was a most entertaining man, with steel-rimmed spectacles and an intense manner. I was reminded how charming he was by the talking trailer for *High Treason* (1929) which was discovered by London's Cinema Museum, and shown just before the feature at Pordenone. Humberstone Wright reads the excellent reviews the film received, and then introduces Elvey. After a few remarks, Elvey looks at the camera and says: 'Of course, all those ladies and gentlemen out there are supposed to think we haven't rehearsed this, whereas, as a matter of fact, we know we have!'

Science fiction is usually unbelievably silly – even *Metropolis* (Germany, 1927) has its embarrassing moments – but Elvey does very well with this play by the colourful Noel Pemberton Billing. In *High Treason*, we see autogiros on the Thames flying over buildings which look remarkably like some of the worst of London's postmodernist constructions. Terrorists plant a bomb in a train travelling through the Channel Tunnel. The enemy is the 'Atlantic States' and we see the bombing of New York by airship.

Elvey's drawback was that he took what he was given, and did not spend time working on the script. This was to undermine his reputation later on, even though he made some talkies which rivalled the best of Hitchcock. Had *The Life Story of David Lloyd George* been released, however, Elvey might even have been hailed 'the Griffith of Britain' and he might have been as well known – and as successful – as Hitchcock himself. Certainly, the Lloyd George film would have been placed beside the best work from America and the Continent and it would not have been entirely overshadowed.

The Americans had achieved world domination by 1918, mainly because the European industries were shattered by the war. They released super-spectacles like *Civilization* (1916) but they avoided the film biography. *The Fighting Roosevelts* – its title changed to *Our Teddy* – was the story of Teddy Roosevelt and it appeared in 1919, just after the great man's death, but it made no impact on the box office. Thus the film biography as we know it today appears to have been a British invention developed by none other than Maurice Elvey. In addition to *The Life Story of David Lloyd George*, he made *Florence Nightingale* (1915) – which is unfortunately lost – and *Nelson* (1918) – which survives incomplete. Elvey's technique of drama-documentary is precisely the same as is used

rman Page as Lloyd George and Alma Reville as his daughter Megan.

today on television, and had his Lloyd George film been released in America – and been financially successful – it might have led to Hollywood embarking on biographical pictures many years earlier than it did.

When I first saw a rough assembly of the film, at the Wales Film and Television Archive in Aberystwyth, I was shocked at my lack of knowledge. Lloyd George emerges from it as the greatest political leader we have had. Churchill is presently in the ascendant, because we can never forget what he did during the Second World War. But while Churchill was a great war leader, Lloyd George combined this with astonishing achievements in time of peace. I never realized that he had brought about improved conditions for merchant seamen, and had been largely responsible for medical insurance and the Old Age Pension. Here was a poor boy, brought up in a Welsh cottage, who became the most important man in the world. The film showed a pacifist, almost lynched for his opposition to the Boer War, who put aside his principles to deal with the threat from Germany. John Grigg, Lloyd George's biographer, saw the film at the same time as I did. He pronounced it remarkably accurate until the war sequences, when its sense of history goes haywire. However, the war scenes include documentary passages John Grierson would have been proud of – the visit to an ammunition factory would make a brilliant short documentary on its own. And although there are no scenes shot at the Front, the battles, restaged in Aldershot and on Salisbury Plain, are imaginatively done, and it is poignant to think that perhaps Elvey's use of reserve troops was delaying their return to France and perhaps saving their lives.

Inspired to read John Grigg's books on Lloyd George,[2] I was further astounded by how much the man achieved, and how little we remember – all the more ammunition for a documentary, if not a documentary series. The cinema once again proves itself to be an excellent educator, if only for sparking one's desire to find out. But television people are terrified of anything their viewers find unfamiliar, for they are now ruled by the ratings. On those figures – as arbitrary as the National Lottery, and as accurate as a tabloid's estimate of a politician's mistresses – depend their careers. So while anything goes after the nine o'clock watershed as far as sex and violence are concerned, they are deeply understanding of their viewers' fear of that seven-letter word 'obscure'. And they keep it at bay with all the weapons in their arsenal.

One could make a case that this is a form of censorship quite as bad as the more common kind. It soothes the ignorant and ensures they remain that way, arousing no awkward questions and disturbing no carefully computed schedules. It is not all that far from what the authorities did in 1918 – removing an awkward film so that the public would not be influenced by it.

The story of how the film was confiscated is told elsewhere in this book. One can only put forward theories about why it was considered necessary. Film in 1918 was still primarily a working-class concern, and what the working class choose as entertainment always has to be 'regulated' in Britain. Initially, I thought that perhaps at the end of 1918, with the war over and the enemy, as in 1945, changing from Germans to Bolsheviks, the objections might have been to Lloyd George's achievements in the social sphere, which might have been regarded as alarmingly socialist. The film gives an excellent impression of Lloyd George's concern for the working man and woman, and his own rise from the rural working class might have presented too much of a challenge. Bolshevism was on the march in Germany and other parts of central Europe, and it was making its voice heard on Clydeside and in the coal-mines of Wales. This theory seemed stronger when Sarah Street, who had first drawn attention to the film when she described Harry Rowson's memoirs in a film-history journal, revealed that one of the two men responsible for suppressing the film was Basil Thomson.[3]

Thomson, who was to Reds what Horatio Bottomley was to pro-Germans, was certain that Britain was seething with revolution. When the Special Branch was expanded into a civil intelligence department soon after the end of the war, Thomson, assistant commissioner of the Metropolitan Police, became its director. Funded with Secret Service money, the new directorate was permitted to operate in the UK and abroad to counter the threat of Bolshevism. In 1919, Thomson wrote a story for a film attacking Lenin, and director Harold Shaw took a company to Lithuania, then part of Russia, to make it. It seems incredible that a film company would take such a risk, for civil war was raging, but evidently Thomson and his associates wanted authenticity. It would not be stretching credibility to imagine that such a man saw a danger in this adulatory story of Lloyd George that others might not.

But now, thanks to Harry Rowson's daughter Janet Davis, I have read the Rowson memoirs and I think the explanation is more mundane. I agree with historian Tony Fletcher that Bottomley's 'revelations' might have been a put-up job, Bottomley's palm being greased to ensure his thorough discrediting of the Ideal company. This would have provided the simplest excuse for withdrawing the film. But Bottomley's accusations were misplaced, and the Rowsons challenged him in court, so – in my opinion – something else had to be thought up. Lloyd George must have agreed to the strategy, for he ended up retaining the negative. He must have been persuaded that the film would give him an unfair advantage in the next election, and this was unacceptable to the establishment. Undoubtedly, it was unacceptable to the Tories while he was heading the fragile coalition, and a threat of non-co-operation from the Tory benches would be enough to make him submit. The war was not over – and the conduct of the war was more important than any film. But in time of peace it would be both unnecessary and highly unsuitable; it was not the way the British conducted politics.

According to Harry Rowson, Simon Rowson, his brother and producer of the film, was summoned by Captain Guest who informed him that Lloyd George did not want the film released – this decision had, allegedly, nothing to do with *John Bull*. Friends of Lloyd George, who strongly disapproved of the cinema, persuaded him that the status of the cinema would be so enhanced if the film were shown that the whole country would be in danger, although they would probably have been more concerned about the damage he might do to himself by exploiting the cheap populism of the 'flicks'. In our era, imagine what would happen if Tony Blair were given the Andrew Lloyd Webber treatment at Wembley Stadium – his participation would be giving unacceptable prestige to an entertainment which most people in authority affect to despise. The damage done to him – as was done to Neil Kinnock after the Sheffield rally in 1992 – would be real enough.

Certainly the ruling class had nothing but contempt for the cinema. A series of letters recently came to light in which Ideal tried to secure permission for the filming of Lloyd George meeting Gladstone at the Gladstone home, Hawarden Castle. Gladstone's son wrote (in private), 'As this involves the grotesque impersonation of my father by a Cinema actor I have had to refuse leave' (letter from Henry Gladstone, 10 September 1918).

Not even Lloyd George had any legal way of stopping the film's release, but Ideal would be paid for their work. Meanwhile, Carl Laemmle of Universal, Harry Rowson's closest American friend, was offering unimaginable sums for the film's release in America. The Rowsons were actually as pro-British as Bottomley accused them of being pro-German. The money was beyond their wildest dreams, but unless they could have the film shown unimpeded in Britain, they would not let it go abroad. 'We knew that if we did, it would be a world scandal – in which Lloyd George and ourselves would be the central figures. Great pressure was brought on us – by our greatest personal friends – to prevent this, at any cost, from becoming a Jewish question – the only way we could look at it.'[4]

The Rowsons were deeply depressed after they lost the film – and one can imagine the effect on Maurice Elvey – but knew they were powerless. If Lloyd George had stated in public that he did not want the film to be shown, who would have booked it? In 1945, Harry Rowson brought the matter up again in a letter to A. J. Sylvester, Lloyd George's private secretary, and in this he wrote: 'The film was never shown to the public because it was intimated that some members of your family and some of your close friends did not wish to be associated with a project they regarded as somewhat "infra-dig".'[5]

That old fashioned expression is not a term one associates with Lloyd George, who was far more democratic and approachable than the majority of politicians of the time. But it sums up the fate of the film. The contempt which the authorities had felt for the cinema, which had led them to ban cameras from the Front, had been replaced by a sense of expediency. But a snobbery still existed – a snobbery which, I suspect, still exists towards this provocative medium. But if it cannot be treated seriously on our television screens, at an hour when people are still awake, then we have not begun to realize the effect such snobbery has on our culture and society.

Fortunately, the film is such an important discovery that its reputation can only increase. And it will not be long before students start writing theses on it. Perhaps at some stage the film will have a CD-ROM devoted to it and even appear on the Internet. Then, thanks to the latest technology, this remarkable film, which nobody was supposed to see, will be visible across the planet.

Notes

[1] *The Independent*, 24 October 1997.
[2] See John Grigg, *The Young Lloyd George: The People's Champion 1902–1911*, and *From Peace to War 1912–1916* (Eyre Methuen, 1973–85; paperback edn, HarperCollins, 1997).
[3] A reprint of Sarah Street's article can be found in this volume.
[4] Rowson, memoir, p.141.
[5] Rowson, memoir, p.145.

Appendix A

Maurice Elvey on
The Life Story of David Lloyd George

(What follows is an extract from Denis Gifford's 1967 interviews with Maurice Elvey.[1] Elvey was eighty and living in London when he gave two or three interviews to Gifford, but he died at the end of 1967 before he could talk about his 1920s silents.)

In 1916 the London Film Company closed down, but Elvey continued to work at the company's former studios with Butchers, International Exclusives and Ideal, run by the brothers Harry and Simon Rowson whose imaginative policy allowed Elvey considerable latitude in the choice of subjects.

MAURICE ELVEY: The London Film Company folded up and all its American personnel returned to the States. I transferred to the Butchers Film Company . . . which had very Dickensian offices in Wardour Street. To my great satisfaction I was able to carry on making films for them.

. . . My next move was to Ideal Films run by a man we called Simi (Simon) Rowson. It was an extraordinarily successful operation for many years.

. . . After making a number of films at the Ideal Film Company [including a version of Galsworthy's *Justice* and the popular *Masks and Faces*] the most interesting film I ever made cropped up: *The Life Story of David Lloyd George*. This I suppose must have been one of the best films I ever made or shall ever make. The part was played by Norman Page, an actor of the period who looked extraordinarily like Lloyd George and who made himself up in the later years to look incredibly like the great man. It took the life of David Lloyd George all the way from the time when his mother and her orphan children got into a pony cart and drove all the way from Manchester, when they were destitute, to Criccieth, north Wales, where they were taken in by his uncle, a remarkable man who was the village blacksmith. The smithy is still there at Criccieth, and I remember shooting there outside this forge, with the actor playing young Lloyd George. And I remember the famous baptism ceremony – the chapel where it happened also still existed in those days – when the young actor portraying the young Lloyd George actually went down to the stream wearing a kind of long night-shirt to be baptised in the Welsh Baptist tradition. I remember quite well a local clergyman, a Welshman, had been watching this for some time and indeed had advised me as to the procedure. Whilst we were in the middle of it, I turned to him and said: 'Now, sir, are you sure that the procedure is absolutely correct?' And he said: 'Yes, but I am very concerned.' I said: 'I'm very sorry about that.' 'No, no, no,' he said, 'it is nothing to do with you, but I am very concerned to understand how you can photograph them if they keep moving all the time.'

Everything was thrown open to us because it was the life of the great David Lloyd George and Wales was at my disposal. The town of Carnarvon [sic] became the scene of an extraordinary event. I advertised in the local papers for three consecutive weeks that on such and such a day and on [sic] such and such a time in the evening the torchlight procession celebrating the Welsh David Lloyd George's election to Parliament [re-election] would be reconstructed and the townsfolk were advised to turn up and take part in it and to bring torches – otherwise they would be provided. And we provided dozens and dozens of torches. Now these had to be specially prepared. They had to be what is called actinic, so that the light would be sufficient for the film stock. They were also very dangerous, so that everybody had to be warned. Nothing deterred the populace from being in this procession. The whole of the main street of Carnarvon [sic] was lit by these torches, with the help of some arc lamps. It was an extraordinary scene. I remember being in a little alleyway, up a flight of steps, with the principal camera (we had as many as three cameras filming this scene). Full of importance, and of course very, very busy, I was conscious that a lady was rather anxious to speak to me. Eventually I gave her of my attention and must have said: 'Well, madame, and what can I do for you?' And she said 'Could you please come round tomorrow and take a couple of sticky-backs of my children?'

The parliamentary scenes in this [film] were done in the studio somewhere. I forget which studio I was using at the time. I am sure it was the best film I ever made, because everything was laid on, there was nothing I wanted that I couldn't have. Unfortunately political opposition stepped in. The film was eventually destroyed. It was contended by the other political parties – or so Simon Rowson told me – that this was an unfair use of Liberal Party funds for political propaganda, when this of course was not done or indeed permitted. And so the film disappeared. I have never been able to ascertain what became of it.

I remember that we wanted to show the young, or fairly young Lloyd George being mobbed by suffragettes, who were of course making a damned nuisance in London at that period. Lloyd George was due to speak in Queen's Hall, Langham Place, and I remember we had arranged for something like two or three hundred extras – people from the labour exchange – to present themselves and to be told to try and mob the hall. We cordoned off the whole of Langham Place from Oxford Street upwards in order that these scenes should be done. By a fortunate coincidence, the day happened to coincide with a police strike. So the only police on duty were the police extras that I had dressed up in uniform for the purposes of my vellum, to control the crowd. And we lined these police along the streets leading to where I was shooting. We even cordoned off Oxford Street for at least an hour. What people thought was happening I have not the slightest idea! The part of the young girl, Megan Lloyd George, was played by that charming lady Alma Reville who was to become Mrs Alfred Hitchcock and at that time used to edit my films for me.

The film included the scene of the attempted storming by the mob of Birmingham Town Hall, when this 'pro-Boer' as he was called was speaking inside the town hall. This was wartime and we couldn't afford all those extras. So we advertised in the local paper for two weeks previously – this was a trick of mine – always the local paper. So we advertised that the scene would be down at such and such a time and the townsfolk were invited to attend and they would hear my voice without knowing where I was speaking from – of course this had to be done by megaphone, there were no tannoys in those days. And we had dressed up about twenty extras as policemen who formed a cordon around the hall, and the crowd was milling around and milling around until I judged they were sufficiently large in numbers. Of course they loved it – it was free entertainment, Saturday afternoon. I got their attention – they never knew where the voice came from. And I said to them: 'When I give you the word, one, two, three, go. I want you to try to get into the town hall. Well, one, two, three, go' – they never got in but three of our policemen had to be taken off to the local hospital. This was really quite a remarkable scene, one of many extraordinary scenes in this film. It is such a shame it has disappeared.

Notes

[1] The interviews were first published in *Griffithiana*, 60–1 (October 1997), 77–125. This extract is from pp.95–9.

Appendix B

The Life Story of David Lloyd George:
Credits, Notes on Players and Studio, Film Synopsis

Credits

Norman Page	(David Lloyd George)
Ernest Thesiger	(Joseph Chamberlain)
Alma Reville	(Megan Lloyd George)
Douglas Munro	(Benjamin Disraeli)

With Thomas Canning, Miriam Stuart, Eric Stuart, S. Leonard Tugwell, Cameron Carr, Beattie Belmont.

Produced by Simon Rowson.

Directed by Maurice Elvey.

From a script by Sir Sidney Low.

Assistant director – Challis Sanderson.

An **Ideal Film** company production by Harry and Simon Rowson.

Notes on Players and Studio

The rediscovered negative of *The Life Story of David Lloyd George* contained no credits and it has been difficult to identify, so long after the fact and beyond doubt, most of the minor players. In the print screened in 1996 only the top three players and their roles were identified. We have verified through the *Kinematograph Weekly Year Books* (principally for 1919 and 1921) the presence in the cast of many of the above players listed. Denis Gifford's invaluable *British Film Catalogue 1895–1985* lists Douglas Munro as Disraeli. Gifford has subsequently identified to us Cameron Carr. We thank Tony Fletcher for providing documentary evidence, since the screening, of Challis Sanderson's involvement as assistant director.

Ideal shot the Lloyd George picture at St Margaret's studio, Twickenham, where the company leased a stage sometime in 1918. In the same year it also leased the old Neptune studios, Elstree – and Ideal moved there permanently in 1921. The company was absorbed by Gaumont in the 1920s.

D.B.

The Life Story of David Lloyd George, Synopsis

The film opens with scenes depicting Lloyd George's humble Nonconformist childhood at Llanystumdwy. His education and his early challenges to authority soon reveal him as one marked to do great things in life. As a young solicitor he takes a daring stance against the Church and wins, making him famed all over Wales as a champion of the underdog. After a visit to the House of Commons he resolves to become an MP. Soon, he realizes his ambition and enters politics. His personal oratory and charismatic personality make him a firm favourite with his electorate who enthusiastically celebrate his 1892 re-election with a magnificent torchlight procession through Caernarfon.

Now in his element – on the political stage – Lloyd George begins to demonstrate the fearless determination to do only what he feels to be right. In 1900 he takes an unpopular stance against the Boer War, provoking a riot at Birmingham Town Hall. Famously, he escapes the terrifying mob by slipping away disguised as a policeman. The resolute maverick is also portrayed as a loving family man with strong Christian principles and a burning social conscience. The popularity of the Welsh Wizard's social reform, in particular the provision of the Old Age Pension, is graphically illustrated with some stunningly poignant images. There is, however, gloomy foreboding as the tide of war approaches. Lloyd George, now minister of munitions, determines to turn the nation's factories to the war effort.

Lloyd George becomes secretary of state for war and in 1916 prime minister. He replaces the unpopular Asquith as 'the man to win the war'. The film portrays the statesman on the international stage and impressing his allies with his gifts of oratory and persuasion. Never forgetting his humble origins, and conscious of the need to boost morale, Lloyd George visits troops in the trenches and listens to anecdotes of war atrocities. The powerful closing images show hundreds of soldiers lining up for the last roll-call, and in a most moving sequence, being transformed from uniformed soldiers to their former civilian status as they are reunited with their families. The lonely statesman is left mulling over the political and social consequences of war.

Appendix C

Diaries, 1918–1919 and 1994–1996

Production Diary for 'The Life Story of David Lloyd George'

1918

21 February
Trade paper *Pictures and Picturegoer* announces Ideal Film Company plan to shoot Lloyd George film *The Man who Saved the Empire*. Noted British historian Sidney Low to write the script. David Lloyd George in this last year of the war is Liberal prime minister of Tory-dominated coalition government.

30 May
DLG picture expected to be in eight parts, or reels, says *Kinematograph Weekly*. Reveals plans to shoot at scenes of Lloyd George's childhood in north Wales.

13 June
Trade press says – prematurely – that trade show is to be held at Cardiff Olympia (the present ABC, Queen Street).

15 June
Interview published with director Maurice Elvey on set of his feature *The Life of Nelson* at Walthamstow studios. Three weeks later *Pictures and Picturegoer* reports fire at laboratory, causing loss of 1,200–1,500 ft reel of *Nelson* and damage valued at £30,000. Retakes required (apparently taking six weeks).

20 August
Actor rehearsals for DLG feature at Criccieth, Portmadoc and Pencaenewydd (*Yr Herald Cymraeg*).

22 August
Ideal company steps up publicity with first of special weekly advertisements in *Kinematograph Weekly*. Company forecast that the Lloyd George film will be 'the picture of the year'.

5 September
Kinematograph Weekly reports filming of fights between pro- and anti-suffragette factions outside Queen's Hall, London. All main scenes for the feature shot in September.

12 September
Kinematograph Weekly reports seeing Alma Reville on set, and Elvey – 'a human dynamo, the electricity of his thought a real live current to the densest intelligence'. Paper says go-ahead now given for shooting of Lloyd George escaping, disguised as a policeman, from mob at Birmingham Town Hall after anti-Boer War speech.

12 September
Trade magazine account of filming torchlight procession through Caernarfon celebrating Lloyd George's re-election as MP for Caernarfon Boroughs, 1892 – stirring scenes with thousands of people reported there as extras and spectators (*Caernarvon and Denbigh Herald*).

3 October
Kinematograph Weekly claims 10,000 extras used in Birmingham scenes. Double-page advertisement says film (with its present title) will be issued in ten episodes, or 'chapters' – one a week from December, 'a strategy planned from the outset'. (This conflicts with 1940s memoirs of Harry Rowson, Ideal co-founder, who claims company had rejected moves by exhibitors to have the film released in instalments.)

5 October
The blow falls. Horatio Bottomley, editor of the powerful *John Bull* – weekly circulation 1.7 million – alleges in article that executives of Ideal are Huns and unsuitable people to make the film.

10 October
Ideal announces writs taken out against proprietors and publishers of *John Bull*.

17 October
Trade show reported fixed for Cardiff's Park Hall cinema (later part of present Park Hotel), for 12 November.

19 December
John Bull and Odhams Press lose contempt of court action against *Cinema and Property Magazine* for publishing leaflets stressing Ideal's fine film record.

1919

30 January
High Court libel action, *London-Ideal* vs *John Bull* settled in favour of film company. Defendant withdraws all allegations and indemnifies Ideal against legal costs. (Harry Rowson's memoirs say solicitors for government – on a date unspecified – took away the film's only copy and negative, paying firm £20,000 – in twenty £1,000 notes – to cover production costs. Film would have made £100,000 from domestic market alone, he claimed.)

Restoration Diary for **The Life Story of David Lloyd George**

1994

April
Screening at Llanystumdwy of A. J. Sylvester's filmed record of Lloyd George's controversial trip to Germany to meet Hitler, 1936. This film had been restored in the previous six months by the Wales Film and Television Archive, in collaboration with German archive and funded by Lumière (Media 95).

May
Lord Tenby, Lloyd George's grandson, who was invited to but could not attend screening, asks Archive to collect and store other Lloyd George nitrate (non-safety) material and 16 mm acetate held in the attic of his Hampshire home. Collection had been there for twenty-five years but Lord Tenby knew nothing of the Lloyd George film and was unaware he held it (in one large container of 137 reels of nitrate).

Wales Film and Television Archive identifies the main film in the collection as the long-lost *The Life Story of David Lloyd George*. Its state was generally good, but some shrinkage evident, severe mould on 30 ft, rest of footage slight mould. Document found with Lloyd George film container was signed by Cinema Traders Ltd, who supervised sealing of the film in December 1920. Wales Archive preservation officer and other staff pleased to discover original 1918 tinting and toning laboratory instructions on the film's leaders and tails.

Also in Lord Tenby's collection – only known complete copy in the world – 'Hepworth Cinema Interviews' (directed by British director Cecil Hepworth) with statesmen (including Lloyd George) and other leading men of the period. Plus various news magazine footage of Lloyd George mainly from *Topical Budget*, *Gaumont*, *Pathé*.

Detailed inspection of the Lloyd George feature begins in Aberystwyth – 14,000 ft to be dealt with including intertitles, out-takes, repeated scenes etc.

August
Copy shipped to National Film and Television Archive, Berkhamsted, for duping, production of fine-grain positive from original nitrate negative and new fine-grain safety-film negative made from positive.

December
First reel back from NFA (reel 2) on safety film. Image quality superb. First modest, but concerted, publicity campaign for the film.

1995

January
Bulk of material returns. Rough assembly made in Aberystwyth, but chronology within film, as first assembled, way out. Alphabet details on tops and tails did not correspond to chronological order. Archive preservation officer soon realized each letter of alphabet indicated a specific colour. It was the numbers on leader which indicated the specific order of the film.

19 April
Kevin Brownlow and other screen historians, Lloyd George biographer John Grigg and Welsh historian Emyr Price view the Archive's first official cut. All advise and make written and oral observations. Subsequently reels 9 and 10 are modified as not correctly reassembled (almost no intertitles on reel 9 when film rediscovered and 10 had none and was roughly cut together).

May–November
Fine tuning. Introduction into film of one or two uncut sequences for sake of clarity and on advice of historians. Indications on negative that certain scenes were missing which were found in the can of uncut material.

December
WFTVA receives first 300 ft of colour, flash-filtered material from the laboratories including spectacular David and Goliath sequences. Eleven different tints on complete print.

1996

March
Final assembly – negative due at laboratory, Film and Photo Design, London.

April
Copy submitted to British Board of Film Classification for certificate.

27 April
Preview of film at Pwllheli – first ever screening.

5 May
World première, MGM Cardiff.

D.B.

Appendix D

The Chief Players

David Lloyd George (1863–1945)

One of the great statesmen of his era, David Lloyd George was Liberal prime minister of a coalition government from 1916 to 1922. Born in Manchester, he was raised almost entirely in Llanystumdwy, a north Wales village, where he was brought up by his mother and his shoemaker uncle, Richard Lloyd. A solicitor from the 1880s, Lloyd George gained fame in 1888 when he defended local Nonconformists who had resisted a Church ban against burying their dead in the local churchyard.

A member of the first ever Caernarvonshire County Council in 1889, he was elected MP for Caernarvon Boroughs a year later, defeating a local Tory squire Ellis Nanney by just eighteen votes. Two years later he was re-elected with a 196 majority, and held the seat for more than forty years, eventually becoming Father of the House of Commons. In 1894 he launched the short-lived Cymru Fydd movement promoting self-government for Wales, but gained a solid parliamentary reputation before endangering his seat with an anti-Boer War stance in the 'khaki election' of 1900. He fought Joseph Chamberlain on the free-trade issue in 1903, fiercely opposing tariffs which hit the working man's cost of living, and in 1905 he became president of the Board of Trade.

When Asquith became prime minister in 1908, he made Lloyd George Chancellor of the Exchequer, and that year Lloyd George brought in old age pensions for the over-seventies. In 1909 Lloyd George's famous People's Budget – to 'declare war' on poverty, unemployment and sickness and involving imposing a supertax of 1s. 2d. in the pound on higher incomes – laid the foundations of the welfare state and the introduction of national insurance schemes. The Budget was rejected by the Lords but became law in May 1910 – after the Liberals had again won power – and the National Insurance Bill emerged the following year.

Embroiled in the Marconi scandal after speculating in shares of the wireless telegraph company, Lloyd George emerged to play a key part in discussions on the vexed Irish question. He became minister of munitions in 1915, turning the industrial system into a war economy before a rebellion against Asquith brought him to power as Liberal prime minister of a coalition government supported by the Unionists under Bonar Law. The war greatly increased Lloyd George's stature, and the coalition won a massive victory, gaining 526 seats in the election of 1918. Lloyd George was criticized for his 'Germany must pay' speeches – in a climate when others insisted that the Germans would be squeezed 'until the pips squeaked' – but he made more moderate demands than the French at Versailles.

The post-war period proved unhappy for the statesman. The Irish peace settlement of 1921 left a legacy of bitterness and permanent scars, and the same year saw even more industrial turmoil than 1918. Unemployment topped one million in 1922, when the coalition lost much of its Tory support and Lloyd George resigned. He was under fire by then for the operation of his personal fund (set up when he broke with the official Liberal party in 1916) and facing allegations that he had sold honours for cash. By the late 1920s the Liberals, divided by clashes between the Lloyd George and Asquith factions, were the third party in Parliament, and Lloyd George never again tasted power, though remaining in Parliament through the Second World War. His wife Margaret died in 1941 and he married his long-time secretary and mistress Frances Stevenson in 1943. He surprised – and disappointed – many by accepting a peerage as Earl Lloyd-George of Dwyfor, awarded in the year of his death.

Maurice Elvey (1887–1967)

No British film director in cinema history can claim more remarkable achievements, from inauspicious beginnings, than Maurice Elvey, who made more than 200 movies in a forty-four-year career from 1913 to 1957 – yet had little or no education and started work at nine, as a London hotel pageboy. Elvey, born William Seward Folkard in Darlington, Yorkshire, was a stage actor before launching his screen directing career with *The Fallen Idol* (1913).

He made around fifty films during the First World War, and around 1918–19 he was astonishingly prolific, moving from one ambitious project to another. After re-shooting part of *Nelson* following a laboratory fire, he moved on to the Lloyd George feature and in 1919 completed a version of Dickens's *Bleak House*. He directed the first of his English 'heritage' biopics, *Florence Nightingale*, in 1915, and for Sir Oswald Stoll's film company he made fifteen episodes of a Sherlock Holmes series in 1921 and two features on the Baker Street sleuth, *The Hound of the Baskervilles* (1921) and *The Sign of Four* (1923), all starring Eille Norwood. In 1923 he directed the ambitious *The Wandering Jew*, remaking it ten years later.

After a five-film Hollywood spell with Fox in 1924–5 he made a buoyant version of Stanley Houghton's popular stage play *Hindle Wakes*, almost a decade after first filming it, and made a series of impressively cinematic silents including *Palais de Danse* (1929) and *High Treason* (1929; reissued with sound 1930). His talkie career began well when he propelled Gracie Fields to stardom in *Sally in our Alley* (1931) and the following year he directed Cardiff's Ivor Novello in the sound version of *The Lodger* (1932), six years after Hitchcock's much-lauded silent version with the Welsh star. Novello also starred in the comedy *I Lived With You* (1933) – perhaps Elvey's finest sound film – from the actor's own stage play.

Other Elvey films to arouse interest and gain critrical acclaim included *The Tunnel* and *The Clairvoyant* (both 1935). Elvey made more than 100 films for Stoll, a studio later berated by historians for its dull lighting and creaky middle-brow literary adaptations, but much of his early work, especially for other studios, gives the lie to the director's detractors. In 1954 he made *The Happiness of Three Women*, a Welsh comic romance written by and starring Eynon Evans, and the following year directed *Room in the House* from Evans's stage play *Bless This House*.

Norman Page (1876–1935)

Who can say what heights Norman Page's screen career might have scaled if his performance as David Lloyd George had not been consigned to limbo in late 1918? For Page gave a masterly performance – the body language was wonderfully expressive and assertive, indicating just how scrupulously he had studied the 'Welsh Wizard' in visits to the House of Commons during the film's preparation.

Nottingham-born Page apparently valued his theatre acting career more than his celluloid forays and in later years he was probably best known as a London stage producer at venues as exalted as the Strand and the Coliseum. His attitude to movies might be summed up by his (probably self-penned entry) in *Who's Who in the Theatre* (1933) which states that in 1919 he was principally engaged in acting for 'the cinema stage'.

Page made his theatre début in 1896 – the first year of projected cinema in Britain. He became associated with Maeterlinck's Expressionist stage drama *The Blue Bird*, first as an actor in 1909, then as producer of a 1912 theatre version in Australia. In 1910 he appeared in Gaumont's film of the play. Later he acted with Mary Glynne (Welsh-born 1920s star with Famous Players

Lasky in Britain) in *The Cry for Justice* (1919), directed by ace cameraman A. G. Frenguelli. In Maurice Elvey's *Bleak House* Page, with his pinched features, is humorously devious as lovelorn clerk Mr Guppy, and he also featured for Elvey in *At the Villa Rose* (1920) and the Stoll version of Conan Doyle's *The Sign of Four* (1923). He popped up in *The Yellow Claw*, a Sax Rohmer adaptation in 1920, and his other movies included two adaptations of Arnold Bennett novels for Ideal – *The Old Wives' Tale* (1921) and *The Card* (1922). The actor was heavily engaged behind the footlights on leading London stage productions from 1922, which explains why his film career petered out before the British screen crisis of 1925–6 and the sound era.

Ernest Thesiger *(1879–1961)*

Thesiger flits through the Lloyd George film in an imperious cameo as Lloyd George's formidable political adversary Joseph Chamberlain. In later years the stage and screen actor became the most successful of all the Lloyd George biopic performers.

Cadaverous and sinister-looking, with a bony proboscis as remarkable in its own way as W. C. Field's snout, Thesiger was wonderfully effective in Hollywood horror movies for Universal, in particular, and was unforgettable as demented boffin Doctor Praetorius in James Whale's *The Bride of Frankenstein* (1935). In 1932 he featured with Melvyn Douglas and Boris Karloff in Whale's stylish black comedy *The Old Dark House* (1932), the first Hollywood sound feature set in Wales (even if filmed in the US). There were echoes of this Universal movie in Thesiger's 1933 British feature *The Ghoul*, made for producer Michael Balcon and Gaumont.

London-born Thesiger made more than fifty movies and played William Pitt for Maurice Elvey in *Nelson* (1919), filmed in the weeks immediately before the Lloyd George shoot. In 1921 he enjoyed a lead role in A. V. Bramble's *The Gentleman's Club*, then appeared as Mr Jingle in Thomas Bentley's *The Adventures of Mr Pickwick*. He was in Hitchcock's first (unfinished) feature *Number Thirteen* (1922), but the pick of his British screen roles was probably his ghoulish mastermind in the 1938 Arthur Woods film *They Drive by Night* (for MGM) in which Emlyn Williams played the chief suspect.

Off-screen Thesiger, a gay actor, was incorrigibly camp and lively. He made little of his First World War service, when he witnessed horrors recounted in his autobiography, *Practically True* (1927).

Alma Reville (1900–82)

One big surprise in *The Life Story of David Lloyd George* is the presence of Alma Reville (later Hitchcock's wife) in her only known screen role, as the politician's daughter Megan. Reville had earlier been editing movies for Elvey at Twickenham and she became best known as a script-writer, adaptor and editor, active in the industry for more than three decades.

The first woman assistant director to work on British features, she was a script/continuity girl on Hitchcock's first completed film *The Pleasure Garden* (1925) and married the director after working as his assistant on his 1926 silent *The Lodger*. Reville first met Hitchcock while editing and acting as script girl on the box office hit *Woman to Woman* (1923), directed by Hitchcock's talented mentor Graham Cutts. She later proved a valuable collaborator on many of her husband's best-known films as director, co-scripting his *Rich and Strange* (1932) and *Young and Innocent* (1937) and penning 'additional dialogue' for the classic train thriller *The Lady Vanishes* (1938). In 1935 she helped adapt *The Thirty-Nine Steps* from the novel by John Buchan, who was responsible for First World War intelligence in Lloyd George's government. In Hollywood she co-scripted Hitchcock's Cary Grant thriller *Suspicion* (1941), and the taut suspense movie *Shadow of a Doubt* (1943). Her career effectively concluded with her husband's British thriller *Stage Fright* (1950).

Horatio Bottomley (1860–1933)

Bottomley, a tub-thumping journalist who seized life by the tail, was an outrageous knave and beguiling hedonist who duped and swindled thousands of those readers who idolized him in his pomp. Could Lloyd George or his fellow ministers in that fragile 1918 coalition government have been so afraid of accusations made by Bottomley in the magazine *John Bull* that they sought to squash the film? The question remains but there can be no doubt of Bottomley's immense public appeal during the years when the magazine was riding high with a circulation of 1.5–1.7 million.

The film trade paper, *The Bioscope*, with only a hint of irony, dubbed Bottomley 'Britain's unofficial Prime Minister' in 1916. The former London orphan boy's popularity was greater than any minister of the Crown could command during the First World War, and he was the most influential journalist of his day, according to his biographer Julian Symons. Bottomley began *John Bull* in 1906, the year he was first elected to Parliament as a Liberal for Hackney, and as the self-proclaimed 'people's friend' he championed the 'poor man', through the magazine's early years, constantly pouring invective on major companies or damning establishment figures by innuendo.

His practised speech-making skills also served him well, extricating him in the courtroom twice when he faced fraud charges and helping explain away for years the various ruses he devised to part gullible readers from their money and sustain his gambling and champagne-quaffing lifestyle and his string of mistresses and horses. He went bankrupt in 1911 but later duped *John Bull* readers with Victory and War Bond schemes which lined his pockets. Discharged from bankruptcy he returned to Westminster as an independent, but his vanity proved his undoing in 1922 when he sued Birmingham businessman Reuben Bigland after a pamphlet – distributed in London, Birmingham and Cardiff by the Midlands entrepreneur wearing a black mask – focused attention on his fraudulent operations, particularly a *John Bull* lottery in which winning numbers, but never names, were announced. Bottomley's own dishonesty could no longer be concealed and he was jailed for seven years for fraud. He died in poverty.

Sir Sidney Low (1851–1932)

Historian Sir Sidney Low, scriptwriter of the Lloyd George film, suffered a double setback in 1918, the year of his knighthood. The Lloyd George feature was shelved after Low spent seven weeks in north Wales writing the scenario but he had already had a bitter foretaste of the paranoia evident in Horatio Bottomley's 'Hun' accusations against the Ideal company.

In January 1918 Low accepted an offer from newspaper magnate Lord Northcliffe, the minister for propaganda, to join his Propaganda Committee for Enemy Countries. In March he became head of the Information Ministry's Wireless Service but in July Ministry of Information secretary Sir Harold Snagge questioned him about his parents (Low's father was Hungarian). Low resigned his wireless post and Northcliffe pointedly read a letter in the Propaganda Committee drawing attention to the historian's central European origins. Low resigned from the committee – ostensibly on the grounds of 'want of time' – and his wireless post resignation was finally accepted in September.

Low's ambitions, despite a full life and years as a respected lecturer in imperial and colonial history at King's College, London, may never have been fully realized. His career also reveals unexpected parallels with Bottomley's. Low, like Bottomley, once edited a noted opinion-forming London publication (in his case the *St James Gazette*) and flirted with movies, suggesting scripts to film men, including an 'actuality' on Serbia and a feature *Attila, the Scourge of God* – and he even sent ideas to German studios UFA in the 1920s. Bottomley was a little more successful – he played the lead as himself, the *John Bull* editor as troubleshooter and paragon, responding to problems in a 1916 propaganda serial *Truth and Justice*, shot at Kew for director Bert Haldane and the Brum company and also appeared, again as himself, in the 1914 thriller *Was It He?*, from the low-budget Hewitt Films. Bottomley found himself an anachronism in the 1920s when his attempt to repeat his *John Bull* circulation success with the magazine *John Blunt* was a dismal failure.

Low, who wrote such books as *The British Constitution* and *The Governance of England*, was a colonialist who had championed such Boer 'heroes' as Rhodes and Milner. By the late 1930s his reputation was already fading and his 1936 biography is called – simply – *The Lost Historian*.

D.B.

Index